THE
CLARINET
AND
CLARINET
PLAYING

THE
CLARINET
AND
CLARINET
PLAYING

DAVID PINO

CHARLES SCRIBNER'S SONS
NEW YORK

Excerpt from Musical Instruments Through the Ages *edited by Anthony Baines, Copyright* © *1961, 1966, 1969 Penguin Books. Used with the permission of Penguin Books and Walker and Company.*

Copyright © *1980 David Pino*

Library of Congress Cataloging in Publication Data

Pino, David.
The clarinet and clarinet playing.

Includes index.
Bibliography
1.   Clarinet–Instruction and study.   I.   Title.
MT380.P56   788'.62   80-19579
ISBN 0-684-16624-0

1 3 5 7 9 11 13 15 17 19 F/C 20 18 16 14 12 10 8 6 4 2

Printed in the United States of America.

FOR
KEITH STEIN,
*the master clarinetist and teacher
who inspired this book in more ways
than he has imagined,*

AND FOR
MY STUDENTS,
who teach me more than they know

Acknowledgments

The ideas as presented in this book are my own, but I have drawn them from many sources—from teachers and students, from books, from friends, from my own experience.

There has been no way for me to avoid frequent mention of the words and the approaches to clarinet playing of Keith Stein, the great clarinetist to whom, along with my students, this book is dedicated. Although several men have had a significant influence on twentieth-century clarinet playing, Stein must be ranked among the most influential of all. I acknowledge his contribution to the book.

It is customary for author-husbands to thank their wives and children for their patience in putting up with the process of writing, and such thanks are certainly in order here. My wife, Carol, and our sons, Aaron and Nathan, have helped me immensely, too, through their patience and interest.

My good friend and colleague Dr. Byron Wolverton has offered me much encouragement and advice. His fine dissertation on Early American keyboard music has sparked my interest in the Early American clarinet—which remains a wide field for further study.

My thanks go to Susanne Kirk, my editor at Charles Scribner's Sons, without whose help—and patience, pleasantness, and encouragement—the book could never have been written. Jacques Barzun, Literary Advisor at Scribners, has my gratitude, too, for his help and encouragement.

For the photographs in Chapter 11, "Reeds," I am indebted to my friend David Herbert, who is also a fine oboist and a fellow member of the San Marcos Woodwind Quintet.

To my mind, the greatest experimenters of all are open-minded students, and—as a teacher—I have been blessed with many. To all my students I give my thanks.

I might add that this book was *not* the result of a grant or a leave of absence from my teaching position; I had not asked for such. Nor was I forced to write by a "publish-or-perish" situation—I was under no such pressure. The book was written because of concerns that will be mentioned in the Introduction and because Keith Stein had been urging me for some time to write my own book on the clarinet.

Finally, much of this book was written here in my study in a fine old Texas-German farmhouse with a wonderful breeze coming in through the windows from across the fields; I feel that the book has been immeasurably helped by being created in such surroundings. My shepherd dog Hilda has been at my feet, wondering when I would stop this infernal tapping and go play with her outdoors, where she believes I belong . . .

DAVID PINO, D.M.A.
San Marcos, Texas

Contents

Introduction

I wrote this book because of my great concern that information about the clarinet should be more widely available. Also, I have long felt that the clarinet and clarinet playing should be better understood on all levels—not merely at the beginning and intermediate levels. Too many advanced clarinetists and clarinet teachers have been holding out on the rest of us, guarding "trade secrets" to an alarming degree, or at least withholding them through neglect. Interestingly, perhaps one of the most closely guarded "trade secrets" of all is the fact that the more advanced a player becomes, the more he or she must rely on the basic and fundamental principles that are, or should be, taught to beginners. Beginners are urged to "use more air," to develop a better embouchure, to relax the arms and fingers, and so on—the very advice that should be given to the professional clarinetist when faced with a particularly difficult passage.

Another concern that led to this book is my belief that many myths about clarinet playing should be struck down. I have attempted not only to do this, but also to replace the myths with constructive alternatives. Nowhere, for instance, have I seen any full discussion of the possibility of adopting a truly workable technique for the double and triple tonguing that would seem natural on the clarinet. The type of multiple tonguing used by brass and flute players who have no mouthpiece or reed in their mouths is not adequate on clarinet in the long run. I have provided an alternative technique in Chapter 7, "Tonguing and Articulation." All tonguing strokes on the clarinet—whether single, double, or triple—must be done on the reed itself.

Similarly, despite the increasing cost and decreasing strengths of commercially made clarinet reeds, nowhere have I discovered a recent, fully adequate description of the making of reeds by hand. Some earlier, and valuable, work was done in reed making by the clarinetist Kalmen Opperman and others, but I believe that I have devised a more direct, less complicated method for making reeds than any I have read about elsewhere.

The tone qualities of American clarinetists in particular are, I feel, becoming smaller and harsher through a combination of several factors; I have attempted to alleviate this problem by offering a variety of possible causes and solutions.

I believe that there is today a need to revolutionize, if possible, the common conception of what it means to *practice* the clarinet. I have seen too many clarinet students—and professionals, as well—almost beating their heads against the practice room walls, and I cannot let this pass without comment and without offering, again, a constructive solution. I feel that both students and teachers should approach the clarinet with a sense of humor because, otherwise, both learning and instructing become emotionally and physically overwhelming.

In the private-lesson situation, the tyrant-teacher and the victim-student are still too often the only actors in an all-too-dramatic "tragedy." In Chapter 10, "Teaching Other Clarinetists," I have offered an alternative approach to the private-lesson session—one that will, I hope, show the way in which teaching and learning can become pleasant give-and-take processes.

Books have been written already, of course, about the history—or "life story," as I have called it—and the literature of the clarinet. Several of these are excellent. Too often, however, such books have been so packed with detail that the reader has great difficulty (to use a well-worn phrase) in seeing the forest for the trees. In Chapters 14 and 15, on the life story and the literature of the clarinet, I have provided the reader-student with a more usable source of this information.

I have become concerned that clarinetists are in general far too close-minded about everything related to music and specifically to the clarinet. In this book I hope to open some of those minds—to free them to experiment more broadly in the clarinet's "problem areas." Above all, I have felt a need for clarinetists to reorder their priorities as both musicians and clarinetists. Such a reordering will be of tremendous help to them, and might indeed revolutionize clarinet teaching.

CHAPTER

1

What
a Clarinetist
Needs

PERSONAL CHARACTERISTICS AND OUTLOOK

Maybe the best way to answer the question of what a serious clarinetist needs is to approach it from another angle: Why does anybody want to play clarinet in the first place? Why play an instrument at all, and why the clarinet in particular? Although these questions may seem largely rhetorical, I have come across a great many players who appear to have never seriously considered them. Just because your Great-uncle John played clarinet in his hometown band during weekly concerts in the park in the early days of the century, you don't have to bring out his old metal Albert-system clarinet from the attic, dust it off, and try to learn to play it. That's not only a poor reason for studying clarinet but also a poor clarinet to try to use. Another poor reason for studying the

I

clarinet is to enable yourself to enter contests, either in the public schools or elsewhere; if you are already seriously studying clarinet, and if, after some progress, you want to enter a few playing contests, that is fine. But the clarinet should not be taken up as a mere way to gather a collection of contest medals. There is more to music-making than that. Instead, you should love music-making in general, and the clarinet in particular, in order to be properly motivated to study the clarinet. That love is the first requirement.

To fulfill that requirement you should have a great desire to play the clarinet for its own sake, but perhaps even more important than that you should possess an intense desire to create, and to become expressive, within the art of music. You should feel personally confident in the quality of your playing and the development of your art. And it is essential to success that you possess what psychologists would call a good self-concept. The creative impulse must come from within rather than from someone else such as a tyrannical teacher or a domineering relative. Many fine players have developed their skills under the external influence of such teachers and relatives, but if that influence is stronger than the player's own inner impulse he will eventually come up against a creative barrier due to the simple fact that he lacks the necessary self-motivation. It all comes back to having an excellent self-concept for, without that, the perseverance the developing player needs will become a chore rather than the immensely rewarding experience that it should be.

Another requirement of fine clarinet playing is "a good ear." This can be said of fine playing on any instrument, of course, for it is absolutely essential. Some people seem to have the idea that anyone can learn to play an instrument well if they just practice hard enough, but that is not true. A violinist I know once told me a story about an adult beginning student who came to him with the idea that if he, the student, worked hard and diligently practiced for exactly 14,000 hours, he would automatically become a first-rate violinist. The man had computed the 14,000 hours by figuring out how much time a child prodigy would have to practice before reaching adulthood, and he felt that if a child could do that, so could he. What actually happened was that this man had to give up the struggle after a few months because he lacked a good ear. He discovered that there is much more to becoming a first-rate violinist than the number of hours spent practicing.

What we call a good ear cannot, unfortunately, be taught; you must be born with it, just as you must be born with any other aspect of "talent." This does not mean, however, that your "ear" cannot be "improved" through study. The clarinetist's knowledge of music and his ability to interpret it are tremendously enhanced by "ear training," as that term is used by music theory teachers today. In fact, such study is essential to fine clarinet playing. You can also train your ear through intelligent listening to your own clarinet playing and that of others. You must be able to distinguish an interval, or the distance between two tones, before you play the two tones in question; you must be able to play in tune with yourself and with others; and you must work toward developing a fine tone quality in the sound that issues forth from your clarinet. All these things are essential to the development of a good ear, and a good ear is essential to the development of these things.

The clarinetist's next requirement is a good teacher. No blanket statement can adequately describe a good teacher, but I strongly feel that the best clarinet teachers are those who can both play and teach. There are fine players who, unfortunately, are unable to communicate with students. Equally unfortunately, there are articulate people who cannot back up their communication skills with good playing experience. It becomes obvious, then, that you should pick for your clarinet teacher a fine player who has demonstrated the results of good teaching through his former students. This represents the ideal situation, of course, and the ideal cannot always be attained. So, if a choice must be made between these two strengths, I recommend giving preference to the fine player. If such a player's interest in teaching goes beyond monetary considerations, he will at least try to explain to the student what he is doing to achieve his fine playing, and he will be able to set goals for you. The good communicator who cannot play well, however, is communicating to you from a very limited frame of reference. In clarinet teaching, there is no substitute for the teacher's knowledge of how first-class clarinet playing actually feels.

Other personal characteristics required of aspiring clarinetists, such as the ability to be endlessly patient with one's own progress (or with the seeming lack of it), will be dealt with later in the book. But, first, let us consider the clarinetist's equipment and accessories, since musicians have material needs as well as intangible ones.

EQUIPMENT AND ACCESSORIES

Quality equipment is as essential to good clarinet playing as it is to any other craft, of course; but it may surprise many people to learn that the clarinet itself is probably not the most important item on the equipment list. The mouthpiece is the clarinetist's most important object. Second in importance is the *condition* of the clarinet and its mechanism. Next in importance may very well be the reed, and we have already relegated the clarinet itself to fourth place on the list of important pieces of clarinetist's equipment. The specific reasons for listing the mouthpiece, the condition of the clarinet, the reed, and the clarinet itself in that particular order will become clearer as we discuss each of those items later on. Suffice it to say here that each of those items must be of the highest quality obtainable.

The rest of the necessary equipment and accessories is listed here in no particular order.

A *clarinet swab* is necessary to clean and dry the bore of the instrument after each playing, and it's a good idea to use it during long playing sessions which allow condensation to collect inside the instrument. More will be said about this when the care of the clarinet is discussed, but for now please note that allowing excessive moisture to gather in the bore of your clarinet is bad for both the wood in the instrument itself and for the pads covering the tone-holes. A variety of clarinet swabs is available in music stores, but the best one of all is one that you make yourself. Clarinetists know the problems and limitations of most commercially made swabs: They are too short to go through the entire bore of the clarinet so you have to take the whole clarinet apart to swab it out; they have little, rough, hard-to-control metal weights that may, and often do, scratch the surface of the clarinet bore; and finally, many of them fail to absorb moisture well. In order to make a superior swab you need three things: a large piece of fabric, a 40-inch shoe- or bootlace, and a piece of wooden doweling about the same length and diameter as a new, unsharpened pencil. (In fact, a new, unsharpened pencil will work just as well.) All you do is sew 10 or 12 inches of one end of the bootlace onto a corner of your material in such a way that it extends straight from the corner toward the center of the material. In other words, sew it on so that when you use it later as a swab, the string will pull a corner of the material into the clarinet first, rather than the middle of a straight side of it. The material can either be a three-sided or a four-sided piece, and of course, the little plastic endpiece on the shoestring should be cut off. After you have attached the string to the cloth, simply sew the doweling (or the pencil) into the interior of the other end of the shoelace. Once it is inside, stitch across the end of the shoelace to keep the wooden piece from falling out, and stitch across the shoelace at the other end of the wooden piece so that it will not fall down even farther into the shoelace toward the piece of material. Your new swab will be ready to use when you make sure it fits through the bore of the clarinet. Drop the weighted end of the swab into the assembled clarinet (minus the mouthpiece, of course) at the bell end, watching for it to emerge at the barrel-joint end, and then try to pull the material through; if it gets stuck in the clarinet, remove it by taking the clarinet apart around it. Then trim the material to size. When the fit is right, hem the material all around the edges so that it will not fray too readily during use. I have a black swab that my wife made for me from a woman's head scarf, and it has worked very well for several years.

A *reed clipper* is indispensable during the processes of reed preparation and adjustment, and its proper use will be discussed in Chapter 11, "Reeds." The best reed clippers are made by the Cordier company in France. There are many less expensive ones on the market, and although none of them compares with the Cordiers, a young student learning to work with reeds can do very nicely at first with a less expensive clipper. Eventually, though, a Cordier reed clipper should be purchased. When choosing one, take along to the music store a few old reeds that you won't be using any more and test the reed clippers to make sure they cut cleanly and evenly.

A few pieces of the finest-grained *sandpaper* are just as indispensable while working with reeds as the reed clipper is. Be sure to get the finest available, such as 600A or something even finer, or else you will tear far too much wood off your reeds, especially when the paper is new. Again, proper use of the sandpaper will be discussed in Chapter 11, "Reeds." Many clarinetists recommend using Dutch rush, or reed rush, for some of the same purposes that I use sandpaper, but I think that a small piece of sandpaper wrapped around the index finger works just as well, and it is much more readily available than Dutch rush.

Next, in order to have something to use the sandpaper on, you will need a piece of *plate glass*. This can be any size from a few square inches on up. Plate glass is a big help in working with reeds, and for sanding purposes it is unsurpassed. When sanding on it, always use the same spot on the glass, since repeated sanding does mar the surface of the glass. Some clarinetists use Plexiglas or some sort of sheet plastic, but plastic seems to me to wear down too quickly if it is used for sanding. When you buy the piece of glass, request that the glass company buff down the edges so that they will not be sharp. If you are thinking of making your own reeds, see Chapter 11, "Reeds," in which I give more specific information on the sizes and thicknesses of glass to buy.

A reed *scraping knife* is absolutely essential if you are going to make your own reeds (see Chapter 11, "Reeds," again). It can be a big help even with commercially made reeds. Any knife, I suppose, could be used if it will take a keen edge on a straight blade. The well-known Exacto knives have the advantage of using disposable blades, eliminating any sharpening process. Many clarinetists use such knives. The serious reed worker, however, should have a fine, straight, beveled-edged knife such as the ones used by bassoonists in making their reeds. The bassoon knives seem handier for making single reeds than do the oboe knives, and there are several music supply mail-order houses that sell both bassoon-reed scraping knives and clarinet-reed scraping knives without bothering to tell the buyer that they are one and the same knife!

A supply of *cork grease* is needed in order to properly lubricate the cork-covered tenon joints of the clarinet. Without cork grease the corks will dry out, crack, tear, and cause air leaks between the clarinet's joints.

A *soft-bristle brush,* such as one of the larger sizes commonly used by schoolchildren for their watercolors, is excellent for keeping dust and dirt out of the mechanism of the clarinet. An occasional brushing under the keys and around posts and rods is a good way to keep up the appearance of your clarinet, and may even help to maintain smooth working order.

A small bottle of *key oil,* or of sewing machine oil, is useful for occasional application to the key mechanism, at the various points where moving parts meet, again to maintain good working order. A stiff or sluggish mechanism simply makes clarinet technique more difficult than it already is.

Just like a fine piece of furniture, the wooden bore of the clarinet needs to be taken care of, and for this you need some *bore oil.* There are various kinds of commercially prepared bore oils, but the best one is probably already in your home: It is olive oil, just as good for the wood of your clarinet as it is for dressing your salads. To apply the oil to the bore of the clarinet you need a special *oiling swab.* This has to be a different swab from the one you use for normal cleaning and drying because, if you use the same one, you will soon have an excessive amount of oil in the bore. Use an old swab that you have put into retirement, or make a special swab as described on page 4, but do *not* use a commercially made oil swab that contains a twisted metal handle! That metal handle can do more harm to your clarinet bore during one use than you might ever do by failing to oil the bore at all. Whatever you use to apply bore oil should be just as soft and smooth as your regular swab is. The proper way to oil a clarinet bore will be discussed in Chapter 3, "The Clarinet Itself and Barrel Joints."

In order to replace any screws that may be working their way out of your key mechanism, you should have a special *repairman's screwdriver*. Or you could use a jeweler's screwdriver, or any other small screwdriver that has a small blade. The screwdriver is especially useful if it has a small but very long blade. It is possible to purchase screwdrivers with a selection of interchangeable blades.

On the list of required materials needed by a clarinetist there must be, of all things, the humble *pencil*. A pencil may seem insignificant but the experienced player knows that when he needs to write something down and he finds himself without a pencil handy, he feels silly. A pencil is very helpful during individual practice sessions, and many ensemble conductors become enraged at players who have nothing to write with during rehearsals. Keep a pencil right beside your other clarinet supplies.

Unless you have access to institution-owned equipment, you must have your own *music stand*. Many parents of young students fail to see why their little clarinetists can't simply prop up the music on the piano (this puts the music up much too high and sometimes causes actual damage when the clarinet and piano keyboard collide) or, worse, they fail to see why the music can't be propped up inside the clarinet case lying open on the bed. Any clarinetist could tell those parents that playing problems can easily develop when a young student is attempting to read his music at an undesirable angle, since it forces him to hold his clarinet at an equally undesirable angle. Get a music stand!

Not as essential as the other items I have mentioned, but helpful enough to be included here, is the *clarinet stand*. Usually made of wood or metal, with one or more pegs mounted on it, it is specifically designed for holding clarinets in a vertical position. Players in symphony orchestras use the two-peg variety on the floor in front of them in order to facilitate changing rapidly from the B-flat to the A clarinet and back again, but even in the home it is better to stand the clarinet up on a peg during a short interruption than to lay the clarinet down on its keys.

Finally, clarinetists should have a *place* to store their clarinets and equipment and to practice without being disturbed and without disturbing others. I have often encountered the sad plight of a young student who has several brothers and sisters, some of them sharing the same room he uses for playing and sleeping. It is no wonder at all that such a student is discouraged from practicing. Even if you are an older, more experienced clarinetist, it is essential that you have a special place to keep your things and to practice your clarinet. It should be a place that is used for nothing else, so that if you are, for instance, working on reeds, you can leave your work where it sits and return to it later, knowing that nothing will come along in the meantime to disturb it. A special table or desk, containing several drawers, is excellent for the purpose, and, better yet, if you have such a luxury available, is a separate room to put it in.

The commercial music supply industry has an endless catalog of clarinet accessories, widely advertised and readily available, but I believe that the items I have listed here are the only ones that are absolutely necessary. To be sure there are products, not mentioned here, that are simply fun to own and that do serve a useful purpose. Perhaps you will enjoy expressing your individuality by owning and using something that nobody else within your circle of acquaintance has. If you get the items I have described here, however, be assured that you are off to a good start with adequate equipment.

CHAPTER

2

Mouthpieces
and
Ligatures

THE MOUTHPIECE

As already noted, the most important part of the clarinet is its mouthpiece. Thus, we will begin our discussion of the clarinet with a description of mouthpieces.

Unfortunately, no two mouthpieces are alike. If we could be sure of a method or system whereby we could duplicate certain existing mouthpieces noted for their high quality, much of our trouble concerning mouthpieces would disappear. There is no such system, however, and, due to the countless factors affecting mouthpiece quality, there probably never will be such a system. In mouthpiece selection, then, we must do the best we can with available knowledge and with intelligent selection. Although mass-produced mouthpieces, manufactured on an assembly line, are made

9

of the same materials and to the same specifications, they are never entirely uniform. Even the mouthpieces made to the same specifications by a master craftsman who specializes in refacing mouthpieces are never exact duplicates of one another, although such a craftsman will be able to come very close to his own ideal.

Let me describe the mouthpiece more fully: The parts of the mouthpiece are the facing, the window, the side-rails and the tip-rail, and the chamber. The facing is the flat part of the mouthpiece on which the reed is placed, and it extends from the bottom of the mouthpiece up towards the tip. Some musicians have referred to this flat part as the "table" or the "lay"; still others have referred to the lower, straight section of it as the "table" and to the upper part that gradually curves away from the reed as the "facing," but I prefer to call the entire flat reed-placement area the "facing." The window is the approximately rectangular-shaped opening in the mouthpiece that leads down into the bore; the side-rails and the tip-rail are the edges of the facing that surround the window at the sides and at the tip; and the chamber is the hollowed-out area inside the mouthpiece.

Clarinet mouthpieces have been made from many different materials such as wood, metal, crystal, plastic, or hard rubber. Wood, metal, and plastic are not recommended since each possesses at least one fatal flaw such as a lack of durability or poor tone quality. Many fine clarinetists advocate crystal, or glass mouthpieces. I have heard excellent tone quality produced with crystal. On the whole, however, I prefer mouthpieces that have been bored from hard rod rubber, and I recommend that you try to select a mouthpiece made from that material. Hard rubber seems to me to possess more advantages and fewer drawbacks than the other materials do, and apparently most good mouthpiece manufacturers, as well as most good clarinetists, agree on this.

MOUTHPIECE SELECTION

To select a good mouthpiece you must first be sure of what it is you want. That is another deceptively simple statement; you may think you know what you want, but do you? If you have not played clarinet for very long, it may be best for your teacher to select a mouthpiece for you. You should do your own choosing only after you are sure of exactly what you want.

The trying-out of new mouthpieces must always be done on a

clarinet that you are used to; otherwise you will have no true basis for comparison. This is also why it is not a good idea to get a new clarinet and a new mouthpiece at the same time; you should get accustomed to one before trying the other.

There are four criteria upon which to judge a mouthpiece: (1) intonation, or its ability to play in tune with itself and with other instruments; (2) tone quality; (3) response, or its willingness to begin a sound exactly when you want it to, or its ability to "speak"; and (4) freedom, or its ease of blowing. These four criteria are all very important and I have not listed them in any particular order. You must be very careful not to allow the last two, response and freedom, to take precedence over the first two, intonation and tone quality. It is easy to be fooled by a very responsive, free-blowing mouthpiece, and you might discover later that you are not pleased with its tuning or with its "sound." Insist upon response and freedom, to be sure, but be certain that you like the mouthpiece's tuning and tone quality first.

To test a mouthpiece for intonation, play octaves, perhaps in long tones, and really listen to them. Are the octaves in tune, or do they sound rather narrow or rather wide? Play slow-moving scales, listening to each interval. It is a good idea to play these octaves and scales at very different volume levels, too, to make sure that the loudness or softness of your playing does not unduly affect the pitch. Finally, enlist the help of another clarinetist and play slow-moving scales with him in octaves and in unison to check the pitch. The final test for intonation is playing duets to see whether you have any unusual intonation problems in a playing situation. Many experienced players would argue that I have forgotten to mention an obvious test for intonation: the use of an electronic tuning machine. It may be a good idea to check your pitch with a machine, but I am somewhat skeptical of that approach for several reasons. The machine may be very accurately calibrated, but it will never make any music of its own! The world's finest players, using their own excellent clarinets, would never be able to match pitches to the electronic satisfaction of the machine, and I submit that they don't have to do so. Among fine players in any ensemble there has to be a certain amount of give-and-take that constantly shifts from one tone to the next. An experienced player knows this and adjusts accordingly, but it is all too easy for a younger player to be mistaken about whether his mouthpiece plays in tune if he takes the machine too seriously. Use the machine to look for glaring discrepancies, if you must (but even there I would claim that if the discrepancies are all that glaring they will show up in normal playing), but take the machine, otherwise, with a grain of salt.

To test a new mouthpiece for tone quality, simply discover whether it is easy to achieve the full range of tone colors that you desire from that mouthpiece. If you like the basic tone quality, something that no one can adequately describe in words and something that is a matter of personal taste anyway, try playing different musical styles at different volume levels, attempting at the same time to be very expressive and mindful of the phrasing, and decide whether you are satisfied with the mouthpiece from those standpoints. If you need a little more guidance on that, I have attempted a description of ultimate tone quality near the end of Chapter 5, "The Embouchure."

To test a new mouthpiece for its response, play long tones in the low and the high ranges of the instrument at both soft and loud volume levels. Then play a familiar piece of music that contains many different types of articulations in varying patterns. Through it all, observe whether the mouthpiece is responding to your wishes.

To test the new mouthpiece for the fourth criterion, freedom, see whether it feels "stuffy" or "sluggish" during your long tones as well as during quicker-moving phrases of regular music. If you require a thinner reed than you are used to, I would recommend rejecting that mouthpiece. The resistance that is necessary in good clarinet playing should be built into the reed, and not into the clarinet or the mouthpiece. This opens up a whole new area for discussion, and to pursue it further see Chapter 11, "Reeds." Meanwhile, though, let's just say that your new mouthpiece should maintain free-blowing qualities while using the same strength of reed that you are already used to, and that, in any case, it should not force you to go to a softer reed. If you have been used to playing on relatively soft reeds and the new mouthpiece requires firmer ones, that may well be permissible and desirable, but don't go the other way in reed strength.

MOUTHPIECE FACINGS

The foregoing description of an approach to mouthpiece selection should be adequate for the purpose; using the four criteria mentioned is of utmost importance. However, more should be said about mouthpiece facings, since they have such an effect upon the playing qualities of both the mouthpiece and the reed. You will find it useful and informative, also, during your gathering up of several trial mouthpieces, to understand how mouthpiece makers and refacers measure and record the differences between various facings.

In the earlier days of the twentieth century there was no standardized method of scientifically comparing different mouthpiece facings, but the refacer Erick Brand of Elkhart, Indiana, came up with a system in the 1920s or 1930s. This method has become well known and works very well. Before describing it, however, one point must be made very clear: The facing is only one of a great many factors affecting the playing behavior of any particular mouthpiece. Some of the other important factors include the mouthpiece chamber's size and shape, the material used in manufacturing the mouthpiece, the reed, the clarinet's barrel joint, the rest of the clarinet, and the player's embouchure and breath support. The facing does have a tremendous effect on reed behavior, however, and also on how easily your clarinet will respond to your playing activities. With the facing's importance in its proper perspective, then, and with our eyes wide open, we will proceed with a discussion of the Erick Brand method of facing measurement.

This method measures two different aspects of a mouthpiece facing: (1) the length of the facing's curve (that is, the distance between the point where it begins curving away from the reed, and the tip of the mouthpiece) and (2) the tip-opening of the mouthpiece (that is, the distance between the tip of the mouthpiece and the tip of the reed). For brevity's sake, these two measurements are referred to as the facing's "length" and "tip-opening," respectively. The length is expressed by a numeral representing the number of half-millimeters of curve length, and the tip-opening is expressed by a numeral that is actually representative of percentage of a millimeter, or which could be thought of as hundredths of millimeters.

We will discuss the method of measuring the curve, or the "length," first. Erick Brand has manufactured a transparent glass gauge that is used in conjunction with metal feeler gauges of the same type as that used by auto mechanics in their work with spark plugs and distributor points. The glass gauge is placed on the mouthpiece facing just as a reed would be (without a ligature, of course) and then four different metal feeler gauges are placed, in turn, between the glass and the mouthpiece to gauge the amount and the degree of the facing's curve. The four feeler gauges are the "constant" here (they are .0015, .010, .024, and .034 inches in thickness) and the points at which they come to rest between the glass and the mouthpiece are "variable" from one facing to the next. The glass gauge has score marks and numerals representing half-millimeters; by looking through the glass at the feeler gauge it is easy to obtain the reading. (At this point I should say that clarinet and soprano saxophone facings are both read in this manner; for larger reed-instrument mouthpieces a fifth feeler gauge is used in addition to the first four; it is .050 inch in thickness.)

To give an example, let us say that you have positioned the glass on the facing, tip to tip, and that you have inserted the .0015 inch feeler gauge between them. If the bottom edge of the feeler gauge is even with the numeral 36 on the glass the curve on that mouthpiece facing departs from its contact with the reed at a point 36 half-millimeters (or 18 millimeters) from the tip of the mouthpiece. (Half-millimeters are used instead of whole ones in order to use whole numbers rather than fractions.) You would write down the 36 and proceed with the .010 inch feeler gauge, which might produce a reading of 22, since it is thicker than the first gauge and won't go into the crevice as far. Next the third feeler gauge (.024 inch) is inserted, and may very well produce a reading of 12. The final feeler-gauge (.034 inch) reading may be 6. Having written down all four numbers in a vertical column like this:

$$36$$
$$22$$
$$12$$
$$6$$

you would be ready to measure the tip-opening, which is the second and final step in measuring a mouthpiece facing.

Remember that the tip-opening of a mouthpiece is measured in terms of millimeter percentages. Two different types of gauges are used for this purpose: One of them is a solid metal taper gauge, and the other is a dial-indicator gauge. Either one will do, and both are, or have been, available from the Erick Brand Company. The taper gauge is used in conjunction with the same glass gauge mentioned in the foregoing section for measuring the curve, and the dial-indicator gauge comes with its own built-in glass base serving the same purpose. Whichever gauge type is used, it will tell you the distance between the mouthpiece tip and the reed tip expressed in hundredths of millimeters.

To give an example of this, suppose you take a reading with your tip-opening gauge (whichever of the two styles you own) and the reading shows 105. This would mean that there is a distance of

1.05 millimeters between the respective tips of the mouthpiece and the reed, or 105 percent of a millimeter. (Once again, avoid fractional values since whole numbers are easier to work with.) You would now write the 105 at the bottom of your column of facing-curve measurements. In our example (which happens to be the facing measurements of my own mouthpiece) the finished, written measurements of the facing would then look like this:

36
22
12
6
105

But Erick Brand's facing measurement system also provides for a sort of "shorthand," abbreviated expression of its results. If an actual refacing job is required, it is good to use the entire list of five numbers such as I gave in the preceding example. But, if you want to know quite a bit about a facing just for your own and other clarinetists' information, it is permissible to express our example, for instance, as one five-digit number: 36105. This combines the full "length" reading (36, here) with the reading of the tip-opening (105, here). Erick Brand claims, and experience bears him out, that the three other feeler-gauge readings (in our case, the 22, 12, and 6) will be taken more or less for granted in nearly *all* mouthpieces whose length is 36; so it is not absolutely essential that those three figures be included. Looking at it another way, you learn nearly all you need to know about a mouthpiece facing by learning the first and the last of the five readings.

The feeler gauges, the glass gauge, and the tip-opening gauge are all available from: Erick Brand, 1117 West Beardsley, Elkhart, Indiana 46514.

SOME ADVICE ABOUT MOUTHPIECES

These facing measurements, of course, have meaning only to someone who has compared the measurements of several mouthpieces. For this reason, perhaps it would be a good idea to attempt to establish what an average or middle-of-the-road facing measurement may be. I have mentioned that my mouthpiece, which is a Sumner model refaced by the artistic craftsman Robert Scott of Lansing, Michigan, has a facing measurement briefly expressed as 36105. I would call this facing a fairly long, fairly close one, meaning that the length of 36 is rather longer, perhaps, than average, and that a tip-opening of 105 is perhaps "closer" than average. To define what "average" actually means here, however, would probably be impossible. Maybe an average length might be 34 or so (that is 17 millimeters, remember) and maybe an average tip-opening might be around 110 (that, remember, is 1.10 millimeters) but these "averages" are pure speculation on my part. The point is, in fact, that the average (34110) is only useful as a point of statistical departure or reference, and I am not recommending that anyone rush out to have his mouthpiece refaced immediately to fit either this 34110 or any other particular facing. You must search for the mouthpiece you like, using the four criteria discussed earlier, no matter what its facing is. I have seen mouthpiece facings ranging all the way from almost no curve or opening at all (about 29088) to those so open that they appear to be almost ready to take a bite out of the player's embouchure (about 38143). And, somewhere, there is probably a player who would be happy with one or the other of those facings. Despite differing players and differing embouchures and tastes, it is possible to make some very general recommendations, and to establish some general guidelines that will be valid for the great majority of serious clarinetists.

I recommend very strongly that you stay away from facings that are either extremely open or extremely closed. Playing problems, particularly in the areas of tone and pitch, are bound to develop while using such facings. Even if you think you are accustomed to an extreme facing, your ability to play in one or another of the clarinet's registers is being impaired to a much greater extent than you realize. The only test for this is to try a mouthpiece that has a more moderate facing, to fit a reed to it, and to give this new setup a fair trial. I predict that the result will pleasantly amaze you.

My theory is that both the long, open and the short, open facings present problems because the reed is forced to vibrate "out of phase," since either way, it will have to be literally bent out of shape to be put in phase by the embouchure. The result, when the reed's natural position has to be so distorted, can only be embouchure and tonal problems. In general, the more open the facing is, the softer the reed it must take. The softer (or thinner) the reed, the less tone. Thin reeds lack backbone, so the very open mouthpiece is inadequate even if it has grown "comfortable."

On the other hand, the short, closed facing doesn't allow the reed enough room to respond and vibrate properly, and results in a relatively sluggish, harsh tone.

Considering all this, I have come to favor a fairly long, fairly close facing (that is, fairly long and fairly close as compared to my theoretical average, which I have set as 34110), and that approach has brought me to my 36105 facing. This type of facing allows the use of a reed with a good heart in it which contributes to a full, beautiful tone, and it also allows for a thin reed tip for good response. I repeat, however, that even a long, closed facing must never be extreme; I recommend that you look for a medium-long, medium-close facing, and that you then play on it with a firm (thick-hearted) but responsive (thin-tipped) reed. For further information on this subject, see Chapter 11, "Reeds."

Fine clarinetists could debate about mouthpieces and facings forever. This is as it should be, since we are dealing with an art form. My only hard-and-fast piece of advice about mouthpieces is to be sure that the mouthpiece you choose was selected on the basis of the four criteria mentioned earlier. Be sure that you really like that mouthpiece because of how it plays for you, and that you did not get it just because someone else had one like it. You owe it to yourself and to your musicianship to maintain your individuality, your intelligence, and your artistic taste throughout your search for a mouthpiece.

After you have found a fine mouthpiece for your own playing, stick with it! Too often players become faddists and begin playing on so many different mouthpieces that they lose track of what they were originally looking for. Conduct a thorough search, and when you have found an excellent mouthpiece, treasure it and use it for all it is worth. The perfect mouthpiece, like the perfect player, doesn't exist.

CARE OF THE MOUTHPIECE

Probably the first rule of mouthpiece care is that you must exercise great caution while placing the ligature (the clamp or similar device used for holding the reed in place) and the protective cap upon the mouthpiece, particularly if you are using ligatures and mouthpiece caps made of metal. The tip-rail of any mouthpiece is extremely delicate, and any denting or nicking will probably prove fatal to the proper performance of the mouthpiece. Ideally the mouthpiece should be stored separately from everything else in the case, including the ligature and cap, preferably in its own cloth bag or in a plastic container lined with a rag. If you feel you do want to keep the mouthpiece in the case with the ligature and cap on it (but with the *reed removed;* see Chapter 11, "Reeds"), be sure to keep them rather loosely fitted together.

The mouthpiece must be kept clean if it is to do its job properly. When storing the mouthpiece after a playing session, remove the reed and dry the mouthpiece inside and out. If you have a completely soft swab without any rough or abrasive part on it, as you should, I recommend pulling the swab through the mouthpiece, bottom to top. If your swab is one with any exposed metal or hard plastic on it, take the advice of many clarinetists and never pull your swab through your mouthpiece. A rough swab could not only scratch the chamber considerably but could, over a period of time, alter the dimensions of the chamber, ruining the mouthpiece. Instead of swabbing, then, you should wash the mouthpiece with mild soap and lukewarm water once a week or so, greasing the cork first to protect it from the cleaning agents. Whether you rely on washing or on a soft swab, be sure to keep the mouthpiece clean; otherwise, foreign particles will alter the dimensions of that chamber you spent so much time and trouble selecting.

An over-tight ligature on the mouthpiece has been known to warp the mouthpiece itself and so, while you are playing on it and while it is stored in your case, be sure to tighten the ligature no more than is absolutely necessary. And consider this: If a tight ligature can warp a mouthpiece, imagine what it can do to your reeds!

A good mouthpiece, regardless of its facing, must never have even a *trace* of a scratch or a nick on the tip-rail or the side-rails; in nearly all cases of damaged rails the mouthpiece is a source of air leaks, reed squeaks, or uneven reed vibration. Please don't "get used to" such a mouthpiece; replace it!

One horror story about damaged mouthpiece rails involved a student of mine, and this is one of those stories that seems funny in retrospect. This student was practicing in his bedroom one evening when he decided to go down to the kitchen for a drink of water. While downstairs he spent several minutes talking with his mother. When he returned to his room he discovered his three-month-old German shepherd gaily chewing on the mouthpiece and reed which were still attached to the clarinet! The puppy had not pulled the clarinet off the chair, fortunately, but the reed looked like a miniature Japanese fan and the mouthpiece rails appeared to have been freshly pressed by a waffle iron.

Sometimes the appearance of a new mouthpiece can be deceiving; shiny, smooth mouthpiece rails are occasionally so warped and uneven that the mouthpiece is unplayable. Another student, who bought a new mouthpiece shortly before he began his lessons with me, complained that he was having a terrible time with squeaks. His mouthpiece looked beautiful, but after I had applied the facing measurement tools to it, the extreme unevenness of its facing became obvious. The side-rails of that mouthpiece were so erratic that they were thoroughly confusing the vibrations of the reed which, in turn, could do nothing but squeak in protest. The purchase of this student's next mouthpiece was negotiated much more intelligently.

LIGATURES (OR HOW TO PLAY CLARINET ON A SHOESTRING)

A clarinet ligature is nothing more than something to hold the reed in place on the mouthpiece in such a manner that the reed will not shift position or fall off. What makes a ligature desirable, then, is its ability to do that and to do nothing else. Every ligature that I have ever seen, no matter what its design, has been able to hold the reed in place, but I have seen very few ligatures that fulfill their proper function without causing some new problem of their own.

The ideal ligature is one that holds the reed on the mouthpiece by exerting only the slightest amount of pressure evenly distributed on the reed. Contrary to popular belief, reed vibrations do not stop at the end of the upper part of the reed while playing; the vibrations continue down into the lower part of the reed where the ligature is placed in a manner that could be described as "follow-through." Just as a tennis player needs a follow-through motion with his racquet after making contact with the ball, the upper part of the reed needs to be allowed the freedom of sending its vibrations down into the lower part of the reed, where they can stop more naturally than they would if they were suddenly clamped off. The placement and amount of ligature pressure on the reed, therefore, can make or break this aspect of clarinet playing. In simplest terms, we need to remember that the reed vibrations are what cause the sound, that the manner in which the reed is held on the mouthpiece will greatly affect reed vibration, and thus the lowly ligature takes on a far greater significance than many players realize.

The most commonly used of all ligatures, the all-metal ones with two adjustment screws, are not very good. They tend to stifle reed vibration even when not tightened too much, because of their inherent rigidity, which results in a very uneven distribution of pressure on the reed. I have seen metal ligatures so malformed that, even with a very slight tightening of the screws, they move the reed over to one side of the facing. An off-center reed will not vibrate properly, and the inexperienced player tends to blame the reed even when the ligature is actually at fault. This uneven clamping of the reed, a fault in the two-screw metal ligature, will also result in a reduction of tonal quality and volume, since it cuts off part of the vibrating overtone series.

If a two-screw metal ligature is used, it should be turned so that the screws are on the top of the mouthpiece; this will prevent pinching of the reed fibers by the screw side of the ligature.

A ligature with only one adjustment screw has the advantage of putting less pressure on the reed, but on the whole it may be even worse than the two-screw type because it does not cover enough of the reed. Because the lower part of the reed dries out unevenly, a ligature with one adjustment screw easily results in reed warpage.

It is worse if a metal ligature has a contoured pressure plate on the inside of it against the bark of the reed, because those pressure plates hardly ever allow the reed to be properly centered on the mouthpiece. If one reed fits that pressure plate fairly well, the next reed will probably not fit, so great is the difference between one reed's contour and another's.

Having said all that, I will turn right around and recommend that for the sake of cheapness, easy availability, and ease of handling the two-screw metal ligature should be used by beginners and by other less advanced players. Accomplished players will also find them useful for preliminary reed selection and for other occasions when quick reed removal and replacement is an advantage, but such accomplished players, in my opinion, would do well to use a ligature of much better design and quality for their regular playing. In short, good players high-school-aged and older should not use a metal ligature, but rather, something less rigid that gives a more evenly distributed pressure to the reed.

There is one exception to my general ruling against metal ligatures, and the only one that has come to my attention so far, and that is a metal ligature marketed by Harrison-Hurtz Enterprises, at P.O. Box 268, Wymore, Nebraska 68466. These ligatures are very costly, compared with the more common type, but if you must use a metal ligature, the Harrison-Hurtz model is the best I have seen. It exerts very little pressure, which is evenly distributed.

Plastic screw-type ligatures, such as those made by Bonade, Gigliotti, and others, are a great improvement over nearly all of the metal ones, mainly due to the much greater flexibility of the plastic material. For me, however, the distribution of pressure remains a problem, and the plastic ligatures with only one screw do not cover enough area of the reed, and may cause warpage while playing.

The ligature should lightly but evenly touch the bark of the reed that lies within the physical dimensions of the ligature. The ligature should be made of some sort of elastic fabric band. Fabric stores sell a product called Velcro, a strip of which can be easily wrapped around a mouthpiece and reed. The two ends, where they meet, will stick to each other, forming a fine ligature that has almost no disadvantages.

Traditionally, the German ligature was simply constructed by wrapping a string around the mouthpiece and reed. The string ligature offers marvelous playing qualities because of its smooth, even, and light pressure on the reed, but the wrapping process is laborious, time-consuming, and annoying. To that inconvenience is added the extra task of having to tie a knot in the end of it to keep it from unwrapping while playing. Considering those disadvantages, it is little wonder that most players have abandoned the idea of tying a string to the mouthpiece.

Nevertheless, when I was a college student I became intrigued by my newly acquired knowledge of the old German string-tying method and, because of its reported advantages, I determined to give the method a try. I first tried wrapping my mouthpiece with regular string but I became frustrated with how long it took to wrap enough string to constitute a good ligature, and I was thoroughly discouraged by my inability to finish it off with a good knot.

Then, the humble shoestring occurred to me. I obtained an ordinary black 27-inch shoestring (the flat, wide ribbon type, not the hard-finished round string type) and cut the little piece of plastic off one end. I began winding it on the reed and mouthpiece from the cut-off end and, because of the greater width of this shoestring, it was only necessary to wind the string around the mouthpiece six times. I then took the loose end, which still had its little plastic point on it, and wedged that point in between a couple of my earlier wrappings. Eureka! I have never used another ligature in my regular playing since.

Years later, I am still amazed at the effect that this string ligature has had on my playing. The reed is held in place evenly all over the entire lower half of the reed, and the pressure is just as gentle as that expected from wrapped cloth. Tone quality, tonal volume, and even the response are tremendously enhanced, all because the shoestring ligature fulfills the criterion for judging a good ligature: It does its job without creating new problems of its own.

The screw-type ligature slips over the mouthpiece more quickly than does the shoestring, but it takes much longer to adjust the reed properly within the screw-type ligature than it does within the shoestring. Thus, the metal ligature carries no advantage over the string in the amount of time it takes to position the reed properly. And while using the string ligature, the reed is easily adjusted without disturbing the wrapping in any way; yet, never once in all the years I have been using the string has the reed ever moved out of position on the mouthpiece.

I will admit of only one minor inconvenience caused by the shoestring ligature: No mouthpiece cap will fit it. But think about it for a moment, and you may realize that you don't really need that cap after all. No serious player should ever need to leave his mouthpiece out of the case when he isn't using it. Even if you need to leave a busy rehearsal room that is full of people milling around while "taking a break," it is a good safety precaution to take your mouthpiece, with or without reed, with you. If you prefer not to take it with you, you can always put it away in the case again and get it out later. That is safer than leaving your abandoned instrument on a chair or on its stand where someone might trip over it.

Whenever I think that a screw-type ligature might be handier to use, I am immediately reminded of the tremendous playing advantages I enjoy with the shoestring ligature; I am tempted no further. If the shoestring sounds to you like a crazy idea, I only ask that you try it before writing me off as a crank because you may also benefit from its advantages. For people who are not accomplished players, or who have either an inferior mouthpiece or an inferior clarinet there is probably no advantage in the shoestring. But if you are a good player with a good instrument and mouthpiece, I heartily recommend the shoestring ligature, the least expensive one (or rather, two!) on the market.

CHAPTER

3

The Clarinet Itself
and
Barrel Joints

My discussion of the clarinet started with the mouthpiece because the quality of the mouthpiece is more important in the long run than is that of the clarinet. Now it is time, however, to look at the rest of the instrument.

THE CLARINET

The clarinet is a woodwind instrument approximately 26 inches long in its usual B-flat version; the A clarinet is about 1½ inches longer. Woodwinds are wind instruments made up of fixed-length bores (unlike the trombone with its slide). Woodwinds produce sound by means *other* than the player's vibrating lips (unlike the brasses) and are *usually* made of wood. Flutes and saxophones are always made of metal today, but they are still considered wood-winds because of other factors and principles involved.

The clarinet and all other woodwinds except the flute produce sound by means of a vibrating reed. The player's airflow vibrates the reed, and the reed in turn vibrates the air column that already exists inside the instrument. The player's fingers lengthen and shorten the vibrating length of that air column by covering or un-covering the tone-holes on the instrument. This action causes the resulting tone to be relatively high or low. The sound that we hear coming from a clarinet is actually caused by the vibrating air column inside the instrument; it is *not* the sound of the reed vi-brating. The vibrating reed is only the sound generator: it causes the air column to vibrate audibly.

Today the clarinet is usually made of grenadilla wood, some-times called African blackwood because it comes from Africa. The metal keys on clarinets are usually made of an alloy of nickel or silver.

All reed instruments except the clarinet use a cone-shaped bore that tapers gradually from the upper end to the "bell." The clarinet has a cylindrical bore that is slightly hour-glass-shaped. It is not a perfect cylinder; makers have found that both tuning and response are improved when the midpoint of the bore is slightly smaller in diameter than are its top and bottom. At the upper end of the barrel joint the bore diameter is not quite 6/10 of an inch (about .585 of an inch). At the middle point (between the upper and lower joints) the diameter is about .575 inch. From there down-ward it flares outward to nearly an inch at the end of the lower joint, and finally to about 2½ inches at the bottom of the bell.

The clarinet is built in five separate sections for two reasons: first, so that the player can take the clarinet apart for storage in its case; and second, so that the sections can be slightly adjusted at the separable joints for tuning purposes while playing. The upper-most section is the mouthpiece. The remaining four sections in descending order are the barrel joint, the upper joint (for the left hand), the lower joint (for the right hand), and the bell. The barrel and the bell are so called because of their appearance. The only two of the five sections with keys and tone-holes on them are the upper and lower joints that are positioned between the barrel and the bell.

The clarinet has a wide range of tones from low to high. It plays almost as high as the flute does and nearly an octave lower. It plays about a sixth higher and a sixth lower than the oboe. Since the saxophone's range is comparable to the oboe's, the extent of its range is also narrower than the clarinet. The only woodwind instrument that competes with the clarinet in the width of its range is the bassoon; both the clarinet and the bassoon can cover a range of nearly four octaves. The bassoon can play a little more than an octave lower than the clarinet, but the clarinet can play a little more than an octave higher than the bassoon.

The clarinet's written range extends approximately from the E below the piano's middle C up to the C above high C, or, in other words, to about three octaves above the piano's middle C. This is the *written* range; the actual sound of the B-flat clarinet is a whole step lower than that (hence its name). Similarly, the actual sound of the A clarinet is a minor third lower than it is written, so that its C sounds like an A on the piano. This practice evolved through music history so that clarinets of varying sizes and pitches could be played by the same player without confusion. The various sizes (such as B-flat and A) were necessary because early clarinets did not have many keys on them, a situation that made it very difficult for the player to play music written in complicated key signatures. The clarinetist's job of playing music written "in flats" was made considerably easier if he played it on his B-flat instrument; the same happy result was achieved if he used his A clarinet to play music written "in sharps." Although today's clarinet key systems make it relatively easy to play in any key, the tradition of using both the B-flat and the A clarinets in orchestral and chamber music continues for the same reason it began a couple of centuries ago. The whole step (for the B-flat) or the minor third (for the A) discrepancy is compensated for on the printed page. If composers write for the B-flat clarinet, for example, they write the notes a whole step higher than they would if the music were being written for piano; the B-flat clarinet, built a whole step lower than the piano, automatically corrects the discrepancy. When writing for the A, the composer writes the notes a minor third higher than he would have written them for piano; the instrument itself corrects the discrepancy because of its size.

At this point you may well ask, "Why not use the clarinet in C and forget all about such discrepancies?" The reason is the C clarinet is so much smaller that its tone quality is thinner and more piercing that that of either the B-flat or the A. Throughout history, players and listeners have come to prefer the longer and larger clarinets with their fuller, richer sounds. Flute, oboe, and bassoon are all built in C, but their tone qualities allow for that. Clarinets and saxophones, however, are "transposing" woodwinds; clarinets are built in B-flat, A, and (occasionally) E-flat, and saxophones are built in varying sizes (or "octaves") of B-flat and E-flat. All three sizes of clarinets are used today in symphony orchestras and for solo work; all clarinets except the A are used in today's bands and wind ensembles. When musicians simply refer to "the clarinet," they mean, almost without doubt, the B-flat clarinet.

Since they are slightly different in size, there is a slight difference in tone quality between the B-flat and A clarinets. This difference is so slight that listeners can hardly ever tell which clarinet is being played. Sometimes even clarinetists cannot tell unless they are playing one or the other themselves. Nevertheless, this slight difference is real, and it results from the fact that though the A clarinet is about 1½ inches longer than the B-flat, its bore diameter is essentially the same as the B-flat's. Thus the A clarinet has, in effect, a smaller bore in proportion to its overall length than the B-flat has.

In any case, the tone quality of the B-flat clarinet, as compared to that of the A, could be said to be brighter, more penetrating, and perhaps just a bit more "edgy." The A clarinet, as compared to the B-flat, sounds darker and mellower with a sort of haunting, hollow depth in the sound. When I was a young student I played on the B-flat exclusively, and I remember the first time that I ever played on an A clarinet. During one of my lessons, Keith Stein let me put my mouthpiece on his A clarinet, and, after playing a short exercise on it, I remember saying to him, "You have talked to me about getting a 'round' sort of tone, but *this* clarinet's tone sounds *oval!*" Mr. Stein's amused approval of my remark encouraged me to listen even more closely to the difference between the two instruments, and to this day I truly relish that slight tonal difference.

To compare the sound of the two clarinets I recommend listening to a recording of the Mozart concerto, K. 622, which is played on the A clarinet, and to any of the recorded solo works for clarinet by Weber, which are all played on the B-flat. To make such a comparison a fair one you really should hear these works played by the same soloist, such as, perhaps, Karl Leister with the Berlin Philharmonic.

Because B-flat and A clarinets have essentially the same bore diameter players can play either clarinet with the same mouthpiece. Players who use both in orchestras simply switch the mouthpiece from the B-flat to the A or vice versa, at the proper times.

There are more sizes of instruments in the clarinet family than the ones I have mentioned here so far, of course. For a discussion of smaller and larger clarinets see Chapter 14, "A Look at the Life Story of the Clarinet."

CLARINET ACOUSTICS

How does the clarinet work?

All musical sounds are made of what is actually a series of related sounds, usually referred to as "harmonics." The tones we hear are usually the lowest tone of whatever series is sounding, or what is called the "fundamental" tone. But the fundamental is not a "pure" sound; it is enhanced and highly colored by its "overtones," higher pitches of which we are not consciously aware. In other words, when we hear a musical tone we are hearing not only that tone but also all or (more usually) some of its higher "relatives" (overtones) that are part of its harmonic series.

That different instruments bring out different overtones above their fundamentals accounts for the clarinet sounding different from the oboe, the oboe from the violin, and so forth.

The harmonic series itself is interesting. As a theoretical example of it, here is the harmonic series based on the fundamental tone of low C on a piano:

I have carried this example only to nine tones; the series actually goes on indefinitely. (Notice that the higher one goes in the series, the closer together the overtones are.) The fundamental and the overtones taken together are known as "partials," the fundamental being the first partial and the overtones being the succeeding partials. Notice also that in this "C" series, the first, second, fourth, and eighth partials are all "C." The same partials in an F series would all be different F octaves, and so forth.

Now, the interesting thing about the clarinet's tone quality is that it is comprised almost *entirely* of odd-numbered partials. Its tonal spectrum is made up of first, third, fifth, seventh, and ninth partials almost exclusively. The sixth partial *is* present in a very weakened condition, but the second, fourth, and eighth partials (those octaves again) are entirely absent. And the clarinet is the only instrument with that peculiar characteristic! All others have a more "complete" series without, of course, giving up their individualities.

Why does the clarinet find the even-numbered partials so elusive? What confines the clarinet's tonal spectrum to the odd-numbered partials? Acousticians tell us that it is because the clarinet acts as a "stopped" organ pipe as opposed to an open-ended one. Stopped pipes also have only odd-numbered partials in their tonal spectra, while open pipes (and all other musical instruments) utilize some combination of both odd and even partials.

But the clarinet is open-ended, just like the oboe. What is this business about "acting as a stopped pipe"? The scientists, with weary patience, reply this time that the clarinet acts as a stopped pipe because its bore is cylindrical and not conical as is the oboe's.

But the clarinet's bore is not a perfect cylinder. It is, in fact, less perfectly cylindrical than the bore of the flute, and the flute behaves like the open-ended pipe that it is. This time there is no really good answer from the scientists. They know that the clarinet's bore is basically cylindrical, and that therefore the vibrating air column inside the clarinet doubles back on itself just as it does in a stopped organ pipe. A full explanation has yet to appear. Incidentally, the clarinet's sound wave's doubling-back on itself does explain why the clarinet can play tones of lower pitch than can either the flute or the oboe, even though the clarinet is of about the same length as those two instruments.

Now we will see how this acoustical peculiarity affects the clarinetist. The clarinet's range of pitches is traditionally divided into three sections or "registers." The lowest register is called the "chalumeau," named after an early instrument that was superseded by the clarinet. The second, or middle, register is called the "clarion" register since listeners thought that the earliest clarinets sounded like clarion trumpets from a distance. The highest register is simply called the "altissimo" range.

The chalumeau register extends from the bottom up to the high end of sounding fundamentals, the clarion register extends from there up to the end of the sounding third partials, and the altissimo register extends from the beginning of the sounding fifth partials on up to however much higher the clarinet will play—into the seventh and ninth partials, and so forth. That is, as the clarinet goes up from its chalumeau register (first partials) into its clarion register, the sounds we hear are the third partials. The fundamentals have completely fallen away, so that we actually hear those third partials while they are still being enhanced by the remaining higher overtones. As the clarinet goes from the clarion register into its altissimo register, we hear the fifth partials, still enhanced by seventh and ninth (and some higher) partials, but *minus* any first and third partials. As the altissimo register climbs higher the same principle prevails; whichever partial is actually sounding is enhanced by higher partials in its harmonic series, but no *lower* partials are sounding any more.

The chalumeau register, the clarinet's register of sounding fundamentals, covers this written range:

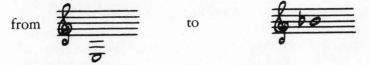

The clarion register, using the sounding third partials without the fundamental first partials, covers this range:

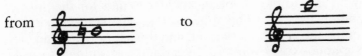

The altissimo register, sounding fifth, seventh, and ninth partials successively as we go higher (minus all firsts and thirds, of course), covers this range:

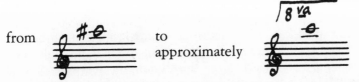

To go further into clarinet acoustics would be to write a separate book; for a more detailed discussion of the subject see the Anthony Baines book on woodwind instruments and their history, listed in the Bibliography.

You may wonder, of course, how the clarinet can have such a wide range of pitches when it is only a small wooden tube and when the player has only ten fingers. The truth is that, basically, all the fingering combinations have to be used over again in each new register. The clarinet fingering pattern is complicated enough to get the player from the bottom note (low E) up through middle-line B-flat, but no further. At that point (beginning with middle-line B-natural) the *same* fingering pattern starts all over again, but this time with the help of a "register key" operated by the left thumb. The register key causes the clarinet to sound its third partials for the clarion register, and to forget all about the fundamental tones it was playing a moment ago down in its chalumeau register. Then, beginning with the C-sharp above the staff, *part* of that same fingering pattern begins all over again, in a slightly altered form, so that the player can convince the clarinet to forget all about fundamentals *and* third partials, and to play in its altissimo register.

HOW TO SELECT A CLARINET

Any musical instrument is expensive to buy today, and clarinets are no exception. However, a clarinet can almost always be purchased for less money than can any other woodwind instrument of comparable quality. Professional-quality flutes and oboes can cost four times as much as professional-quality clarinets. It would probably be easy to buy six or eight fine clarinets for the price of one topnotch bassoon. The soprano and alto saxophones cost about double the price of a clarinet, and the larger tenor and baritone saxophones cost even more. Clarinets are simpler to make than the other instruments; they have the most easily constructed bore and mechanism of any woodwind instrument. In the long run this is a great blessing to clarinetists not only because it helps keep costs down but also because it makes finding a really fine clarinet a little easier.

Generally speaking, manufacturers make clarinets in three different price ranges: student models, intermediate models, and professional models. Nearly all of the student models and some of the intermediate ones are available in a choice of either plastic or wooden bodies. The choice should be carefully considered; wood is generally considered the superior material, but if a student-line clarinet is going to be taken out on the marching field in bad weather (or even in good weather, for that matter) I am dead set against the use of wooden instruments. If there is anything worse for a wooden clarinet than the hot sun, it would be rain, sleet, or snow, one of which you are sure to encounter on almost every outing. In this case, then, the plastic student-line clarinet may be the better choice. Wooden clarinets are superior from the standpoints of tone quality and response, but any harsh weather conditions can easily crack the wood. Technology has advanced far enough now so that plastic clarinets are far better than they used to be.

I have little use for the intermediate-model clarinets today, not because they aren't any good (many of them are excellent) but because they are not superior enough to the student models to warrant such an increase in price. I think that if money is to be spent on a clarinet, the buyer might just as well make an investment and purchase a fine, professional clarinet. Remember that top-quality clarinets do not depreciate in value to any significant degree over the years, though both of the less expensive models become almost worthless in only two or three years.

So, as with the purchase of anything of value, the buying of a particular model of clarinet should be determined by the needs and the goals of the individual player who will own it. For the young player who is solely interested in being a good "band member" during his school years, a good student-line clarinet may be adequate. For the clarinetist who is serious about becoming an excellent player, a professional-model clarinet should be bought no matter how young or old the student is.

As with mouthpieces, a clarinet is chosen by trial. Play several instruments to test them, using a reed, mouthpiece, and ligature combination that you are already familiar with. Also like mouthpieces, some specific criteria should be considered while selecting a clarinet: (1) intonation, (2) tone quality, (3) response, and (4) freedom.

Before considering these four criteria in detail remember that a good clarinet *can't* be selected unless you have a good mouthpiece, reed, and ligature to which you are already accustomed. If you feel unsure, have a more accomplished player select a clarinet *for* you. That would be better than proceeding in ignorance. No matter how accomplished you are, it helps to have another good player, whom you respect, confirm your choice (or choices) of new clarinets. The two of you should each play as the "finalists" in this "contest," and each of you should write down the ranking of the choices by serial number. Later, get together and compare notes. The chances are that you will have agreed on your choices. If there is disagreement, of course, stay with your own choice, because you are the one who will own the instrument.

SELECTION PROCESS I:
Intonation

Today clarinets are built so that, when "warmed up," they will play best "in tune" when the barrel joint is pulled out from the upper joint about ⅛ of an inch. (For further discussion of this, see Chapter 8, "Musicianship," especially its passage on intonation.) When selecting a clarinet, first pull out the barrel about ⅛ of an inch, then play each clarinet by yourself and see if you detect any tuning discrepancies. If not, and if the clarinet is entirely agreeable to play, move on to sterner tests.

When you have narrowed your immediate choices down to about three, play duets with your teacher or with another good player, for tuning purposes. Play scales in octaves with the other person, slowly. Since clarinets are constructed in "twelfths" (the musical distance between the two lower registers, at any given point of similar fingering, is known as the interval of a twelfth), playing in octaves with another clarinetist is perhaps the most telling test to put a clarinet through as a check on its tuning properties, or its evenness in pitch. One particular trouble spot to look for in a clarinet's tuning is in the lowest notes; these notes, at the bottom of the chalumeau register, tend to be quite sharp. A good clarinet is built to minimize this problem.

There are other pitfalls to watch for concerning a clarinet's intonation or tuning. The altissimo D, written above the staff, can be too sharp. An unbearably sharp high C at the upper end of the clarion register might develop if that note's fundamental, thumb F, is even the slightest bit sharp.

On the other hand, there is at least one situation where a tuning discrepancy could be considered an advantage in the long run: If the barrel is pushed all the way in, the throat tones at the top of the chalumeau register should be slightly sharp so that when the barrel is pulled out after warming up, the throat tones will not go flat.

SELECTION PROCESS II:
Tone Quality

A musician's judgment of clarinet tone quality is such a subjective matter that it is most difficult to talk about. Certainly a player should select an instrument whose basic, natural sound is one that he likes. Musical tone is so important within the artistic framework of clarinet playing that the clarinetist must be positive that any new instrument will allow him the freedom to produce the type of sound that he appreciates most. It should be remembered, though, that the tone quality of a new clarinet will improve gradually as the instrument is "broken in" during its first few years.

In Chapter 8, "Musicianship," there is a more detailed discussion of what I mean by the term "tone color," so I won't go into it too much here. You will get the general idea, though, by putting your prospective clarinet through the following tonal tests. Does the clarinet play this passage both very brightly *and* with a darker, more ominous quality?

Does the clarinet also play this next passage in one and then the other of those two extremes?

Notice that I have marked both of the preceding passages to be played "forte" rather than "piano" in order to make certain that you test the clarinet for its extremes of tone color and not merely for its extremes of volume level. Naturally, it would be a good idea to play the same passages again, still testing for tonal color, but this time to play as though the dynamic marking were "p" rather than "f."

SELECTION PROCESS III:
Response

When wind instrumentalists use the term "response," they are referring to the instrument's "willingness to speak when called upon." Some clarinets are reluctant to cooperate with the player in this regard, and response is a most important factor in clarinet playing. Response problems are far more often to be blamed on the reed than they are on the instrument, but still, if you are testing a new instrument, you should be aware that some clarinets are rather unresponsive. Assuming that an unresponsive clarinet is in good mechanical repair, its unresponsiveness is most likely the fault of its bore. In that case, nothing can be done with it; select a different instrument. If the pads look rather worn, however, replace them and test the clarinet again before completely rejecting it for its lack of response.

Test for response by playing isolated long tones; see if those tones begin when you want them to. Play these long tones in all three registers of the instrument, and play them both loudly and softly. Also test the response by playing a piece of music with which you are familiar, listening at all times for accuracy of tonal entrance. Discover whether the clarinet responds with relative ease while you are tonguing rapid passages.

SELECTION PROCESS IV:
Freedom

A clarinetist often hears the phrase "freedom and response" used as though the two nouns were interchangeable. In clarinet playing the two words are indeed related, but they must be distinguished. Response refers to the beginning of a tone; a clarinet's "freedom" reflects what the *rest* of that tone feels like, physically, to the player as he plays it. In short, is the clarinet easy or difficult to blow on? Is its natural resistance to the player's airflow something that remains even and constant over its entire range from low to high, or are some tones noticeably more "stuffy" than others? A clarinet with uneven resistance will not only present its own difficulties but will also be very difficult to fit with a good reed.

A most important point to make here is that a certain amount of resistance to the airflow is *required* in clarinet playing. However, that resistance should be built into the reed and *not* into the clarinet itself. More will be said about this in Chapter 11, "Reeds," but it is important to choose a clarinet that plays evenly from top to bottom, one that is free-blowing rather than stuffy. Your clarinet must give you the freedom to perform the kind of musical, artistic tasks you want to undertake in your clarinet playing.

GENERAL IDEAS
ON CLARINET SELECTION

Do *not* pick an instrument on the basis of appearance; shiny keys, for example, do not mean that the clarinet is a *good* one. Do not pay extra for anything that serves only a cosmetic purpose. To do so is to waste your money. Clarinetists must always be more concerned with the playing qualities of their instruments than they are with how they look.

You may wish to purchase an old clarinet. It is important to be sure that any clarinet, even a new one, is in good playing condition before you test it, and that is especially important in the case of a used clarinet. If the instrument has been played on by its previous owner for a long time, a repairman will need to look at it before you will be able to give it a fair test.

Often players are tempted to buy a clarinet equipped with "extra keys," if only for the sake of novelty. This is usually a mistake. The normal Boehm-system clarinet, with its seventeen keys and six rings, possesses all the keys that are really needed. The overwhelming majority of professional clarinetists prefer this key system. The more keys that are added to a woodwind instrument the more that instrument becomes a mechanical nightmare. I heartily recommend that you stay with the normal Boehm-system clarinet and that you resist the urge to buy a "full Boehm" or any clarinet with a key mechanism that lies somewhere between those two.

I am often asked, usually by parents of high-school clarinetists, what brand-name clarinet should be purchased. From the early 1900s onward, three manufacturers of clarinets have found favor with most American clarinetists, both students and professionals. These three manufacturers are Buffet, Selmer, and Leblanc. All three have their own loyal adherents. My own preference is for the Buffet model R-13 both in B-flat and in A; I believe that a majority of American clarinetists would agree with me in that choice. But clarinetists must remember that Selmer and Leblanc have always made excellent instruments and that the brand name in any case is just a point of departure. Clarinets are to be chosen individually and not by a maker's name; no maker is completely consistent and therefore there are many Selmer and Leblanc clarinets that I would prefer over some individual Buffet clarinets. So, when selecting a clarinet, be sure to do so with an open mind, using the four criteria already described: intonation, tone quality, response, and freedom.

The reign of the big three brand names in America is being challenged by makers from all over the world, especially from Japan. There should always be a ready market for fine French and American clarinets, however, as long as their price stays low.

CARE OF THE CLARINET

A player takes good care of his clarinet for two reasons: The instrument will perform better, and he will be protecting a good investment.

Let's begin by knocking down two myths about clarinet care. First, clarinet keys do not have to be polished. Do not try to maintain a high, shiny gloss on the finish of your clarinet keys by polishing them with a chemically treated cloth! The dried chemicals in such a cloth become powdery when the cloth is briskly rubbed on the keys. This powder flakes off the cloth and falls into (or on) the pads, the tone-holes, and finally into the bore itself. These chemicals also find their way into the key mechanism. Polishing will eventually "gum up the works" of your clarinet. If you must polish your keys, do so with a very clean, lint-free, untreated cloth. Personally I do not polish my keys at all. If your clarinet is worked on periodically by a good repairman, as it should be, buffing the keys on the repairman's wheel will keep them shiny enough. Remember that the functioning of your clarinet's keys is far more important than their appearance.

The second myth concerning clarinet care is that every good clarinetist should be able to do all his own repair work. That notion is so oversimplified that I consider it dangerous. Obviously a good clarinetist who is also mechanically inclined may well be able to maintain his instrument in a fine state of adjustment. Much can be learned from experience, too. But unless you know what you are doing, and unless you are already a good player, *do not attempt anything* in the way of mechanical repair on your clarinet. Instrument repair has been elevated to a high art today and, generally speaking, it should be left to those artisans who have made it their life's work. Even a slightly unseated pad installed by the inexperienced can drastically alter the playing qualities of a clarinet, causing it to "squeak" and to play with entirely too much resistance. The adjustment of the bridge key between the upper and lower joints is especially foolhardy for the amateur to undertake. Still another adjustment to eschew is that of the long extension keys on the lower joint; that particular adjustment is so delicate it should never be attempted by anyone who has not had long experience in clarinet repair. I do not mean that any clarinetist should remain in ignorance as to the mechanism of his instrument, but that mechanism should be respected and treated as the precise machine that it is.

Obviously there are several things a clarinetist *should* do to keep his instrument in good working order. He may easily be able to make fewer trips to the repairman by adopting a program of simple but effective maintenance. To begin with, a fine wooden clarinet is really nothing more than a mechanized piece of wood, and it must be treated like any other fine piece of wood. It must not be allowed to dry out completely or it will crack and leak. To avoid drying and cracking, the bore of the clarinet must be occasionally oiled (see page 37).

Spread out a sheet of newspaper on a table and prepare to oil the four sections (barrel, upper joint, lower joint, and bell) separately. (Do not oil the mouthpiece, of course; it isn't made of wood!) Put just a few, separated drops of oil on the swab and slowly draw it through the barrel joint. The barrel is usually in the greatest need of oil. Slowly and repeatedly draw the lightly oiled swab through the barrel joint until the bore, when it is held up to the light, looks fairly shiny. It should only look shiny; it should never glisten with excessive amounts of oil. Be sure the coating of oil is thin enough so that it will not form running droplets at any time. Also, do not oil the outside of the clarinet; oil only the bore. Enough oil soaks into the wood from the inside out to make oiling the exterior of the clarinet's body unnecessary. The oil is harmful to the pads.

Repeat the process on the upper joint, the lower joint, and the bell. Then leave all four sections on the newspaper to air-dry overnight. Do not play the clarinet until the next day.

How often to oil a clarinet is a subject open to much misunderstanding. Assume that a newly purchased wood clarinet is dry, and oil its bore. Then oil it again about a month later. Oil it a third time two or three months after that, and a fourth time after about six more months have passed. Thereafter, once a year should probably do it.

Always be watchful, however. If you live in a very dry climate or one with cold winters, make sure that atmospheric conditions have not dried out your clarinet. Heated buildings during very cold winters are subject to dryness, and so are air-conditioned buildings during hot summers. When you are in doubt, give the clarinet a light oil treatment, but never over-oil it. Over-oiling saturates the wood and the pads, ruining the pads and causing a lifeless tone quality. Above all, do not set up a regular oiling schedule such as once a month or once every two weeks or any other such nonsense. If you do that, you will certainly saturate your instrument with oil and may even permanently damage it.

Keep an optimum amount of "cork grease" on the cork tenons between the various sections of the clarinet. Use enough grease so that the clarinet assembles easily, but not so much grease that the clarinet tends to fall apart while you are playing it.

While assembling your clarinet, try to keep from putting any twisting pressure on the keys. Fine key adjustments, the hard work of a good repairman, can be ruined by too much pressure on the keys. The use of enough cork grease should help prevent key damage resulting from this sort of twisting pressure.

Never subject your clarinet to temperature changes. Even if you are only going from one room in a building to another part of the same building, put the clarinet back in its case and reassemble it upon arrival. If you have had it outdoors in wintertime, in its case, the clarinet will be cold. If you open the case too soon the instant temperature change can very easily crack the wood. The same principle holds for having had the clarinet outdoors in very hot weather and going inside an air-conditioned room. Always give the clarinet time to adjust *before* you open its case.

The best insurance you can buy for your fine clarinet is a *second* clarinet of cheaper quality, preferably made of plastic, to be used during marching band sessions or for playing outdoor concerts. If you own such a clarinet you need never use your best instrument outdoors. Your "outdoor" clarinet should be kept in perfect playing condition, however. It can be rained or snowed on, or it can be baked in the hot sun, without ruining anything but its pads. A good wooden clarinet can be *entirely* ruined by such treatment. These plastic clarinets can often be bought very cheaply from sixth-grade beginners who "quit band" in the seventh or eighth grade. When I was in high school and college I even had an old *metal* clarinet that I used for all my outdoor playing; I had a good repairman put it into playing condition and it served the purpose very well. (Incidentally, that old metal clarinet is still serving me well, but in a new capacity; it is now sitting on my desk in the form of a unique and beautiful lamp base!)

It is well known that a clarinet should be swabbed out after each playing, and during each playing if the session is a long one. This is more because of condensation than it is because of an accumulation of saliva, but any kind of direct moisture on the wooden bore should be removed by swabbing.

If, while you are playing, water does get into a tone-hole, not only endangering the pads but also embarrassing you with a gurgling sound, do not hesitate to blow it out! Then swab out the clarinet and, finally, put a corner of an absorbent paper towel in between the pad and the tone-hole. This will effectively get rid of the unwanted water droplets. You can keep a paper towel folded up in your clarinet case just for such emergencies.

Put an occasional drop of key oil on all working parts of the mechanism. Remember that key oil is a completely different substance from bore oil.

Remove dust and dirt from underneath the keys and from the interior of the tone-holes with a small soft-bristle brush, such as a child's large watercolor paintbrush. If anything sticky gets into a tone-hole it can often be removed very well with a pipe cleaner.

Beyond this level of routine maintenance, however, leave

everything else to a good repairman! He will appreciate your concern, respect you for it, and perhaps even be readier to serve you well, knowing that you really care. Nothing makes a good repairman sicker than seeing a fine instrument mechanically fouled up by an amateur, even if the amateur is a professional player. *You* play it, and let *him* repair it; that is what he is there for.

How do you find a repairman you can trust? You must look for one who applies high standards to his work, is interested in players and instruments, and shows a desire to give good service. Such men are almost never connected with large music shops. If a repairman is really good and well established, why should he share his profits with a music shop? Almost without exception the best repairmen are in business for themselves. Large music shops usually offer an instrument-repair service, but their repair work is nearly always done by the most inexperienced people in the trade, sometimes in a deplorable manner. Service is usually slow, unreliable, and often downright sloppy. Buy your music in the music shops, but if your clarinet needs repair take it to a respected independent artisan who knows what he is doing.

BARREL JOINTS

Clarinet barrels remain a great mystery. We know some things about them, enough to realize that the unknown is greater than the known. We are certain that a clarinet's barrel will have a most critical effect on the rest of the instrument if only because of its position directly under the mouthpiece, leading into the bore of the clarinet. This effect is so critical, in fact, that many fine clarinets have been rejected by good players who didn't realize that the only thing wrong with the instrument was an inappropriate barrel. It is possible that, fitted with a proper barrel, that same clarinet could be ranked among the very best anywhere.

First of all, make sure that a standard-length (66 mm.) barrel is provided with any new clarinet you buy. In former days, players could be sure that the barrel joint provided by the maker was the best one available for that clarinet; sometimes the barrels were even cut from the same piece of wood as was the rest of the instrument. Fine adjustments in the bore were carefully made by craftsmen who "custom-made" the entire clarinet while sitting at a workbench wearing an eyeshade. Alas, those days are gone! Today even the finest French clarinets arrive in America without barrels, bells, mouthpieces, and even cases to put them in! That's right, only the upper and lower joints (the only two sections of a clarinet marked with serial numbers) arrive intact! It is the American wholesaler who provides, from separate bulk shipments, the 66 mm. barrels, the bells, and the mouthpieces, chosen at random. Finally the wholesaler puts a complete clarinet into an American- or Japanese-made clarinet case that, of course, has been imprinted with the brand name of the French clarinet manufacturer, and then puts the whole package on sale. At this rate, clarinetists are fortunate that the makers are still matching upper and lower joints to each other and are still putting serial numbers on them.

Thus, the barrel joint that comes with your new clarinet, while it is probably the right length, may very well *not* bear any further direct relationship to that particular clarinet. This would not matter if (and here we come to the crucial point of all this) the *bores* of barrel joints did not vary greatly in both size and shape! If the bore size and shape are fairly well matched between the barrel and the upper joint of your new clarinet, you are lucky; if they don't, you aren't. There is still cause for hope, however, and I will be specific about this in a moment. At present, let's assume that your barrel has proven satisfactory enough to use on your new clarinet for some time, and go on to observe some of the problems that arise between players and barrels.

Many players who are plagued by chronic sharpness in pitch believe their problem will be solved by a longer barrel, but actually the sharpness is caused by a pinching embouchure. Many others, suffering from chronic flatness, believe a shorter barrel will solve the problem, but actually the flatness is caused by an inadequate airflow or an undeveloped embouchure. Furthermore, if you get a shorter barrel in order to raise the pitch of the throat tones (the tones found at the top end of the chalumeau register), you will find the lower tones drastically high in pitch, perhaps unbearably so. A longer barrel to lower throat tones is almost as bad; it usually results in some flat throat tones. In addition, you will find it almost impossible to play in tune with an ensemble which has "warmed up."

In short, my advice is to use a 66 mm. barrel regularly, assuming you are fairly happy with it; but it might be useful to have an extra barrel or two in slightly differing lengths to take care of special tuning problems. For example, if you are a member of a community orchestra that consistently plays sharp, you may want to have a 64 or 65 mm. barrel to use while playing in that group. Stay in possession of the barrel you decided on first, however, even if you decide to use a different barrel regularly, because you will need it for purposes of comparison.

If it were only that simple! It is *not* that simple.

Remember that barrels come not only in different lengths, but also in different bore sizes and shapes. Therefore you should, ideally, use a barrel whose bore tapers properly from the bottom of your mouthpiece to the top of your upper joint. As may be expected, there is a gauge designed to measure barrel bores. It is called a "clarinet plug gauge," and it is currently available from the Jack Spratt Woodwind Shop, P.O. Box 277, Old Greenwich, Connecticut 06870. This gauge is a very slightly tapered plug with score marks and numerals, expressing thousandths of inches. The gauge will measure the diameter of bores ranging from about .565 inch up to about .610 inch. Since most barrel-joint diameters seem to range from about .580 inch to about .590 inch this works very well.

When using this gauge, the novice receives an almost immediate shock. He discovers that the lower end of the barrel's bore is *smaller* in diameter than the upper end is! The reason becomes clear once you realize that, in spite of being basically cylindrical, most clarinet bores are slightly hourglass shaped, as I mentioned earlier.

While measuring barrel bores you may want to bear one other thing in mind. We know that a generally small-bored barrel will tend to flatten a clarinet's pitch, while a generally large-bored barrel will sharpen it. The trouble is that a barrel's length also affects its pitch. Overall length and bore size may cancel each other out, then, and we know very little about the relationship between those two factors. Furthermore, there is the matter of bore shape; even that may vary somewhat, and our problem is further compounded.

Barrels are so individual, and our knowledge is so scant, that all you can do is search for the barrel that "plays the best," regardless of these conflicting physical factors.

In any case, the plug gauge can be useful in learning more about your barrel joint. If the bottom of the mouthpiece chamber measures .587 inch and the top of your upper joint measures .583 inch, then, ideally, the barrel bore that fits in between the two should also taper from .587 inch down to .583 inch. Just as a mouthpiece's facing is only one factor entering into its quality, so a barrel's bore size is only one factor among many that affect the quality of the barrel. Thus, if you have a barrel that you are happy with but that has "terrible" measurements, go ahead and use it anyway, at least until you find something definitely better.

I have recently had an experience with barrels that shows how mysterious they really are. My B-flat and A clarinets are both several years old now, and both were selected from quite an array of clarinets, which in turn had been preselected, and so forth. I have never played on a clarinet that I liked any better than this B-flat, and have always felt that my A runs it a close second. Each of these fine clarinets has a barrel joint whose bore measurements are not as exact as they should ideally be, yet both clarinets have always exhibited superior playing qualities. This is slightly mysterious, but recently the mystery considerably deepened when I began experimenting with measuring the bores of other clarinet barrel joints. A repairman allowed me to borrow about twenty barrels from him, some new and some used, and I determined to play on them all after I had recorded their measurements, just to discover whatever might be learned. I spent several days playing with those barrels on both my B-flat and my A. These twenty barrels varied greatly, both in overall length and in bore size.

This experiment, though in no way scientific, was very interesting to me. Some barrels made the clarinet play in a very "stuffy" manner and others were not resistant enough to suit me. All the extra-long, small-bored barrels resulted in the clarinet playing hopelessly flat, and all of the very short, large-bored barrels resulted in the clarinet playing hopelessly sharp.

When I was about two-thirds of the way through these barrels a very exciting thing happened. I came to a certain 68 mm. barrel and happened to put it on my A clarinet first. I was stunned by the realization that my already excellent A clarinet was playing better than it had ever played before! Eagerly I put the same barrel on my B-flat and even *that* clarinet played better than it had previously.

Now, that's what I call a real mystery. Here are two clarinets with rather different bore sizes, and here is a barrel that is 2 mm. longer than normal; yet, here also is a barrel that actually *improved* *both* clarinets, two instruments that were both excellent to begin with. And the bore measurements of that barrel do not really "fit" either clarinet any more closely than their original barrel measurements did.

For quite some time I strongly suspected that the situation was too good to be true, and so I kept retesting my initial reaction. But the same happy situation continued, and has continued for several months now. I can no longer say that my A runs the B-flat a close second because the clarinets are equally great now, and both are even better than my B-flat used to be. It has also become far easier for me to make a rapid switch from one clarinet to the other because I no longer change only the mouthpiece; I change both the mouthpiece and the barrel as a single unit. Since the barrel goes with the mouthpiece I need never worry about changing from a warm clarinet to a cold one; even the cold clarinet is instantly provided with a warm barrel, where the warmth for tuning is most important anyway. Needless to say I have since purchased that barrel and have returned the other nineteen to the repairman, both of us having been made happier and wiser by the experience.

It must be understood, however, that a barrel that will do equally well on both your B-flat and your A clarinets is a very rare find. Most players must keep using the original, separate barrels that came with their respective clarinets, switching back and forth with the mouthpiece only. And whenever anyone asks me how I can get away with using the same barrel on both clarinets, I have to say that I simply do not know the answer. It was an accidental and happy discovery.

To sum up the barrel situation: If you do not think that your barrel joint is beyond suspicion, measure its length and bore size to look for an obvious discrepancy. If you find such a discrepancy, search for a new barrel. If, on the other hand, you are happy with your barrel joint in all respects, stick with it no matter what the measuring gauges tell you. There are too many unknown factors involved to do otherwise.

CHAPTER

4

The Two Basics

in

Clarinet Playing

The most fundamental aspect of playing clarinet or any other wind instrument is a proper state of *relaxation* in the player. Until a player is relaxed, problems will develop that will have to be corrected later. Young students who have not had the years and years of experience it takes to achieve proper relaxation may expect such remedial work in the normal course of learning the instrument. If a talented and promising young clarinetist were naturally relaxed and well coordinated, he could probably learn to be a very fine player in several months or a few years. Hardly anybody is sufficiently relaxed at all times, however, so it usually takes several years to train our minds and bodies to play the clarinet well. Ideal relaxation must be given time to develop and mature.

The other most basic aspect of clarinet playing has to do with the clarinet's being first and last a wind instrument: It is what I prefer to call the *airflow*. Next to relaxation, the airflow is the most important part of clarinet playing.

In introducing relaxation and airflow I have mentioned them in a specific order, and I believe that it is probably the correct order. However, since achieving the proper state of relaxation involves a knowledge of what a proper airflow is, I will discuss the airflow first.

THE AIRFLOW

Some players make the mistake of thinking that the embouchure is even more important than what the air is doing; this is a mistake because no embouchure, no matter how good it is, will have any effect if an unimpeded airflow is not traveling through it. The embouchure, in fact, is nothing but a sort of doorway through which the sound-generating airflow must pass; it is a very important doorway, to be sure, and it must be of the right shape to refine the airflow for beautiful tone quality, but it remains only a doorway through which the star performer, the airflow, comes into view on the stage of sound.

And the embouchure is not the only aspect of playing that is subordinate in importance to the airflow. The truth is that *all* other aspects of playing should be considered less important than airflow because they actually *depend upon* it.

Doubting this, some players may think that technique, for example, is just as important or even more important than the airflow. To them I point out that technique is reduced to just so much finger-wiggling, unless the airflow has been fully established first. Technique, in fact, arises only from a good airflow.

Could tonguing be as important as airflow? Tonguing is probably the least important of all the major aspects of clarinet playing. What is a clarinetist going to articulate if he does not have a good airflow?

Rhetorical games are sometimes fun, and I definitely do not mean to underestimate the significance of the roles played by embouchure, technique, and tonguing, but it is essential to understand the supreme, overriding importance of what literally gives the clarinet its breath of musical life, the player's airflow.

In clarinet playing the player's airflow can be compared to the bow as used in violin playing. If the travel distance of a bow across the string, during a tone, is not great enough, the sound coming from the violin will be too small or too faint. Its tone quality will suffer tremendously, and the listener will cry inwardly for a more generous use of the bow. The clarinetist must think of his airflow as his bow, and as such, it must *travel* in the same manner.

When teaching a clarinetist how to achieve a properly traveling airflow, I have found it is best to be subjective rather than rigorously scientific. It is not so much what the muscles are actually doing to support the airflow that matters to the player, but, rather, what it all *feels* like.

The airflow, or the player's use of the air generally, can be thought of as having two qualities: (1) pressure, which is a "constant," and (2) speed, which is a "variable."

The pressurized aspect of the airflow, caused by the proper muscular action of the player in the area of his waistline (and which will be discussed in more detail later on in this section) is indeed a constant, never-changing thing. The muscular pressure upon the airflow is what musicians commonly refer to as "breath support," which is a good enough term to use, perhaps, for professionals, but I think that when a teacher tells a young player to "support," the teacher is not being explicit enough. Although the player may very profitably think of never changing the pressure under his airflow, he must not forget the ever-changing *speed* of the airflow. Some clarinetists remain confused about breath support for many years, simply because they have observed that it is necessary to make some change in the airflow when they go from playing a loud, high tone to playing a low, soft tone. When they notice this difference in airflow demanded by the various ranges of the clarinet, and when those differences are not explained to them, they begin to take the whole business of "supporting" with a grain of salt, with disastrous musical results.

So, while maintaining what feels like constant muscular pressure to support the airflow, the player should also experience definite variation in his air speed (or, again, what *feels* like variation in the air speed). To understand this concept better, one can compare the necessary changes in the air speed (coupled with a constant, unchanging amount of air pressure) to two different, but equally powerful, vehicles commonly seen out on the roads.

The playing of low, soft tones on the clarinet is like a large, heavy road roller at work, smoothing out the freshly poured tar onto the roadbed. This machine is doing its job powerfully, and yet it is moving very slowly indeed. In spite of its slow speed, the workers on the road are well advised to get out of its way because of its immense power. This is comparable to playing low, soft tones on the clarinet: The air does not have to move rapidly, but it still must move with great force.

The playing of loud, high notes can be compared to a huge semitrailer truck speeding down a freeway. We could say that it is no more powerful than the road roller is, at least for the purposes of this analogy, but in addition to its great power it has tremendous speed. So it is with loud, high notes on the clarinet.

These analogies are only meant to convey the ideas of constant air pressure and of variable air speed, ideas that I have found very useful in teaching. Actually, it may even be that the pressure goes up as speed goes down, and that as speed goes up the pressure goes down. Nevertheless, I have better luck in teaching when I present air pressure as something that is ever-present in an unchanging form. Otherwise, the young student has a difficult time trying to make his airflow do two opposing things at once. It seems better to think of a constant coupled with only one variable. In any event, it works in nearly all cases.

For tones in the more moderate range of the clarinet, and for tones played at moderate volume levels, the player needs to make a subjective judgment as to how fast to move his airflow. Once he has some idea of the dynamic range of the clarinet, he will be better able to judge what he should do for any given tone within its own context.

There are always some exceptions clouding the issue, of course. Certain intervals, when played on the clarinet, temporarily require the player to go against the general rule. An increase in the air speed is required, for instance, when the clarinetist wishes to play smoothly downward, if that downward interval carries him over a "register break" in the instrument. Many other exceptions to the given rule also exist, but all the exceptions are just that, and the general rule remains. The subtleties come with experience.

How should the player feel when his airflow-supporting muscles are doing a good job? Inhalation comes first: Compare the inhaling process to the idea of having a balloon inside the confines of your waistline, which is then suddenly filled, through the mouth, by a helium pump. You should expect this balloon, when filled as quickly as possible, to expand your belt. The concept of a balloon confined to the waistline is also very good for preventing young students from raising their shoulders while inhaling, a practice that accomplishes nothing except an increase in bodily tension. The idea is to fill the balloon and then to put pressure upon it with the surrounding stomach muscles, holding it in readiness for the task of sending it traveling at the proper time.

You will notice, by the way, that I referred to the stomach muscles and that I have not yet mentioned the diaphragm muscle. This touches upon one of the most common misconceptions among players of wind instruments, many of whom believe that it is the diaphragm muscle that supports or pressurizes the airflow. While it is true that the diaphragm is the muscle at the base of the lungs, it is also true that the diaphragm is not a muscle over which the player has any direct control of his own; the diaphragm is merely a muscle that is caught in the middle while the muscles below it press upward toward the area of the lungs. In any case, it is very helpful to know that if it feels as if your stomach is the muscle doing all the work, you are taking the correct approach to supporting your airflow. The entire abdominal area, in fact, should feel as if it is putting forth a great amount of effort, but the effort should feel as though the stomach is at the center of it all. Chest expansion will take care of itself without any real or conscious effort by the player and, as I said earlier, any attempt to raise the shoulders or to tighten the throat will be counterproductive, to say the least.

In Keith Stein's book on clarinet playing, he says "Breath has weight." Beautiful! If a clarinetist will remember what he learned in science class about the weight of the earth's atmosphere, he will realize that all he has to do is to keep his air passages open, expand his waistline, and allow himself to receive the air as it comes rushing in with the weight of the atmosphere behind it. It should be as though a vacuum tube were suddenly opened to the air.

The exhalation process takes place during playing, of course, and its comparison with a violin bow must be remembered. The use of the airflow is as important as the use of a violinist's bow, with all its subtleties of "strokes." The airflow must be under control at all times; the player should, in other words, maintain strict control over exactly what his airflow is doing and over exactly what else is going on in his body to help or hinder the airflow. The throat must be kept relaxed and open, for instance, and the embouchure must not be of such a "biting" kind that it restricts the airflow. Control must also be exercised to make certain that the player is not "over-blowing"; that is, he must be sure that he is not trying to overfill the instrument with an excessive volume of air at any given moment. Such over-blowing results in a lack of control over tone quality, pitch, and articulation.

Through all of this it is sometimes easy to forget that the true purpose of breathing is to keep our bodies alive; breathing to play the clarinet is of secondary importance. It may seem almost comical to put it that way, but I am often amazed at the thoughtlessness and inefficiency that characterize some students' playing. They may play just a few phrases and find themselves worn out. Then they complain that they have no "endurance." I tell them they must remember that their bodies require oxygen to keep on going, and that, if their breathing literally leaves them breathless, their bodies will rebel. Stale air in the lungs must be completely exhaled between phrases or the result will be a lack of space for fresh oxygen. Without a good supply of oxygen the muscle tissues throughout the body cannot properly renew themselves, so that, in wind players, the embouchure may well be one of the first things to go. My experience has been that such inefficient breathing is not even good for technique, because the player begins worrying, perhaps subconsciously, about where he will get his next breath, and he begins to miss notes.

A tremendous help in overcoming the problem of such erratic breathing habits is to enlist the aid of the music's rhythmic flow. When there is a rest between phrases, even if it is for one beat or a half-beat, the player should mentally split that rest into two parts; during the first part of the rest he should exhale completely, and during the last half he should inhale quickly and properly for the next phrase. This sort of "rhythmic breathing" is an extremely valuable technique, and oboists, who share this problem with clarinetists, have used such a technique for generations. Clarinetists who try it will find their endurance is immediately and miraculously enhanced.

A final word on the subject of the airflow: Such things as leg-crossing and leaning against a chair back have *nothing* to do with whether a player will be able to breathe properly! A player's legs are not in any way connected with his breathing apparatus. It doesn't matter what a player has done with his legs, or where he has placed his back. What matters is whether he has constricted his abdominal muscles. This means, of course, that no wind player can sound like one while he is slouching in his chair, or when he is bent over sideways, but neither does he have to maintain the position and bearing of a Prussian general. The player's physical comfort is the important thing, since that will have a direct effect on how easily he can remain relaxed, and relaxation in clarinet playing is absolutely essential.

Some of the finest clarinetists in the world play in symphony orchestras. If you watch them play you see that nobody is standing up, and, while nobody is in any way slouching in his chair, nobody is clicking his heels in a salute, either.

At ease, then. You'll play better for it.

bore; (2) the *technical system,* consisting of the exterior of the clarinet (the keys and tone-holes), the tongue, arms, and fingers; and (3) the *computer,* which is your mind and its musical thought processes, and which governs or runs the activities of the first two parts of the musical machine.

Notice that those first two parts involve areas of *both* the clarinet and you, the player. Considering this hypothetical music-making machine, one can easily see that a fine clarinetist needs to consider himself at one with his instrument. He must make it a part of himself while playing.

Think of a fine singer. He was born with his instrument, and there is no question that his instrument is part of him. The instrument used in clarinet playing must be considered in the same way; the clarinet is merely an external voice instead of an internal one.

This is the essence of relaxation, for it is more than just a lack of tension. It is the realization that the clarinet is an extension of yourself; and through the absence of tension, it can become a new, beautiful, portable voice. Remember that anything tense, anything not completely relaxed beyond the simple alertness in the four areas mentioned earlier, will restrict your full use of that same, great external voice, your clarinet.

CHAPTER
5

The
Embouchure

What is an embouchure, and what job does it do? An embouchure is nothing more than the properly shaped and reinforced *doorway* through which the airflow must pass to be properly received by the instrument. This is why the clarinet embouchure is different from that of the other wind instruments, and why the embouchures for all wind instruments differ from one another. Different wind instruments require different airflow doorways.

The only job the embouchure must do is allow the airflow to act upon the clarinet so that the best possible quality of sound results. The embouchure itself does *not* cause good quality sound; only the airflow, with appropriate help from the embouchure, can do that. The embouchure, by acting as the ideal doorway leading into the clarinet, simply refines the quality of sound that the airflow produces. As such it must remain at all times secondary in importance to the airflow! It's unfortunate that so many clarinetists place the embouchure at the top of their list of playing priorities. It is tremendously important, but it will do the player no good if he has an inadequate airflow going through it!

Before we discuss embouchure formation, one more thing must be said: No embouchure will do any tonal good without a reed that has enough "heart" in it to withstand the proper airflow. If the reed is too thin-hearted the player will be driven out of his mind, as it were, trying to compensate for the lack of tonal potential, the instability of pitch, and the reed's inability to respond properly to softly played high notes. (See Chapter 11, "Reeds.") But for the present I will assume the presence of a good reed, and continue with the embouchure.

So, exactly what *is* this ideal airflow doorway? It is to be thought of as a prescribed series of muscular impulses and alertnesses, and *not* simply as a series of lip stretchings. Keith Stein calls it a combination of "sets and draws," meaning that you set some muscles and draw (or pull) others. But *none* of this should be characterized by rigidity; flexibility must be built in along with the desired muscular alertness.

One basic embouchure setting is all that is needed for the entire range of the clarinet (if the reed is doing its job), but, at that one setting, it remains constantly flexible and alive, very sensitive to what your brain tells it to do. Subtle, minute changes in the muscular structure of the embouchure can result in constantly refining intonation and in varying tonal color (which is very important), all by refining the airflow's doorway. The nature of this subtle flexibility will be discussed later on in the chapter.

EMBOUCHURE FORMATION

1. Start by being relaxed and comfortable, preferably sitting in a good straight chair that has its seat and back padded for greater comfort. Standing up does nothing but greatly increase the danger of muscular tension. By all means, sit down and make yourself comfortable. (If it were possible, which it isn't, to lie down on our backs while playing, that would be the way to do it!) To be comfortable is to be able to combat tension.

2. Put the clarinet together, complete with a good reed (at least a No. 3; see Chapter 11, "Reeds"), mouthpiece, and ligature. Then remove both mouthpiece and barrel as one unit, and put the lower part of the clarinet momentarily aside.

3. Holding the assembled mouthpiece and barrel in one hand and resting them in your lap, relax your body and think of the following muscular process:

4. Airflow muscles, windpipe, embouchure, reed, and clarinet are the sole members of the sound-generating system within the music-making mechanism. So, alert muscles anywhere else must be relaxed *now*. Muscles in and around the windpipe, especially in the neck or throat, and the tongue, must also relax totally.

5. Still sitting in the same position, now think specifically of the embouchure: With lips lightly but firmly closed, move the jaw lower and forward so that the two sets of teeth are vertically in line with each other and so that it feels as if about a ⅜-inch space has been created between the upper and lower teeth.

6. With the teeth vertically in line and with the mouth still closed, bunch up the lower lip as if you were going to try to put all of the lower lip on top of your lower two front teeth. This will have two results: (a) the lower lip should be full of wrinkles and creases, and (b) the corners of your mouth will automatically be drawn toward the center of the mouth. At this point, many people wonder what they are going to do with all that lip under the reed. Nevertheless, the correct embouchure will form if the player is meticulous about keeping the lip firmly against the upper edge of the lower teeth. He must not let the lip protrude as though he were a pouting child or trying to imitate the appearance of a pitcher spout. If a protruding lip does result, more definitely firm the lower lip muscle in against the teeth. Usually a too-limp lip muscle will firm up almost automatically when the mouthpiece is inserted and when the corners of the mouth firm in against the sides of the mouthpiece. Help solve the protruding problem even more by stretching *downward* with the center chin skin, as if you were trying to pull it down to your lap. The whole effect should be a feeling that you have formed a *vertical oval,* anchored at the lower lip on the lower teeth.

7. Now, make sure that the lower lip has formed the bottom half of a circle. If you look at it in a mirror, the lower lip will not look much like the bottom half of a circle, but it should feel exactly like that. This is a most important point, so it may be helpful to think of further analogies; this sensation in the lower lip should feel as if you are preparing to: (a) put your lips around the end of a broom handle; (b) put a soda straw in your mouth; (c) place a large, round cigar in your mouth; or (d) blow up a balloon. Remember that the mouth is still closed at this point and, while it remains closed, you are ready to try inserting the mouthpiece.

8. With the mouth closed, take the assembled mouthpiece, reed, ligature, and barrel, and holding it at about a 35- to 40-degree angle (45 degrees is too far out), place the tip of the mouthpiece and reed on the center of the lower lip.

9. Still without opening the mouth, slowly and carefully work the tip inside the mouth—allowing the reed to pull the bunched-up lower lip with it to some extent, if necessary—and continue this slow, gradual insertion until the top of the mouthpiece meets the bare edges of the upper two front teeth. At this point remember that the two sets of teeth should remain vertically in line. Also make sure that (a) the lower lip is still resting on the top of the teeth, and has not been pushed into the mouth; (b) the lower lip still feels as if it is bunched up (but not protruding) under the reed; (c) the corners of the mouth, the upper ends of that bottom half of a circle, are pointing upward, or in against the sides of the mouthpiece (the corners should feel as if they point toward the eyes, not the ears); and (d) the upper lip closes down upon the top (and sides) of the mouthpiece like the *top* half of a circle, and that it bears a little of the upward pressure of the mouthpiece against the top teeth.

10. You have now achieved the basic embouchure setting and are ready to try making a sound. (Later, more will be said about embouchure subtleties; there must be something there to work with first.)

TONE PRODUCTION

If you feel that you have properly positioned the mouthpiece and reed upon the lip cushion, which is resting on (and being supported by) the lower teeth, and if you also feel that the mouthpiece is firmly anchored against and behind the edge of the upper two teeth, then do the following:

1. Relax the corners of the mouth just enough to allow you to take a breath. Throughout the entire tone production process, of course, remember the correct breathing techniques discussed in Chapter 4, "The Two Basics in Clarinet Playing."

2. Take a breath through the corners of the mouth (*not* through the nose; that is too slow and is a bad habit to develop), a deep enough breath to expand the waistline; and firm the corners of the mouth in against the sides of the mouthpiece once again.

3. Now begin the exhaling process through the mouthpiece, blowing very slowly at first. Maintain the firmly expanded waistline, the studiously set embouchure, and completely relax the throat area and the tongue muscle. In this manner, with your muscularly supported airflow, continue blowing evenly through the oral cavity into and through the mouthpiece and barrel.

4. Gradually increase the speed of your airflow. As the air speed increases, the reed will eventually vibrate and make a sound. Don't stop there! Keep blowing, making the sound louder and louder, but never allow the air pressure to distort the careful positioning of the mouthpiece or the carefully structured embouchure. Make sure that you are not over-blowing or overpowering the reed; just fill the room with sound. That last point is terribly important: You need to fill the room with free-blown sound. You may not find that sound pleasing, but remember that when you later put the mouthpiece and barrel on the rest of the clarinet, the instrument will make it sound much better.

5. After you reach a full but controlled volume, slowly begin to decrease the speed of the airflow. Continue this gradual, even decrease until you are barely breathing into the mouthpiece; then the reed vibrations will stop. Then, *you* stop. Be very sure that your controlled blowing pressure stops only after the reed has stopped vibrating.

If you set about achieving the right embouchure, you should be able to produce a tone that sounds about the same as the second F-sharp above "middle C" on the piano. Repeat the tone production process, as given in the preceding section, this time matching your pitch to that particular F-sharp on a piano; do not allow your pitch to vary with the volume level. I must emphasize this point: If you are using proper breathing techniques as described in Chapter 4, "The Two Basics in Clarinet Playing," your volume level should vary greatly from soft to loud and to soft again, but your pitch should never vary too much, if at all, from that of the second F-sharp above middle C on a piano.

If your mouthpiece-and-barrel pitch is slightly sharp, or higher than that F-sharp, don't worry about it. If, however, it is *very* sharp, you are pinching the reed and mouthpiece too much with your embouchure. If your pitch is flat, or lower than that F-sharp, you are lacking some "muscular alertness," and you must decide whether that lack lies somewhere in your airflow or somewhere in your embouchure.

The foregoing five-step method of achieving tone production shows that: (a) the tongue does not make the sound; (b) the airflow does make the tone; (c) the embouchure must be properly set to obtain the correct type of tone and pitch with controlled air-flow; (d) control of the full dynamic range of the clarinet is en-tirely regulated by the speed of the airflow and not by pinching and unpinching the lip muscles; (e) the embouchure is secondary only to the airflow. (See Chapter 13, "The Clarinetist's Order of Priorities.")

Perhaps, in fact, all the points just mentioned can be boiled down to one indispensable rule of fine, expressive playing: *breath control.* The chief advantage, then, of the five-step approach to tone production is that right from the very first sound produced on the mouthpiece and barrel, the player is forced to control his airflow. Any clarinetist who learns this essential technique early, and who is not allowed to forget it, is a most fortunate clarinetist.

EMBOUCHURE SUBTLETIES
AND REMEDIAL TECHNIQUES

Once tone production is achieved and established, check into the embouchure a little further. First, be sure that your teeth are ver-tically in line, and that the bunched-up lower lip is forming what feels like the bottom half of a circle resting on the top edge of the lower teeth.

The clarinet goes into the embouchure at a 35 to 40-degree angle, and so, much more reed than mouthpiece top should be in the mouth. Be sure that your mouthpiece wedges in at an angle.

Also, the cheek muscles should not only give firm support against the side teeth, but should also support the corners of the mouth which, in turn, lead into the sides of the mouthpiece.

Make certain that the chin skin is pulling firmly downward as if you were trying to pull the cushion of lip off the teeth.

Check the overall effect of the embouchure. When you con-sider the lower lip cushion on the teeth, with the corners and cheeks leading into the sides of the mouthpiece, with the upper lip closing off all air leaks, and with a relaxed tongue, you should be able to tell yourself that you have formed what feels like an oval-shaped, vertical embouchure.

Think of the lower lip as a reed cushion and never as a stretched-out bar across the face of the reed. Because it increases the amount of reed cushion, bringing the corners of the mouth inward makes the exact positioning of the lip on the reed perhaps a little less critical than it might otherwise be.

Remember also that the upper lip has an important function to contribute to the embouchure. Too many clarinetists feel that for the upper lip to seal off air leaks around the edges of the mouthpiece is enough. But, just as the center of the lower lip is being drawn downward by the chin skin, the entire upper lip needs to be drawn downward. Even the nostrils should feel that they are being pulled down toward the top of the mouthpiece by the muscles of the upper lip area. As mentioned earlier, you should have the feeling that the upper lip is sharing, with the upper teeth, some of the upward pressure of the mouthpiece. All of this contributes to an overall roundness in the embouchure, and fixes it so that the vertical oval shape will do the tone quality even more good.

The so-called double-lip embouchure (sometimes called the "French" embouchure) can sometimes be used as a temporary remedial technique to stop jaw bite and to open up the oral cavity of a tense, pinching player. The only difference between double-lip embouchure and the one already described is that the upper lip is placed between the mouthpiece and the teeth instead of placing the teeth directly on top of the mouthpiece. Such an embouchure makes it more difficult for the player to bite or pinch the mouthpiece and reed with his jaws. Many fine players use a double-lip embouchure exclusively, maintaining that it is the best way to achieve openness and freedom in tone quality and response. At the very least, it represents an excellent remedial technique; after the double-lip one has served its purpose, most players prefer to return to the normal embouchure.

It surprises many players to learn that, while they are playing, the *relaxed tongue* should be *low and forward* at all times. The tongue's position should actually be considered part of the embouchure, since it is located in the oral cavity and contributes to refining tone quality and response. Many players feel that they should somehow raise the tongue for better response in the high notes, not realizing that this will actually make high-register playing much more difficult. When the tongue rises it tends to close off, or at least to restrict, the oral cavity, which in turn restricts the airflow. Any restriction of airflow is also a restriction of tone and response whether the player is playing in the high register or not. My experience has been that far greater tone quality and response can be achieved in all registers of the clarinet, even the high one, when the tongue is placed low and forward in the mouth. The tongue, like the rest of you, should stay relaxed at all times; you may not consider the tongue part of the embouchure, but what the tongue does, even where the tongue is, will greatly affect the embouchure.

ANOTHER LEGITIMATE EMBOUCHURE

Many clarinetists have differing ideas about the embouchure, and many of those clarinetists become quite emotional in their defense of their own ideas. There may be, in fact, as many fine embouchures as there are fine players. The embouchure I have described is the one I use and advocate, and it is the one which, in my opinion, achieves the greatest results.

There is another embouchure, however, which is prevalent enough, and certainly good enough, to deserve mention here. It resembles the embouchure described earlier, but has one essential difference: The main thrust of the corners of the mouth is *outward,* away from the sides of the mouthpiece, instead of inward, or toward the mouthpiece. Fine players throughout several generations used this embouchure to beautiful advantage, and many are still doing so, although in somewhat decreasing numbers. This might be called the "corners-back" embouchure as opposed to the "lip-cushion" embouchure.

I do not like the "corners-back" embouchure because when the corners of the embouchure are pulled back, the tone tends to sound the way that embouchure looks: thin and stretched out. A small amount of lip touching the reed results in a tone that is mostly "edge" without much "body." The player can point to his tone and say that there is nothing bad in it, but then I can point to it and say that neither does it have *enough* good in it. When you have a thin, hard lip on the reed you are, in effect, putting a *bar* across it, cutting out a good share of the overtone series. The tone is, then, comparable to the tip of an iceberg. The tip is perfectly good but incomplete and the rest of it cannot be seen or, in this case, heard.

I suspect that pulling the corners back was originally taught as an indispensable part of the embouchure in the days when the thin, bright French sound was in fashion. Many older-generation French clarinetists were, in fact, absolutely first-rate players. It is highly probable that when the Americans asked these fine, old French clarinetists about embouchure formation it was the first time that such a direct embouchure question had ever been asked of them. The French clarinetists, trained in the conservatories of their native land, had been taught almost entirely by example; it could well be that they had never really analyzed their embouchure technique. Any muscular alertness in the corners of their mouths could easily have been misunderstood as a pulling back.

Usually this corners-back embouchure is taught in conjunction with the essential technique of pulling the chin skin down, but the combination results in leaving the mouthpiece and reed with very little muscular support.

I do not mean to belittle the corners-back embouchure, since it is used by many good players who are working toward the bright clarity of sound that was prevalent during the early twentieth century in the French school of woodwind playing. But I can only submit to those players that the lip-cushion approach would give them an opportunity to maintain what they have already achieved, and it would afford them a potential for greater tonal variety, expression, and power.

If you are an advocate of the corners-back embouchure, cherish what you have—namely, a beautiful, clear sound with plenty of that ringing "edge." But you can keep that, and add to it in tonal variety, expression, and power, by trying the lip-cushion approach to embouchure. If an idea promises no loss and great gains, why not give it a try even if you are initially skeptical?

ULTIMATE TONE QUALITY

Ultimate tone quality is a goal based upon musical and artistic taste. The first prerequisite to beautiful tone quality is to have your tonal goals in mind. This means that you must be in possession of a highly developed *tonal concept*. And having a tonal concept means simply that you know what a clarinet sounds like; you know certain famous players whose "sounds" you don't care for, and you know other players whose sounds seem to represent, for you at least, the ultimate in clarinet tone quality. Once you can discern these tonal differences between players and once you can say that you have certain preferences, you are on your way to developing a tonal concept.

The clarinetist's concept of what he ultimately should sound like is terribly important to his development as a musician. If a student tried to develop a beautiful tone quality exclusively from his reading about embouchure, he would not get far. A verbal or literary description of clarinet embouchure formation cannot possibly convey to the aspiring clarinetist the aesthetic, ephemeral, and thrilling concept of beautiful clarinet sound. The verbal or literary description can only be a place to start the search for such an understanding.

To establish tonal goals, then, be sure to listen to excellent clarinetists, both on recordings and in person. Try to put into words exactly what you appreciate in the tones; even though you will never achieve an adequate verbal description of clarinet sound, the attempt is tremendously valuable in crystallizing your ideals. Then, listen for those same admirable tone qualities in your own sound.

Keith Stein recommends playing scales, long tones, and memorized passages while standing in, and facing toward, the corner of a room, trying to hear individual overtones in your sound. This is an excellent approach to tonal development. Listening for overtones is a little like searching for a verbal description of clarinet sound again; you may not hear the overtones, but the search for them is invaluable for tonal development.

As if the quest for a tonal concept and its manifestation were not difficult enough, there is a dangerous snag along the route. Invariably, the clarinetist will hear his own sound differently from the way his listeners will hear it! Not only must the player develop and manifest a fine tonal concept, but he must do so in such a way that the sound he wants is the one that is projected to the listeners, and that it is *not* the one projected only to himself as he plays. It takes years of experience and musical development to solve this problem.

To explain more fully: While you are playing, your reed is sending all sorts of vibrations and extraneous sounds into your head, some of which project to the listeners and some of which do not. You may have had a similar experience with your speaking voice; nearly everyone is amazed that a tape recording of his voice sounds so different from the way he hears it as he speaks. I mentioned earlier in another context that the clarinet could be thought of as an external voice; this idea is particularly applicable to the present discussion. Your clarinet sounds different to others than it does to you.

So, listen to your clarinet sound as it is played back to you on a tape recorder, preferably through a very high quality sound system. Most students who do this are amazed or dismayed. Some of them say, "Do I sound like *that?*" When you hear your own clarinet playing you will hear both what you expected and what you did not expect.

To compensate for the difference between how you sound to others and how you sound to yourself, just about all you can do while you are actually playing is to try to project yourself into an imaginary audience some distance away from where you are. You are then playing the roles of both performer and listener. With practice, it is not as difficult as it may seem. With some imagination (good-humored self-delusion may be a better description) it becomes easier all the time to perceive your own sound as it is perceived by others.

You may find it helpful, during your search for your own ultimate tone quality, to think of beautiful clarinet sound as having two desirable aspects: a firm, full body, or core, and, *around that,* a clear, penetrating, or carrying "ringing edge." If you have a small, thin, yet not unpleasant sound, your tone may lack something in its body or core. If your sound is big but "spread out," the body may be fine, but you probably lack that ringing edge.

Get the opinions of others whom you respect. Do they say that you have a beautiful, expressive tone, or do they say that it lacks something? If your tone does seem to lack something, do not despair; remember that it takes years of experience to approach your goals. Also, no matter how serious your playing problems are, there is almost always a cure for them.

THE PROBLEM OF UNEVEN TOOTH STRUCTURE

Many clarinetists have slightly uneven teeth. If the upper two front teeth are uneven you have to hold the clarinet a little off to the right or left. If the teeth are frightfully uneven, it may be necessary to have a dentist even them up.

The lower two front teeth present an even greater problem since pressure is exerted upon the center of the lower lip, which is caught between the lower teeth and the reed. This small amount of pressure should not be enough to bother a player if his teeth are entirely even, but a slight unevenness in the teeth will result in an undue amount of pressure on one small spot on the interior side of the lip. In such a case it is permissible and even desirable to place some sort of soft pad over the lower teeth in order to avoid slight but annoying pain in the lip. A piece of paper is temporarily effective; a small cutting of leather lasts a little longer. Most durable of all is a plastic dental plate made by a dentist to fit over your teeth, but such a plate is often very expensive. A piece of paper, leather, or formed plastic may also be put on the upper teeth of those who are using the double-lip embouchure.

If you have some sort of tooth structure problem, remember that anything that helps the lip by contributing to the reed cushion can do no harm.

CHAPTER

6

Technique

WHAT IS TECHNIQUE?

It is with great caution and care that I approach the subject of technique, because I feel that this is the most widely misunderstood aspect of clarinet playing, especially when considered in conjunction with tonguing and articulation. Not only do many clarinetists misunderstand the proper approach to technique but they also place it far too high on their list of priorities. Clarinetists must understand that how "good" a player is is determined by his expressiveness, his phrasing, his tone quality, his accuracy, and his faithfulness to the intentions of the composer—*rather* than by how many notes he can play in a given short period of time.

Perhaps technique is best thought of, then, as being the manner in which hands, fingers, and tongue, acting upon the exterior of the clarinet, coordinate their actions with those of the air and embouchure. In other words, technique is really nothing more than *control,* and *control* is really nothing more than *coordination!* To have good technique means that you must have adequate control of yourself, your instrument, and the music you are playing.

In Chapter 4, "The Two Basics in Clarinet Playing," I mentioned three systems within one large music-making whole: a sound-generating system, a technical system, and the brain or the computer system. Good technique is the coordination of the technical system (keys, tone-holes, tongue, arms, fingers) with the sound-generating system (airflow muscles, windpipe, embouchure, reed, clarinet bore). Keith Stein describes technique especially well: He says it is a commanding, overall "control" rather than a "grass-cutting" approach that would plow through or mow down a piece of music. It follows that you should not primarily think of "technique" in its narrow sense when you practice. You should analyze what you need to perform the music well. Analyze how you can achieve both physical and musical control of the music. Very rarely, if ever, is the problem an inherent lack of speed. You *may* lack speed, but if you do, that lack comes from poor control and coordination. It is a mistake to *say* that you lack speed, because that lack is only a symptom of some other and more basic lack. The real problem is usually in the areas of airflow, relaxation, rhythmic steadiness, or in the simple coordination of the fingers with the tongue.

That is often a terribly difficult concept for young clarinetists to grasp, because they have always thought that speed itself is what makes a good player, and that to approach music *means* to work for greater and greater speed. Work for control, coordination, relaxation, but not for speed! The speed will automatically come along with the improvement of all those other, far more important, aspects of clarinet playing.

I always shudder when I hear a good student (usually a pianist but sometimes a clarinetist) refer to his "technique books." I know that the student is thinking he has to practice what is in those books at very fast tempos, for sheer speed. All too often this means that he is practicing bad habits at an ever-increasing rate. For teachers and students alike, I say that if your book is a scale book, or a book of intervalic exercises, *call* it that, and don't use the term "technique book." This latter term not only encourages sloppy attempts at speed but it also makes the student tense, which in turn promotes a vicious circle of sloppiness and tension. Certainly there are books to be used mainly for the improvement of technique, but before referring to them as technique books you must first understand that "technique" is not synonymous with "speed." The player's entire being must enter into the consideration of technique, not just his fingers and his tongue.

HANDS, FINGERS, AND HOLDING THE CLARINET

It seems that the nature of technique forces me to talk more about what not to do than what to do. So it is, specifically, with the physical handling of the clarinet; you must be very careful about what not to do.

Fortunately for clarinetists, wind instruments, unlike the keyboard, are built so that all the keys (and in this case the tone-holes also) are within easy reach without the player's fingers ever moving from one basic position. Clarinetists, even very young ones, must *begin* playing with the idea that they shouldn't have to *reach* for anything. This means that since the clarinet was built to accommodate human hands and fingers we have only to adapt our hand position to the clarinet to establish, quickly and easily, the proper hand position.

The first point to be made is not specifically where to put the hands and fingers, but where and how to hold the clarinet. (Beginners, by the way, should be taught how to hold the clarinet only *after* they have successfully achieved tone production on the mouthpiece and barrel.) First, consider the right thumb. The right thumb is the *only holding support* given the clarinet! The embouchure merely keeps it from falling off the thumb. If the clarinet is held at any points other than at the thumb and at the embouchure, perhaps the bell can be rested on one knee or the other, assuming the player is tall enough for this to be feasible.

The clarinet holding position of most young beginners needs to be closely and continually watched. Some children hook the upper side of the right-hand index finger under the bottom side key (E-flat–B-flat key) to help hold the instrument. Or they hook the little fingers *underneath* the clarinet's body, for the same purpose. While holding the clarinet otherwise properly, the young player often tries to rest his right arm on his right leg. This restricts his right-hand movement and curves his torso too far forward. The head should be held upright, looking straight forward at eye level without casting the eyes upward or downward. Often young players aim their heads downward, in the same direction as the clarinet, causing embouchure problems. But neither should the clarinet come straight out from the embouchure, even with the head held correctly up. Start with the clarinet's bell pointing directly at the floor, and the mouthpiece pointing directly at the ceiling, then bring the mouthpiece in towards the mouth to the proper 35- to 40-degree angle. *None* of the fingers besides the right thumb has *anything* to do with holding the clarinet. They should be able to move freely up and down, or to and fro, all over the place, without changing the position of the clarinet and without disturbing the embouchure.

Once you are sure that the right thumb is securely holding the clarinet under its thumb-rest on (or near) the side of the first knuckle, lightly place your fingers in their *approximate* positions, and hold the clarinet up in the air until you have the middle joint at eye level. Then slowly lower the clarinet to a playing position without allowing the position of the fingers to change much from the position they held while you had the clarinet up in the air. Your fingers should come at the clarinet from about a right angle, but not quite. There should be a slightly upward angle leading from the fingers up the wrists and arms. Wrists should be comfortable but rather low. Many young students raise their wrists far too high, and make it very difficult for the left hand to get in and out of the throat tones. The right-hand little finger can hardly reach the four lowest keys when the wrist is too high.

Each finger should have a slight bit of rounding in its knuckle. The fingers should never flatten out and lock at the knuckles while you are playing. Tone-holes should be covered by the soft ball of the finger.

The left-hand thumb should cover its tone-hole at about a 1:30 clock position (or perhaps you could say that it should point northeast) with just enough skin left hanging off the upper side of the hole to be able to open slightly the register key by flexing the first knuckle just a bit. If these left-hand thumb instructions are closely followed, very few register problems relating to the thumb need arise.

The first note I teach beginners is bottom-line E-natural (sometimes called "throat E") which uses the thumb-hole and hole for the top finger. In this way the student learns to cover holes right from the beginning, but not too many holes all at once. If open G is taught first there is too great a tendency for the student to want to hold the instrument with his left hand, usually at the barrel. Playing E forces the left hand to stay in its proper position just as the thumb-rest forces the right hand to stay where it belongs. Starting on E means that the student can play up to throat F and G by merely lifting fingers, and it does not usually tax him too much to play back down through F and E to D and C. In that way he can cover an entire perfect fifth without too much trouble, assuming of course that he has already successfully produced sounds on just the reed, mouthpiece, ligature, and barrel.

THE USE OF THE FINGERS WHILE PLAYING

During the stress and strain of playing, especially during difficult passages, tenseness tends to creep into the fingers (sometimes it *barges* in), and the fingers start grasping at the keys and rings. Often when this happens the fingers start hanging onto, and even holding, the clarinet. This is a danger that must be avoided. Relaxation must be immediately reinstated. Each of the eight fingers used on top of the clarinet must maintain a slight arch in each joint while playing; stiff fingers automatically lead to technical problems.

At all times remember that the fingers are not making the sound; the airflow is doing that. All the fingers do is lengthen and shorten the vibrating length of the clarinet bore, so tenseness is a detriment, not an advantage. The finger ends themselves are *pads* and need not close the holes any more tightly than the other pads do.

While playing, the fingers themselves must be thought of as individual, relaxed, rather heavy weights that are raised and lowered solely by the one joint (in each finger) that is attached to the palm of the hand. The outer two joints in each finger never flex, do any work, or take on any alertness.

To see how the fingers should work, let us use the example of an F major scale, in the low register only, descending first: Start on "thumb F" and completely relax all over again while holding that one note. Slur down that F scale for one octave, very slowly and with a full tone, and, as each finger goes down to cover its tonehole, think of it as *falling* into place because of its own *heaviness.* You will immediately see what the advantages are to this approach. Its result is a sound indicating *lightness,* not heaviness, simply due to the total absence of tension. Fingers should never be *pushed* into place.

Now try the ascension of that same scale, from low F up to thumb F. Lift each "heavy" finger from its joint nearest the hand,

and only far enough to clear the tone-hole. If the finger is lifted higher than that the tone-hole will be harder to find the next time you want it.

This is the essence of good finger movement, and it is easy to carry over to other music what you experienced with the low F scale. The next step is to use the same finger-movement approach in the other registers of the clarinet while playing scales; then try scales in thirds, arpeggios, and wider intervals. Think of finger movement continually, of course, while playing music from the printed page.

PRINCIPLES OF CLARINET FINGERING

The player's fingers can't do any more than lengthen and shorten the vibrating length of the clarinet bore. The placement of the fingers is therefore determined by the acoustical properties of the clarinet itself. The acoustical properties of any instrument are determined by how that instrument produces, or responds to, the tonal "harmonic series." For a discussion and explanation of the harmonic series, see Chapter 3, "The Clarinet Itself and Barrel Joints." Here, I will only reiterate that the clarinet is unique among all instruments because it is incapable of producing the even-numbered "partials" (in any usable way), and it is limited to producing fundamental tones and their odd-numbered partials. The low (chalumeau) register is entirely fundamental tones; the middle (clarion) register is entirely third partials; and the high (altissimo) register is made up of fifth, seventh, and ninth partials.

A knowledge of how these registers relate to the harmonic series is most valuable in improving one's clarinet technique; a player can understand certain intervals better and can experiment and search for new fingerings.

The *basic principle* behind the choice of fingering is to take the easy way out every time! When any given tone can be produced with more than one fingering, the easiest fingering will vary with the context.

A *second principle* of clarinet fingering is to avoid *sliding* a finger from one key to an adjacent key. Use alternate fingerings to avoid finger slides. This principle usually affects the use of the two sets of little-finger extension keys; alternate little-finger keys, note for note, unless for some reason they just won't "come out even" in some passage. In that case, sliding is unavoidable, but it must be done with a relaxed finger, quickly and crisply.

A *third principle* of clarinet fingering, one that is more often overlooked than not, is to avoid exchanging fingers (lifting some up while others go down); instead, try either to add fingers to or subtract fingers from the existing fingering combination. This principle is more ideal than real since it is not often possible to put it into practice during the heat of a playing situation. Nevertheless it is a good one to remember for those occasions when it can be followed.

A *fourth principle* of clarinet fingering is, simply, to move as few fingers as possible between any two given tones. All four of these principles, taken separately and together, will help promote greater smoothness and more mechanical efficiency in everyone's clarinet technique.

"Harmonics" (upper partials not normally used) can be useful for special effects since they sound unusual; sometimes they can even be used in an otherwise normal passage in order to avoid a difficult fingering pattern. This is an example:

Clarinetists are familiar with the fingering for the B-natural that is written with one ledger line above the treble staff. This fingering involves the left thumb covering its tone-hole while also depressing the register key, plus the covering of the top tone-hole with the left index finger. That is the most usual and useful of the fingerings for the B-natural. Sometimes, however, the music calls for a trill from that note to the C-sharp a whole step above. Normally the B-natural is a third-partial (above the fundamental first-line E) and the C-sharp is a fifth-partial (above the fundamental low A). The clarinet finds it all but impossible to trill rapidly between those two differing sections of a harmonic series, so that trill presents a real problem. It is usually solved by holding the B-natural and using a trill key, but clarinetists know that trill keys are sometimes unstable and unreliable.

I have sometimes used an alternative solution to this problem, one that involves "harmonics," to very good advantage. The principle involved here is to put both notes on the same partial above their respective fundamental tones, and in this case it works out very well to make both notes become fifth-partials: The B-natural above the fundamental low G, and the C-sharp above the fundamental low A as it is normally. In this new way the trill is accomplished in exactly the same way as would be a trill between fourth-line D and fourth-space E, with the exception that the player also holds open (during both notes) the bottom side key with the side of his right index finger. The result is a very fine B-natural to C-sharp trill with an interestingly dark and mellow tone quality. Incidentally, a good "harmonic" fingering for the C-natural in between those two tones can be achieved by fingering fourth-space E-flat while holding open the bottom side key. This can be played, too, at a very quiet volume level, making it a useful possibility in passages that call for a quiet, dark high C. Again, in this case all we have done is change that C from its usual status as a third-partial (above "thumb F") to a new status as a fifth-partial (above the low A-flat).

Actually, the idea of "harmonics" has been extended in recent years to include what have become known as "multiphonics," a subject so theoretically broad, and yet so realistically limited in its potential application, that it is beyond the scope of this book. Multiphonics could be called intentionally "cracked" tones, or sounds that are produced by forcing the clarinet to *try* to sound more than one partial in a harmonic series simultaneously. Some attempts are more successful than others, and the whole realm of multiphonics remains experimental. Some clarinetists have achieved the simultaneous sounding of three, four, or even more partials, resulting in what sounds like a chord; usually most of the partials involved are very weak and raspy and are heard at much less than a full tone. Multiphonics are used extensively in some new music that employs other "extended techniques" right along with multiphonics. As is always the case in works of art, the result should be judged by its ultimate aesthetic effect and not by the artistic materials used in its creation. My own feeling is, however, that multiphonics are much less successful on clarinet than on any of the other woodwinds, simply because the clarinet is incapable of sounding even-numbered partials. When multiphonics are attempted on clarinet the player is immediately by definition limited to odd-numbered partials, whereas the players of any of the other woodwinds have the lower end of any given harmonic series entirely at their disposal. This can make a tremendous difference. In any case, books such as the Bartolozzi book listed in the Bibliography now deal adequately with multiphonics as well as with other extended techniques.

The whole general subject of clarinet fingering is a broad and open one. I have included an appendix that deals with clarinet fingerings. Experiment with the fingerings you are unfamiliar with, and try to find new ones based on your knowledge of how the clarinet is affected by the harmonic series. If you discover a "new" fingering you will not only have a new technical possibility to work with but also a sense of accomplishment.

HOW TO PRACTICE

The great British clarinetist and teacher Frederick Thurston says this about practicing:

> Five-minute periods will probably be found quite long enough at the very beginning: you will find your endurance developing of its own accord with time. But do not on any account over-practice: you cannot concentrate when you are physically and mentally tired, and you will do your playing as much harm as by not practicing at all.

Thurston has written a great truth. A beginner is well advised to practice very briefly two, three, or more times a day. Doing "a half hour a day," or "an hour a day" cannot be anything but counterproductive if done by a beginner all at one sitting. For intermediate and advanced players it is often said that it is not how long you practice that matters, rather it is the quality of your practice session. This is very true! Two or three hours a day of tense, exhausting playing, feverishly drilling and drilling over rough passages, cannot possibly do as much good as one mere hour of intelligent, relaxed practice can do.

I have never advocated long hours of practice for my students. In fact, if a student is convinced that he must practice for three or four hours or more, he is almost sure to begin that session with his brain turned off. Some students may say, "What about the best professionals who must play four or six or eight hours a day!?" Nonsense! They may be in scheduled rehearsals and performances for that long a time, but they are never actually playing their instruments continuously during that time. Sometimes rather long periods of rest occur while the conductor's attention is turned elsewhere, affording the clarinetists time to relax and refresh their embouchure muscles. The extreme fatigue sometimes felt at the end of a long rehearsal is much more likely to be emotional than physical, because of the pressure of having to do a fine job rather than the physical aspects of actual playing.

If a clarinetist feels the need for several hours of practice each day, he must do it in two or three separate sessions, and never attempt it all at once.

Something else we have all heard is "Practice at least a little every single day." I cannot agree. In general, of course, it is a good policy to try to practice every day, since playing the clarinet is such a personal, physical business. Muscles must be built up and maintained in peak condition for any physical activity whether it is clarinet playing or athletics. However, just as in sound athletic training, an occasional day off can be most beneficial. Players can be much refreshed by taking, say, Saturday or Sunday off after a good week of practice. Both Saturday and Sunday should not be taken off, though, since some of the value of previous practice sessions begins to wear off if the player misses more than one day of practice in a row. The only reasons for missing two or more consecutive days of practice are illness, severe overpracticing on previous days, or extended travel during which practicing is not feasible. Even in the case of travel, however, practice should be resumed if at all possible whenever you reach your destination; try not to wait until you have returned home. And, if you do not practice for a few days in a row, even for a very good reasons, you should bear in mind that you will have a lot of concentrated work to do once you return to your instrument.

Before I discuss the individual practice session, an essential philosophy regarding practice *must* be understood. Without a firm grasp on this piece of philosophy you will become, and will remain, frustrated as a clarinetist.

This philosophy has three steps. The second one seems to cancel out the first one, but the third puts the first two in perspective: (1) Strive for absolute perfection in your playing, whether it is during practice sessions or during a performance. (2) In the knowledge that you are a human being, you must remember that you *will never attain perfection* as a player. (3) Knowing *and accepting* the fact that you are a human being striving for perfection as a player, you know also, in all good humor and in all good faith, that the end result will be nothing less than your best.

No one ever expects you to do better than your best! Your teachers, conductors, and listeners want you to strive continually to improve, of course, but the human element is a factor, and a big factor at that. The very best professional players are not perfect, as they would be the first to admit. They make mistakes, and you must be able to forgive yourself for your own honest mistakes. The key words there are *forgive yourself,* because, believe it or not, you are probably a more severe critic of yourself than are your teachers, conductors, and listeners. Work for constant improvement, but maintain your sense of humor, your sense of perspective, and your knowledge that nobody is perfect.

During the individual practice session, then, what should you do? Be sure to have handy all your clarinet equipment, music, and anything else you need, so that you don't have to jump up in the middle of playing to find them. What you need will depend upon what music you want to practice. (By the way, if you are working toward a solo recital, that is a different matter entirely. For recital practice procedure, read Chapter 12, "Public Performance.")

Clarinetists and other reed players usually do not require a systematic, regular "warm-up routine" in the same way that flutists and brass players do. Nevertheless, it's a good idea to play something first, just to get going. You need to feel your way into the practice session carefully, so that you can relax and so that you can find out how your reed is doing that day. Start out with some sort of scale book, perhaps playing just a page or two from it. The famous scale page from the big, old Klose book is ideal for this, but there is, of course, a wide choice. And you don't have to open with scales; you might play a movement or a complete piece that you have known and played for a long time. If, during your initial playing, you discover that your reed is inadequate, stop and work on it or use a different one. If you find that your playing is especially tense that day, don't try any fast, technical passages until you can convince yourself to relax again. (See Chapter 4, "The Two Basics in Clarinet Playing.") If you find that your embouchure is especially tired that day, don't tax it too much. If it is terribly tired, stop playing and take that day off from practicing.

Once you are well into your practice session and you feel relatively comfortable with the way you and your instrument are playing, begin work on your music.

Let's say that you are beginning work on an etude that you have never played before. Take a good look at the whole piece and then begin just plain old sight-reading; but *slowly!* At this stage, disregard any mistakes you know you are making; the idea is just to get through the piece in order to familiarize yourself with it. You should have a pencil handy to mark in anything that you think you might forget on future playings of that same music. Many students are told that it is "unprofessional" to make penciled reminders of fingerings, accidentals, tempo changes, and so on. Just the opposite is true! Professionals know better than to make some sort of memory game out of increasing the accuracy of their performances.

Go through the piece a little more carefully now, still slowly of course, and continue marking special reminders in whatever way is the clearest for you. Very clear breath marks must be put in according to phrasing. Always put in your breath marks! You will actually make fewer mistakes because many mistakes are caused by subconsciously wondering about where the next breath will come. In music where the phrases are clearly defined, such as those that regularly occur every four bars with a beat or so of rest between them, breathing places present no problem. In places where you think "there is no place to breathe at all," you must find such places, even for very quick breaths.

Here are some thoughts on selecting a breathing spot: (1) Seldom should you breathe at a bar line; it completely upsets the rhythmic (metric) flow of the music. (2) breathe right before a pick-up note, or before a short group of pick-up notes; or (3) breathe right *after* landing on a strong beat. In fact, in some music (especially Baroque transcriptions) it may be advisable to leave a note or two out of a weak part of a weak beat in order to take a breath. *Anything* not to upset rhythm, meter, or phrasing. For more on phrasing, see Chapter 8, "Musicianship."

After an initial playing or two of your new piece, and after putting in all the necessary markings, put it away and wait until the next day to begin working on it in earnest. How to proceed in future practice sessions to continue working on your new piece will be taken up in a moment. First, I will deal with the rest of *this* practice session.

Continue now with other studies you have been working on or go directly to your solos. "Solos" present a special practice problem requiring some additional things to think about while practicing. First, always remember that there is a piano accompaniment (or, in more cases than many people seem to think, a piano part equal in every respect to that of the clarinet!) whether or not you will be actually accompanied by a pianist later. In other words, remembering that there is a piano part will help you account for something that "sounds really strange" when you are playing your part all by itself. Also look for possible ensemble problem spots and think about how you could work them out with the pianist.

Dynamic markings are never to be viewed as little gods, but be especially skeptical of them in solos until you rehearse with a pianist. I feel very strongly that dynamic markings have been elevated in importance by many musicians to a position they do not merit and that rigid adherence to such markings is almost always a detriment to fine, "musical" playing. Dynamic markings should never be ignored but, after careful consideration, many of them should be dispensed with and thoughtfully replaced by something better. (See Chapter 9, "Musical Interpretation," for a further discussion of this problem.) If something is marked "p," then, in your clarinet solo part, you may have to play it out quite strongly if the piano part is full and sonorous at that particular point. In any good piece of music for clarinet and piano there are spots where the clarinet should play a subservient role to the piano, but to play so softly that the clarinet cannot even be heard is obviously a violation of the composer's intentions. Dynamic levels such as "forte" and "piano" are all relative to each other; they are not predetermined by some fixed system of volume levels. Be guided initially by the printed dynamic markings, but the end result must be "musical" no matter what is on the page. For a more complete discussion of how to rehearse with a pianist, see Chapter 12, "Public Performance."

After putting in a good work session on your solos, your practicing should end for that session. None of the foregoing means that you just "play through the music without really practicing." Work intelligently on the spots that need it but never resort to mindless drilling! That teaches nothing but "finger memory."

So now we take up the working on music in your various practice sessions, whether it be on studies or on solo parts, from the beginning session until the piece is "worked up" or "polished."

I have already said what to do with a piece of music upon first attempting it: a couple of slow, careful sight-readings, using a pencil liberally throughout, and never attempting full tempo if it is a "fast piece."

In subsequent practice sessions on a particular piece, merely *familiarize* yourself with the music; never work it into the ground! It must have a relatively fresh sound in your ear every time you play it. In a solo, of course, leave out the multiple bars of rest where the piano is supposed to be playing alone, but, where your rest is less than a measure (or two) in length always count out the rhythm to yourself; otherwise you can easily get into a bad habit of shortening the rest.

In fast passages with complicated fingering patterns, use what I call the "metronome notch-by-notch" system, section by section. This is a system I adopted when I was faced with one particular advanced study rather late in my development as a clarinetist. I am referring to Etude No. 14 in Paul Jeanjean's *Sixteen Modern Etudes* for clarinet, and any accomplished clarinetist who knows that study will also know that it has quite complicated fingering patterns. I broke the first page of the study into four or five sections of fairly equal length, and then I began working my way through the first of those sections alone. After a couple of careful sight-readings and marking in various strategic reminders with a pencil,

I decided upon a slow tempo at which I could be fairly sure of playing the passage without committing too many errors. I set the metronome at that tempo and played through the passage while strictly adhering to the metronome's incessant clicking; sometimes it seemed that I was wasting my time by playing so slowly, and at other times, at that same tempo, I thought that the metronome had speeded up on me! This illustrated to me how much musicians can be influenced, as far as tempo is concerned, by how easily they can play a certain passage.

When I was relatively satisfied with my playing of the first section at that slow tempo, I moved the metronome dial so that the machine would click one notch faster, in a new tempo minimally different from the first one. It was hard to tell the difference, and I had no more trouble with the passage at that tempo than I had had at the first tempo. I continued this process, notch by notch, for quite some time; occasionally I had to play the section at the same tempo twice in a row, but in general I proceeded up the metronome one notch at a time. At the end of only ten or fifteen minutes I was *amazed* at how easy it had become to play that section, and to play it at a much faster tempo than had been possible to begin with. I moved the metronome back to its original setting and went on with the second section, using the same notch-by-notch system. I was amazed again by the rapid rate of technical progress. After about four days of practice sessions on that Jeanjean No. 14 I could play all of it at a fairly respectable tempo; I used the rest of my practice time that week working on improving various passages that had presented more difficulties, all the time using that same metronome method. During a second week of study, I spent more time trying to make the piece sound expressive than I spent on rhythmic accuracy and fingering problems, simply because my earlier careful practice improved my rhythm and my fingering. At the end of the second week my teacher and I were very pleased with my playing of that study, but I was even more pleased with the metronome notch-by-notch system. It is a good approach to practicing anything with complicated fingering patterns, and it is very effective. I have had students at both intermediate and advanced levels achieve the same sort of results by using that method, and I am sold on it. The chief reason for its success, I think, is that the player is forced to refrain from increasing his tempo too rapidly. Large increases in tempos that occur too suddenly are apt to bring on great amounts of tension and a sort of frantic feeling in the player. Obviously, players who feel tense and frantic will not play as well as they are able to play.

Another reason for the success of the system is that the player *familiarizes* himself with the music gradually, always at a tempo where he can think ahead easily. This process of familiarization is the key to success; what I referred to earlier as "mindless drilling" can never accomplish as much familiarization as the notch-by-notch system can, simply because that system is not a mindless one. By rehearsing passages carefully and gradually (and yet surprisingly quickly!) the player is never put in a position where he feels frantic about what the next group of notes will bring him. Relaxation can be maintained, and that is the most important consideration of all.

One point should be added: In a solo work, if you have already occasionally begun rehearsing with a pianist, be sure in your individual practice sessions to work in any new knowledge of the piece you have gained while rehearsing with the pianist.

HOW TO JUDGE YOUR OWN PROGRESS

Judging one's own progress is a matter so complicated, and yet so important, that I believe it warrants a section all its own. Nearly always students think they have to rely entirely upon their teachers to be the sole judges of how they are doing. Naturally you should listen to what your teachers say and take those words to heart; indeed, a student should assume that his teachers' assessment of his progress is more accurate and valid than is his own opinion. But many students, perhaps a majority of them, have such an overriding sense of insecurity that they cannot believe even a teacher whom they respect when he tells them they are doing well. Students very often are such harsh judges of themselves that they become discouraged to the point of quitting the clarinet even in the face of nothing but praise and encouragement from their teachers. This is a psychological problem and not a musical one, but it is so important that it deserves discussion in any book on the clarinet. Teachers often claim that they can do nothing with unmotivated students, and that is a valid claim. No matter how good a teacher is, and no matter how talented a student is, an unmotivated student will not make progress. Not all unmotivated students suffer from laziness or lack of interest; many of them become discouraged simply because they are incredibly insecure. And since the outward symptoms are often the same, it is very difficult for the teacher to tell what the true cause of the lack of progress is. The prevalence of this problem would disappear if teachers and students alike knew how to recognize and how to avoid student insecurity.

If you are a young student in a good junior high or high school band, you will find yourself especially prey to such feelings of insecurity. It is logical to judge your own progress according to what "chair" you hold in the clarinet section of the band, but it is a superficial judgment, not to mention a bad mistake. You should never judge your overall progress, or your potential as a player, by the results of your band's last "tryouts" or "challenges." If you are not sitting very close to the top of the section, be assured that your fate as a clarinetist does not begin and end with what happened to you during tryouts or challenges last week, this week, or next week, next month, or even what happens to you next year. The rate of progress varies greatly from one individual to the next, and progress on a wind instrument must take place over a long period of time. Try to look at the long view and don't judge yourself too much on short-term results.

Progress not only varies between individuals but also varies within each individual. Progress is not, in fact, a slow and gradual build-up as you probably think it should be, but rather, it goes in spurts that are few and far between. Many people think of good progress as a long, evenly inclined ramp, heading ever upward into the sky. Instead, it should be thought of as a series of steps, or long terraces or plateaus. You may think that your practicing is getting you nowhere, but almost overnight sometimes, you will find yourself on a new plateau. The next plateau may not be reached for several months or more after that, but when it comes it will come without warning.

Most young students are still growing; people of all ages experience emotional growth and increasing maturity. Students should never become discouraged because they "can't do" something on the clarinet that they think they should be able to do; if such students only give themselves a little more growing time and stop judging themselves by the achievement of their peers, they may soon find that those same peers will fall behind them. As a ninth-grader, or as a college freshman, for example, it may be very difficult to see your own clarinet playing in the long view, but you must try. Students must learn to be very patient; they must give themselves time.

Sometimes young students think that their teacher, who is a fine player, was *always* a fine player! Your teacher, whoever he is, was once a young student, and he, too, experienced exactly the same kind of discouragement. And when that same teacher praises your playing and says that you are doing well, believe him! He has come along the same route that you are now traveling and he has not forgotten what the road looks like.

There are some more specific indicators to gauge your own progress. If you are playing accurate rhythmic patterns and are playing them in tempo, you are demonstrating to all who hear you that you have a strong potential for making fine music. Rhythm may well be the most basic and most important element in music, and to be able to execute a piece of music in a rhythmically accurate manner is to be able to do something well worth doing; you should feel very proud of your ability.

If you are told that you play with a good, strong sound on your clarinet you have been handed a very high compliment indeed. So often student insecurity manifests itself in a very small sound, and if your tone quality is good it means that you have another reason to feel proud of your abilities.

Fairly advanced students should know that some of the studies assigned to them by their teachers are not pieces of music that can be mastered overnight. If your teacher assigned you a complicated piece of music he is expecting progress on it, of course, but he does not expect you to be able to exceed your own abilities on it. Most good students take two weeks or even more on an advanced study, and this is as it should be. Music takes a while to settle into the blood, as it were, and a good piece of musical performance, like a good student, does not ripen in just a few hours or days. Again, be patient with yourself and be diligent in your efforts. No one expects you to do better than your best. True improvement will be easily noticed by both you and your teacher when you reach that next plateau, whenever it comes.

CHAPTER

7

Tonguing
and
Articulation

Earlier I said that a clarinetist's technique should be lower on his list of priorities than are the more important aspects of his playing such as relaxation, airflow, and embouchure. I will now put tonguing and articulation even lower than technique on that list of priorities by pointing out that the player's use of his tongue is only one aspect of his technique.

It is a great shame that many clarinetists, even some of the professionals, place the three aspects of clarinet playing, "tone, fingers, and tonguing," on an equal footing in their minds. I sympathize with clarinetists who believe this because I know how they arrived at such thinking: No doubt the players concentrated on these three aspects of playing during their many years of practicing. Still, I maintain that they are mistaken. Tonguing is *not* as important as relaxation, airflow, or embouchure, and tonguing is not as important as "technique" since technique includes tonguing. Tonguing should be thought of only as a means to greater subtlety in phrasing; it must always remain in a subservient position. Tonguing can even be thought of as an "assistant" to technique since it simply cleans up the beginning of a tone that was not slurred into from the preceding sounds. Since this is its sole role it is definitely at the bottom of the list of a clarinetist's physical priorities.

Articulation refers to the *manner in which* tonguing assists technique. In wind instrument playing a tone is always begun either with the use of the tongue (called "tonguing") or without the use of the tongue (called "slurring"). Articulation is the artistic combination of playing certain tones within a phrase tongued and certain others slurred. It is psychologically better for clarinetists to think of articulation this way because of two factors: (1) As the player develops, articulation becomes a far broader term than "tonguing"; and (2) as the musical role of "articulation" expands in the player's mind, as he begins to think of articulation as one of his musical tools, then the whole concept of "technique" becomes less formidable to him. This is especially beneficial when the player realizes that everything involved with the three terms, technique, tonguing, and articulation, is completely and totally *dependent upon,* and can only be achieved as a direct *result of,* relaxation, airflow, and embouchure.

It is a terrible shame that the young student tends to conjure up visions of a solid page of note heads when tonguing is mentioned; all those black note heads on the imaginary printed page are connected by big, equally black, multiple beams illustrating rapidly tongued sixteenth or thirty-second notes. Students become apprehensive because so many teachers make such a big issue of the importance of rapid tonguing that the student is led by the teacher's own words and manner to believe that an absolutely frantic tongue is the very key to good clarinet playing. The whole business of tonguing is presented in such a way that the student blows it all out of proportion in his mind; he tenses up for every note he plays, whether the notes are tongued or slurred; and all of the other, and basically more important, aspects of fine clarinet playing go right out through the mental window and into oblivion.

The word "attack" is one of the most harmful words in the English language when used to present proper tonguing to the student. And the younger the student, the more harmful the word. Older clarinetists, including teachers, often use that term to describe the player's action in beginning a tone with the help of the tongue. This is understandable because "attack" is a short word very quickly and easily grasped. Far better, however, would be to speak of "the beginning of the tone," or perhaps best of all would be to accustom the student to the term "tonal entrance," whether or not the tone in question will enter tongued or slurred. Anything is better than the term "attack." If a player, especially a young one, thinks of "attacking" a tone with his tongue, there is almost no way that he can avoid becoming very tense, even before he starts the tone.

Students and teachers alike must remember the basic, incontrovertible fact: Airflow is what causes tonal entrance. Nothing else causes it. The tongue's role is a relatively minor one of helping achieve cleanliness and accurate timing at the beginning of the tone. The tongue's role may be less important than that of the airflow, since it is possible to begin a tone satisfactorily with just the airflow. The only reason for using the tongue at all is that it is easier in the long run to learn to begin a tone cleanly and accurately with the help of the tongue than it is to expect the airflow alone to time precisely the beginning of a tone.

If I give the impression that tonguing is unimportant, good! That is what I set out to do. When it is compared to the other aspects of clarinet playing and of music-making, tonguing is unimportant.

But there is, of course, another level on which tonguing must be considered, and even I will have to admit that on this level tonguing takes on much more importance. The new level I refer to is that of the *correct use* of the tongue in clarinet playing. If only because of its relative unimportance, tonguing has the power to corrupt all the other aspects of playing. When it does this, it does so through distracting the player from more important things. Indeed, incorrectly executed tonguing is perhaps the worst enemy of relaxation. Once improper tonguing has been allowed to distract the player from his state of relaxation, his airflow will suffer. When his airflow has become restricted, the player will try to compensate by tightening and "pinching" with his embouchure. From that point on, things go from bad to worse until finally (and all of this happens very quickly) the player is completely tense and he must stop making any pretense of performing well.

Proper tonguing *must* be mastered in order for the player to be able to concentrate on the more important aspects of his playing. But remember that tonguing is only a part of articulation; articulation is only a part of technique; and technique is less important than relaxation, airflow, and embouchure.

NORMAL TONGUING

Many people have heard that clarinetists' tongues must be able to accomplish all of the same articulatory effects that are available to violinists through the use of their bowing techniques. This is very true, and it is a tall order because violinists have a wide range of bowing techniques at their disposal, all with formidable sounding French and Italian names. Unfortunately this has often given students the idea that clarinetists' tongue strokes must vary greatly, and the truth is that, like the way a violinist holds the bow, there is no variation in that part at all!

Basic tongue position should never vary; at rest, during tones, it should be *low and forward* for best tone quality and for best muscular relaxation. Varying articulatory effects are accomplished by the manner in which the tongue *leaves* the reed.

Again, articulation may vary to the same extent that it does with violin bow strokes, but basic tongue position and relaxation should be compared with basic bowing *position:* It doesn't vary in the slightest.

What is the correct tongue position? I have said that it must be low and forward at all times, and completely relaxed; it is only the front portion of the tongue that takes on any muscular alertness, and then only to reach the reed tip. Do not raise the back of the tongue! Brass players and singers claim they must do this, and they may be right, but raising the tongue on the clarinet will only result in a closed throat and impaired response in the high register. Keep the tongue low and forward at *all times!*

Next comes the question of the tongue stroke itself. Many students have been told to place "the tip of the tongue on the tip of the reed." That is usually correct, but sometimes it is only half correct, due to the greatly varying sizes and shapes of people's tongues. We are all familiar with some children who delight in being able to "stick out" their tongues to an almost alarming extent; we are equally familiar with children who cannot place their tongue tips outside the mouth to any extent. This illustrates how very different tongues can be.

Clarinetists with very short or with average-length tongues should indeed remember to place the tip of their tongues on the tip of the reed just prior to executing a tongue stroke. Actually, the phrase "tip of the tongue" can be interpreted loosely to mean that those players should use any comfortable point between the extreme tip of the tongue and another point about $\frac{1}{4}$ to $\frac{3}{8}$ of an inch back from the extreme tip. In a moment I will say more about how to find the best spot on your tongue to use in clarinet tonguing.

Some players, of course, have very long tongues. Occasionally, this means that the player, keeping his tongue in a basically low and forward position as he should, finds that his tongue tip feels greatly restricted when he attempts to place it on the tip of the reed. For such a player, a technique known as "anchor tonguing" may be in order, because at no time should the tongue act upon the reed at any point other than at the reed's own tip.

Anchor tonguing is simply a way of getting a too long tongue tip out of the way. To try this technique, point the tongue tip downward toward the floor of the mouth and move it forward until it braces, or "anchors," itself against the inside edge of the lower front teeth. Having done that, "tongue" on the reed tip with whatever portion of the tongue is nearest to it. It feels as though you are tonguing with the middle of your tongue on the reed tip, when actually you are making contact with the reed tip at a point about 1 inch or so back from the anchored tongue tip.

Please understand, however, that anchor tonguing should be used only by those who have great difficulties using the tip of the tongue on the tip of the reed. As a rule such people usually have extremely long tongues. I have known several excellent clarinetists who employ anchor tonguing exclusively and who achieve beautiful results with it. Personally I find the whole concept horrifying, mainly because I have a rather short tongue; if I tried anchor tonguing the listeners would hear me playing nothing but slurs since there is not enough tongue in my mouth to bring off that technique. Anchor tonguing remains a very effective approach for some players, however, and I heartily recommend it to those with long tongues.

One thing about tonguing that should *never* vary from player to player, though, is the other half of the contact point, the tip of the reed itself. Every clarinetist *must* articulate with his tongue by contacting the reed tip itself, and must *not* make contact with a point on the reed that is lower than its tip. This is why I said earlier that the old saying "tip of the tongue on the tip of the reed" may be entirely correct or it may be only half correct in some cases; while the tongue's contact point may vary from player to player, the reed's contact point must never vary. Some part of the tongue must always contact the reed tip and *only* the reed tip.

The reason for making such an issue of the reed tip's importance is that, after all, the vibrating reed generates the sound. Remember that the airflow causes the reed to vibrate, and the vibrating reed generates sound by activating the clarinet's air column. If the tongue touches, say, a point on the vibrating reed about halfway between its tip and its uncut bark, it is like trying to split the vibrations in the middle. The vibrations will stop, but, from a musical standpoint, it is much cleaner to act upon the reed at its tip where the vibrations begin. If the tongue acts upon the reed at any point lower than the reed tip, the resulting sound will be a dull "thud." The object of tonguing is clean, accurate tonal entrance; the sound of the tongue itself at work should never be audible to a listener. So, be sure to contact the reed tip exclusively.

Now I will get back to that problem of discovering just what point on your own tongue is the one to use for best results in your particular case. This is perhaps best done by relating the whole procedure to a story.

Begin by playing a good, strong second-line, open G. While holding that open G concentrate on completely relaxing the interior of the oral cavity and the throat and neck muscles. Now imagine that your tongue, lying relaxed on the floor of the mouth, is like a baby whale that has become temporarily beached between the shore and two boating docks. The baby whale, asleep, and totally relaxed, is your tongue; the three-sided barrier formed by the shore and the two boating docks is your line of lower teeth.

Take a new breath and again play open G, quickly reestablishing complete relaxation in the tongue, or the baby whale, or whatever it is. Now imagine that the water level around the baby whale begins to rise slowly as the tide comes in. The baby whale very slowly floats upward between the shore and the two boating docks. Compare this to what you actually do next: Allow your still-relaxed tongue to rise very slowly in the mouth. As the tongue rises, suddenly the tip of the vibrating reed tickles the first spot on the tongue to make contact with it. That tickled spot is, no doubt, the very spot on your tongue that should be used, during tonguing, to make contact with the reed tip.

To end this analogy we will hope that the water rising underneath the baby whale allowed him to rejoin the herd out in deeper water, and we will also hope that your clarinet playing can stay *out* of deep water by your contacting the reed tip with the "tickled" point on your tongue while tonguing.

All the rest of the tongue, of course, should remain totally relaxed at all times, no matter what style of tonguing you may need at different times, and again, its position is always low and forward.

THE TONGUE ACTION
ITSELF

The first two criteria of good tonguing, then, are to establish relaxation and to find the point on the tongue that should contact the reed tip. All articulation that takes place with the tongue's help must occur while the player maintains these criteria.

Remember that the tongue stroke makes no sound. Only the airflow vibrates the reed. The fierce hammer-stroke tonguing style of some young players shows that they unfortunately have the "attack" concept of starting a tone. Clarinetists must guard against this at all costs.

Instead, a player must be completely prepared for a tone before that tone is tongued. Relaxation, airflow, embouchure, and fingers must all be ready to play their roles before the tongue can even begin to assist with the tonal entrance, a hard fact often forgotten by clarinetists in playing situations. In plainer language, tonguing should be the very *last* of the player's preparations for producing a tone. Far too often it is one of the first, especially among inexperienced players. Think of it this way: How can it possibly be time to tongue a new tone if you aren't relaxed, if your airflow isn't pressurized yet, if your embouchure isn't formed, or if your fingering isn't yet in position? Remember that the tongue has nothing to do with producing a tone. It merely helps do the job a little more cleanly.

Whenever you tongue, make your airflow "think" that you are still slurring. Tongue each of your tongued notes as though they were all positioned in the middle of an ongoing phrase, whether the tongued note is actually at the beginning of a phrase or not. And, before tonguing, make sure that your fingers really are in place. You may think that you tongue and finger simultaneously, but actually the tongue must come last of all.

When practicing this technique, try to exaggerate it for emphasis: Slur a full-toned low F scale downward from "thumb F," then play it again at the same tempo tongued, trying to tongue as late as possible. Remember that the tongue action, when it does occur, must be relaxed: The little muscular alertness near the reed tip merely *brushes* the reed tip, and gets quickly away again.

Thus, the tongue action is relaxed, quick, and *late*, just as short and quick and relaxed a motion as is required of the fingers themselves, except that the tongue action comes later.

COORDINATION OF TONGUE
AND FINGERS

Many students complain that they can tongue rapidly on a repeated pitch, but that they cannot tongue fast enough on moving-
finger passages. From what I have said, it is easy to see the problem: The tongue is coming too early in its zeal to "get ahead."
When the tongue stroke is made after the fingers are in position,
rapid tonguing can occur, for it will coordinate with the action of
the fingers. It is pointless to tongue a note whose fingering is not
yet in place.

Whenever a student makes repeated mistakes in a technically
difficult passage involving tonguing, I have him play the passage
all slurred. The student almost always plays it successfully, much
to his surprise. Then I tell him that his tongue has been coming
too soon to its tasks, and that he should instead make it come in at
the last split second. When airflow and fingers continue as in slurring, and tonguing comes in *later,* the student usually plays the
passage correctly with relative ease. In each clarinetist's "technical
machine," all the "parts" related to tonguing are those that easily
go out of adjustment; it requires constant vigilance on the part of
the "operator" to see that they do not slip in too early.

TONGUING STYLES

You may easily gather that I advocate nothing but "legato tonguing"; that is, very light tonguing during a passage, tonguing so light
that the general effect is only a very little different from what it
would be if the player had actually been slurring the passage. Since
musical tones are primarily made of sound and not of "tonal entrance," the player should tongue as lightly as possible while he
stays within the proper musical context of the moment. The effect
of the clarinetist's tonguing must be as wide-ranging as that of the
violinist's bow but I repeat that the basic relaxed, quick, and light
approach must be maintained at all times, and in all musical contexts. Strong muscular "attacks" upon the reed by the tongue must
be abolished forever.

But how is the clarinetist to make audible any differences between one style of tongued articulations and another? The answer
takes us back to the airflow, that most basic of all the clarinetist's
physical activities. I have already described how legato tonguing is
accomplished: The airflow continues as though the player were

actually slurring, while the tongue lightly brushes the reed tip at the beginning of each tone, creating a very smooth and sensitive effect. All other tonguing styles, ranging from legato tonguing to "staccato" (the other extreme), differ only in how the airflow is used to accomplish them. If a tone is to be played "marcato," the player should accent the tone with his airflow as he tongues, but his tongue action should remain the same as ever. It is true that sometimes tones in rapid passages need to be played with some noticeable separation between them, and in that case the tongue may linger on the reed tip between the tones a little longer than usual, but the tongue action itself remains relaxed, quick, and light.

To understand the tremendous effect that the airflow has on tonguing, think of "conveyor-belt breathing." This concept places the burden of style upon the airflow, where it belongs, so that the tongue does not have to tighten up in futile effort. In clarinet playing, the tongue should not *end* tones; it should only begin new ones. In passages where tones should be separated, the ends of tones should be tapered off by the airflow, and that is where conveyor-belt breathing comes into the picture.

To grasp the idea of conveyor-belt breathing, play a tone on the clarinet, using the tongue on its beginning as though you were pronouncing the syllable "tah." To end the tone, keep the supporting stomach-muscle pressure firm and solid, but stop the *flow* of air. Remembering that the airflow has two aspects (pressure and speed) as discussed in Chapter 4, "The Two Basics in Clarinet Playing," keep the pressure in effect while stopping the speed of the airflow.

Now begin a tone a second time in exactly the same way you did the first one: Tongue the beginning, keep the air pressure and speed going strongly during the tone, and, at the tone's end, keep the pressure but stop the airflow from any further motion. This should again result in a nice "tah." Now if you play that tone a third time the same way, and a fourth time, and so on, with increasing frequency, you will notice that the airflow is stopping, flowing, stopping and flowing, so that you are creating a series of "tahs" that are appropriately tongued on the beginnings and are beautifully "breathed off" on the ends. This resembles what the airflow would be doing if it were indeed a conveyor belt, moving from tone to tone on an assembly line. The air pressure (or stomach-muscle pressure, or the "support") remains constant both during and between tones, but the actual *flow* of the air is what is doing your articulating for you; the light, relaxed, and quick tongue motion is merely helping the airflow clean up the beginnings of the tones.

The entire range of tonguing styles, then, can be brought about primarily through the efforts of the airflow, and secondarily through those of the tongue. It would be fruitless for me to try to describe in detail here exactly what the airflow and the tongue must do in relation to each other to achieve all of the articulatory effects that are possible on clarinet; such an explanation would take far too long, and it would miss the point in any case. Each new passage is a new and different artistic challenge. What the clarinetist really needs is a basic grasp of the proper *approach* to articulation, no matter what the context.

If the player remembers to rely primarily on the airflow, while helping it out with a relaxed and light tongue on the beginnings of tones, he has already gone far toward achieving beautiful articulation. In some passages, either fast or slow, conveyor-belt breathing is most appropriate and effective while used in conjunction with a light tongue. In some other passages, either fast or slow, the flow of the air as well as its muscular support (or pressure) should never slacken, but should continue flowing unabated, still being helped, on the beginning of tones, by that famous relaxed, light tongue. In some rather fast staccato passages the tones need more separation between them than normal, and the tongue may remain on the reed tip between tones slightly longer than usual as long as it remains relaxed and light.

Incidentally, the word "staccato" does not mean "short"; what it really means is "separated." Separation of tones at a fast tempo does tend to shorten the tones themselves, a fact that has led to the widespread misunderstanding that to play staccato means to play a series of very short tones, no matter what the context. This misunderstanding is perpetuated by ensemble directors who call out "Short!" to the clarinet section while they are in the midst of a staccato passage. He wants them as *individual* players to play shorter tones so that the general *section* effect will be separated, but the individuals involved should not take that to mean that they should play such short, "bitten-off" staccato tones in their own solo or chamber music playing. To do so would be to play in a most insensitive manner. The watchword here, as it is in all tongued passages in all styles, is *tone;* remember that the listener should always be treated to the sound of your tone, not to the sound of your tongue.

Articulation results from the player's artistic combination of (1) the behavior of his airflow, and (2) his unwavering use of relaxed, light, and quick tongue strokes on the beginnings of tones. Also, all tongue strokes must be executed a split second *after* all other preparations for that tone have been made. Remember, too, that the musical role played by the tongue is amazingly unimportant in itself, but that it has the power of undoing you as a player if tonguing is not done correctly. The bad result of improper tonguing is twofold: The playing will be unsatisfying and the player will become tense.

If you as a player force yourself, as in "mind over matter," to keep tonguing in perspective, your tonguing problems should be few indeed.

THE MULTIPLE-TONGUING IDEA

I know from personal experience that there are some clarinetists who tongue correctly, but who simply cannot get up enough tonguing speed to articulate certain passages properly. For players who are absolutely certain that their approach to tonguing is a properly relaxed one, for players who know that their tonguing is being helped rather than hindered by their airflow, but whose tongue will nevertheless not "make it" during the fastest tonguing passages, the idea of multiple tonguing may be the answer. I must hastily add, however, that I do *not* refer to the type of multiple tonguing used by brass and flute players; stay as far away from that approach as you can, for reasons that I will discuss in a moment. First, let me tell the history of my multiple-tonguing idea from the beginning.

Although it has been nearly thirty years since Keith Stein gave me my first clarinet lesson, I was privileged to study with him continually over fifteen years. It soon became obvious to both of us that I had a tremendous problem with tension, and that the chief manifestation of that problem was in my tonguing. I was unsure of myself as a young student, insecure and quite uncoordinated. When I played the clarinet my throat was constricted, my arms and fingers moved stiffly. Looking back on it, I suppose I was lucky to have been able to tongue at all. Professor Stein was extremely patient with me throughout the entirety of my study with him, a lesson in itself that I have never forgotten.

As the earliest years passed I was able to overcome most of the tension; my shoulders, arms, and fingers relaxed for the most part, and I was usually able to keep my throat from closing up by consciously relaxing it. My tongue relaxed somewhat, but it remained slow. Professor Stein used every pedagogical device known, and then threw in a few more of his own invention, to keep my tongue from becoming tense and to increase the speed of its activity in passages demanding fast tonguing.

Eventually Professor Stein's long and patient work with me brought my tonguing to the point where my tongue's action was definitely correct, at least almost all of the time, but it continued to lack speed for the faster passages. Professor Stein and I were both forced to conclude that for the time being I would have to content myself with what little tonguing agility I had. We hoped that I would "grow into" better coordination within the next few years.

From the standpoint of my tonguing, however, those next few years were a disappointment. All other aspects of my playing did improve greatly, and I was able to take a clarinet teaching position of my own, but, even as a professional performer and teacher, I was plagued by my tongue's basic slowness. I was forced to change some of the tongued articulations found on the printed page, removing some of the staccato markings or adding some slurring marks where there had been none before. I became quite adept at deception, and I believe I disguised my slow tonguing problem so that few listeners could have detected it with certainty.

But I knew the problem existed, and it began to bother me more and more. It became a real challenge to me, one that I could not ignore, and one day I decided that I would set about finding a solution to the problem once and for all.

The players of flutes and brass instruments have made use of a very simple technique that allows them to tongue rapidly whenever rapid tonguing is called for, and they have used that technique for generations. The technique is called multiple tonguing. It breaks down into two distinct processes known as double tonguing and triple tonguing. Double tonguing is used for fast notes that are rhythmically grouped into twos or fours, and triple tonguing is used for fast notes rhythmically grouped into threes and sixes. I should emphasize, however, that even brass and flute players *normally* use the approach to tonguing that is essentially the same as that used on clarinet, an approach that could be described as "single tonguing," the same approach discussed earlier in this chapter. The only difference is that since brass and flute players have no reed in the mouth, their tongue strokes are directed at the roof of the mouth rather than at the reed tip. Single tonguing as I described it earlier in this chapter is, then, the type of tonguing used by players of *all* wind instruments at slow and medium tempos. Players of the reed instruments (oboe, clarinet, bassoon, and saxophone) have had to use single tonguing at *all* tempos, whether fast or slow. Only brass players and flutists have been able to use multiple tonguing when the tempo becomes too fast for single tonguing.

Brass-and-flute multiple tonguing operates as follows: In double tonguing, the player's tongue pronounces the sound of the letters "t–k–t–k," and so forth, which, in effect, "doubles" the type of tongue stroke and greatly increases the speed of the player's tonguing. In triple tonguing, these tongue motions are used: "t–k–t, t–k–t," and so forth. Some players of these instruments prefer to use "d" and "g" instead of "t" and "k," but the idea remains the same.

Brass players and flutists have been able to use that style of multiple tonguing successfully because no part of their instrument is inserted in the mouth. They can articulate with the tongue upon two different points on the roof of the mouth so that there is no audible difference between their single and multiple tonguing strokes.

Clarinetists and players of other reed instruments must, however, stay away from that type of multiple tonguing, because they *do* insert part of the instrument in their mouth, and while the "t" part of it is perfectly all right (acted upon the reed tip), the "k" part of it results in musical disaster! Remember I have stressed that all tonguing done on a clarinet *must* act upon the reed tip; there is no way that a "k" or a "g" sound can be acted upon a reed tip. When a clarinetist pronounces a "k" or "g" sound while tonguing, an air pocket forms behind the tongue which, when released, fails to act upon the reed instantaneously enough for clean articulation.

In a sense, the situation seems hardly fair. Clarinetists, no matter what style of music they play, are expected to tongue just as rapidly and cleanly as are the flutists and brass players. While the latter have been able to go into a sort of "high gear" (multiple tonguing) in fast passages, the clarinetists have been stuck with having to cover the entire tempo range with nothing going for them but single tonguing.

So, in the search for the solution to my too-slow-tonguing problem, I knew that whatever that solution might be, it would have to involve some form of multiple tonguing that was (1) *different* from the traditional one used by brass and flute players, and (2) solely acted upon the reed tip. One day, after I had been a solo clarinet recitalist and a university teacher for several years, I set about developing a system of multiple tonguing on the clarinet that would fit those criteria.

ON-THE-REED MULTIPLE TONGUING

In the past, some attempts to discover a good system of multiple tonguing on reed instruments have been made with varying success. Keith Stein himself, in his book *The Art of Clarinet Playing,* refers to the possibilities of a sort of "paintbrush" stroke in which the tongue moves both up and down, making contact with the reed tip both ways. I have spoken with other reed players, and it appears that a number of instrumentalists, particularly oboists and clarinetists, have attempted something similar to the "paintbrush" idea that Stein wrote about, so I pursued that idea first.

I began with a single tone, during which I tried "painting" the tip of the reed with the tip of my tongue. The upstroke presented no problems, but the downstroke was strange indeed. I stuck with this technique, however, for just a few minutes each day for a couple of weeks, until finally I was able to make that up-and-down tonguing stroke sound the same as very rapid single tonguing. That, after all, was the whole object, and I was most encouraged by the accomplishment. It showed me that if the technique could be refined enough to sound like normal, rapid tonguing during a single long tone, then perhaps it could also be refined to allow coordination with rapidly moving fingers. I had great hope for it, but I knew that this next step would be a tough one.

So as not to tire my tongue too much, I was careful to spend only a few minutes of my daily practice session on the technique. By the time another month had passed, I was able to coordinate this type of on-the-reed multiple tonguing with my moving fingers. I was thoroughly delighted with the result, and I began incorporating it into my technique. I knew that I had found the answer to my slow-tongue problem and that, with further work, I would be thoroughly satisfied with it.

The last section of this chapter consists of a procedure that any clarinetist can follow to learn this technique. It is essentially the same procedure I taught myself, and the instructions include step-by-step details. I will not go into the details here, but I should make some cautionary and explanatory comments on it.

First, remember at all times that nothing about this on-the-reed multiple tonguing represents any change in approach from normal single tonguing. The tongue must *still* remain relaxed and light at all times. If you think about normal tonguing for a moment, you will realize that the tongue does make a sort of double action: It must approach and make contact with the reed, and then it must get *away* from the reed tip. The great thing about on-the-reed multiple tonguing is that it harnesses, so to speak, that double action of the tongue, simply by contacting the reed tip in both directions. This can mean doubling the effective speed of your tonguing!

Next, keep in mind that this technique should never be considered a substitute for regular, normal tonguing; in fact, many clarinetists have no use for it at all since they already possess very fast and agile tongues. This new technique should not even be attempted by anyone who has not mastered the normal method of single tonguing on clarinet. On-the-reed multiple tonguing is, rather, a *supplementary* technique to be used by those players whose tongues are naturally slow, and even then it is only to be used during very rapidly tongued passages.

Some clarinetists have expressed needless worries about this technique that should be dispelled. In no way, for instance, does this on-the-reed multiple tonguing present a danger to the reed tip. The tips of reeds are thin, of course, but they are never so thin that a fast-moving, light, and relaxed tongue tip could do them any harm. Similarly, there is no danger to the tongue itself. As long as the tongue is relaxed, and as long as the technique is not indulged in for too long at one sitting, no harm will befall the tongue tip.

In the procedure that follows, you will note that I have recommended the use of the syllables "Tuttle-uttle-uttle-uttle," and so on, as a basic pattern of tongue movement to be used while learning the technique. Those are the syllables that seemed to help me the most in my efforts, and they have been equally helpful for some of my students who have developed on-the-reed multiple tonguing; however, you may find some other set of syllables that has more meaning for you. Any set of syllables is acceptable as long as it gets the tongue moving over the reed tip, up and down, in a typical paintbrush motion.

The procedure that follows is to be used at your own pace; in that sense, it is a "programmed textbook," as many other books are today. The learner should not only go at his own pace, but he should also be very careful not to go ahead to the next step before he has mastered the earlier ones, all of them, in order.

I have discovered through experience that the double tonguing part of the technique is not only easier than the triple tonguing, but it is also more useful. I use triple tonguing wherever it is appropriate, of course, but double tonguing is needed more often. For this reason, if you have much greater difficulty with the triple tonguing, you should forget all about it until you have practiced on-the-reed double tonguing for quite some time. Let several months pass, if necessary, between learning double and triple tonguing. For some clarinetists, of course, triple tonguing will present no more problems than double tonguing.

Finally, if you have terrible difficulties coordinating the tonguing technique with your moving fingers, the cause of the trouble will be, almost invariably, the tongue's moving far too quickly! It is your tongue that is *ahead*, not your fingers that are *behind*. Remember that you have literally doubled the effective speed of your tongue tip. You must remind yourself that you have become capable of tremendously fast tongue speeds, while the tongue itself should feel lazy, relaxed, and slow. I had one student whose only difficulty with double tonguing, from the very first day he tried it, was to slow it down enough so that his speed could be measured on a metronome! After several minutes of experimentation he finally slowed it down enough that, while he held a long open G, I "clocked" his double tonguing tempo at four beautifully tongued notes per beat at a metronome marking of 160.

On-the-reed multiple tonguing, as I have described it, continues to please me very much. I have now used it for several years and I have taught it successfully to players who have been interested in learning it. I spent most of one summer gaining a command of the technique, and during that time I never let it take up too much of my practice time at any one sitting. During the following fall, I felt confident enough to use on-the-reed double tonguing during one of my solo clarinet recitals. My naturally slow tongue need never be a problem again, and that is gratifying!

THE PROCEDURE FOR LEARNING ON-THE-REED MULTIPLE TONGUING

PART I:
The Introduction to the Technique

Record the metronome markings at which you can single-tongue repeated open Gs both four to a beat and three to a beat.

Momentarily putting the clarinet aside, simply sit in a good playing position and say the words "Tuttle-uttle-uttle-uttle" (etc.) making sure that the tongue remains low, relaxed, and wide across the middle; not pointed.

Take up the clarinet and single-tongue a few repetitions of open G again, this time at only a medium tempo. This is just to become reacquainted with the reed, and to relax the tongue.

Begin a fairly long open G with a regular single-tongued stroke, taking care to pronounce it "Tuh" as in the first syllable of the word "Tuttle." Do this a few times, totally relaxing the tongue during each held tone.

Begin another open G with "Tuh" but this time finish the word "Tuttle" by returning the tongue to the reed after "Tuh" in the manner of "tle." This second stroke should carry the tip of the tongue up past the tip of the reed to the roof of the mouth, and it should leave the middle of the tongue relaxed and broad across the bottom of the mouth.

Staying relaxed, return the tip of the tongue to its resting position by passing it *downward* over the tip of the reed, pronouncing the syllable "Uh."

The tongue is now ready for another upward stroke, as in pronouncing another "tle," and to be brushed past the reed tip again on its way towards the roof of the mouth.

Now another downward stroke, brushing past the reed tip again, to return to the resting position in the bottom of the mouth.

Repeat this whole process, quicker but still without extreme speed; in other words, do a very relaxed, smooth, and even "Tuttle-uttle-Uh." The last syllable could also be "Ah" if desired.

Remove the reed and mouthpiece from the mouth and say again, "Tuttle-uttle-uttle-uttle" (etc.).

Replace the clarinet into the embouchure and do it again on the open G, this time adding another stroke: "Tuttle-uttle-uttle-uttle-Uh." *Stay relaxed throughout;* aim for evenness.

Keep practicing this on open G until the double tonguing begins to sound like very fast single tonguing, very smooth, even, and homogeneous. The tongue *need not move quickly* to achieve this similarity.

At this point you should stop practicing this technique. It is very important to let the tongue rest now. Normal practicing, using only the usual single tonguing technique, may be resumed.

Follow the same procedure again later at other practice sessions, still using open G only, until you are satisfied that the effect is a good one, and that the up-and-down strokes sound identical to a listener.

After you are satisfied with the effect, record the metronome marking at which you can tongue four open Gs to the beat by using this form of double tonguing. Compare this with your fastest tempo for single tonguing four notes to the beat. (Triple tonguing comes later.)

PART II:

The Development of Double Tonguing

Extend the procedure (a long tone followed by "Tuttle-uttle-uttle-uttle-Uh," etc.) from open G to thumb F, low C, low F, thumb F again, top-line F, fourth-space E, throat E, low E, low F again, low C again, and finally thumb F again.

After doing that exercise on thumb F, do the following also on that note: "Tuh-tuttle-uttle-uttle-Uh" in the rhythm of:

Repeat the foregoing exercise, and then *slur* this passage:

Now, using the double-tonguing technique, play the following exercise:

The next step is to repeat the last exercise, this time tonguing every note in all four measures rather than slurring the last two. In this manner, double tonguing has been accomplished while rapidly changing pitches.

Now do the following *two* four-measure exercises (first, the one containing a slurred scale; second, the same one played all

tongued) up a whole step, thus transposing them from F major to
G major:

Transpose all eight measures (the two exercises together have
become one longer one) down to E pure minor in the lowest octave of the clarinet's range.

Now transpose the eight-measure exercise back to F major,
then to G major, and then to E minor again. A rest for the tongue
should occur here; put off further practice of the technique until
another occasion.

The next transposition of the eight-measure exercise is to G
major in the second octave. In other words, play the exercise as it
is printed above, in the key of G, but take it up an octave.

When satisfied with that, next do it in F major down a whole
step, so that its range begins on top-line F and ends on thumb F.

The next step is to transpose the same exercise into *any* or *all*
descending one-octave major or minor scales, but *avoid* the range
above G on top of the staff. Do this until crossing the "break"
downward is satisfactory.

Having become satisfied with your execution of one-octave descending major and minor scales over the "break," double-tongue
the following exercise. In syllables this exercise would be pro-
nounced "Tuh-tuttle-uttle-uttle-Uh, tuttle-uttle-uttle-Uh."
(Again, the last syllable could be "Ah" if that seems more natural.)

Double-tongue this last exercise as *slowly* as possible *and* as *fast*
as possible. Rest from this by throwing in an occasional run-
through at a medium, comfortable tempo.

Transpose it now up a step to G major, and then to G *minor* at
the same pitch. For variety, do all three forms of G minor.

Now transpose it up an octave to G minor beginning on the G
on top of the staff. In this manner you encounter double tonguing

over the "break" *ascending.* (Do *not* try that particular octave yet in
G *major.*) Now rest the tongue.

When rested, or at a later practice session, transpose that exercise down a step to F major (not F minor yet). Make *that* work
satisfactorily by employing the same over-the-break principles
you have always used: Keep the fingers relaxed, the air flowing
smoothly, and use as *little finger movement* as possible. It will probably help to put the right hand down when ascending from B-flat
to C-natural at the "break."

Next, go back to the G scale up a step again, this time playing it
in *major.* Now the "break" will occur between A-natural and B-
natural. Employ the same principles of smoothness and relaxation.

After this can be done to good effect, transpose the same exercise to any and all major and minor scales for one octave, using the
range again from low E up to no higher than G on top of the staff.

Continue exactly the same thing, but now extend the range of
the scale exercise higher, going no higher than high C-natural.

Now the exercise must be *reversed:*

Take this new exercise up one octave.

Now take it up *another* octave, which will extend your double-
tonguing range to high F.

Now up one step to G major, which extends the double-tonguing range to high G.

Next, practice two- and three-octave major and minor scales,
four notes to the beat, all over the range of the clarinet. Begin
each new octave of the scales with this rhythm:

Double tonguing has now been accomplished over the entire
range of the instrument, since it will be quite easy now to extend it
even beyond high G. You are now ready for the printed page.

Obtain a copy of Reginald Kell's *Seventeen Staccato Studies* (International Music Company) and look at the first study. Disregard
the words at the top of the page, which are directed toward single
tonguing only.

The entire study reiterates the "eighth-and-two-sixteenths"

rhythmic pattern. Practice the study first *all slurred* to become completely familiar with the notes.

Next, at a comfortable tempo, practice the piece using the usual single tonguing. Do not bother to make much, if anything, of the dynamics in order to concentrate on smoothly flowing air.

When you are thoroughly familiar with the piece, *completely disregard* the *dynamics* this time, and apply double tonguing to it in this manner: "Tuh-tuttle-Uh-tuttle-Uh," and so on. Maintain a good *forte* volume throughout.

If you feel musically and technically ready, you could try playing the piece observing the dynamics now; however, it will be absolutely necessary to use continuous breath support as well as concentrated tongue control. Dynamic variation, executed simultaneously with double tonguing, will become easier to achieve later on.

PART III:
How to Practice Double Tonguing

On-the-reed double tonguing should now be established. Proceed with the Kell Study No. 2, one beat to the measure, after practicing it first slurred and then single-tongued, just as you prepared No. 1 earlier.

Systematic practice should proceed essentially as follows: First, with a metronome, find a comfortable tempo at which you can double-tongue four notes to a beat, and do the following exercise at that tempo, using the metronome:

Now set the metronome only *one notch faster,* and do the exercise again.

Continue setting the metronome one notch faster and repeating the exercise until you cannot double-tongue any faster on that exercise.

Now set the metronome one notch *slower* and repeat the exercise.

Continue setting the metronome one notch slower and repeating the exercise. Soon you will be back to your starting point on the metronome, but *continue* setting it one notch slower and repeating the exercise until your double tonguing cannot be slowed down any more. By following this procedure you will greatly extend the tempo range of your double tonguing.

Also extend your new double tonguing to the solo literature for clarinet. Try tonguing the long sixteenth-note passages in the fast movements of the Mozart Concerto and in the various solo pieces of Weber, for example.

When this sort of thing happens in music:

you must put the tongue "in gear" by single-tonguing the first note (E) and beginning the "Tuttles" on the next notes (F and G).

In addition to using the clarinet's solo literature, applying double tonguing to other music will be profitable. Use more of the Kell Studies, other studies, and ensemble music.

PART IV:

The Development of Triple Tonguing

We must first be *certain* that on-the-reed double tonguing is comfortable for the player before he attempts triple tonguing. The more comfortable the former, the easier the latter will be.

In the rhythm of triplets (and *without* the clarinet in the mouth), say the syllables "Tuttle-tuh-tuttle-tuh-tuttle-tuh-Tah." The rhythm would be:

Although the process will be considerably shorter than it was for double tonguing (since the player has now developed facility with "Tuttle"), we must go back to using the open G. On the clarinet, then, tongue "Tuttle-tuh-tuttle-tuh-Tah" etc. on open G in the rhythm of triplets.

When the triple rhythm on repeated open Gs sounds smooth enough, play the following exercise several times using the syllables "Tuttle-tuh-Tah":

Once that works, extend it in the following manner, using "Tuttle-tuh-tuttle-tuh-tuttle-tuh-Tah":

Next, using the same syllabic pattern, extend it in this manner:

Now add a triplet to the beginning of the last exercise:

(etc.)

Finally, add one more beat at the beginning, making a complete three-octave descending F scale:

(etc.)

After the descending three-octave F major scale sounds satisfactory, do a descending three-octave G major scale, also in triplets, of course, and also saying "Tuttle-tuh-tuttle-tuh," etc.

Next, triple-tongue this:

Now do the same exercise up an octave. It will include going over the "break," of course. Keep the air well supported and fast-moving. Forte!

Take the same exercise up still *another* octave, and you will be going over the upper register break. Fortissimo!

Transpose that exercise to whatever major or minor key you wish, and to whatever range you wish. (Keep resting the tongue whenever necessary.)

When you feel ready for the printed page, look at the Kell

Study No. 4 and proceed with practicing it as you did other Kell Studies: First slur it, then single-tongue it at a comfortable tempo.

When you are thoroughly familiar with the music, speed it up a bit to a comfortable tempo for triple tonguing. (Again, do not worry about the dynamics yet.) Fortissimo!

PART V:
How to Practice Triple Tonguing

Continue applying triple tonguing to the printed page. This could take the form of practicing Kell Study No. 7 in the usual way: first, all slurred; second, all single-tongued; and third, at a suitable tempo for triple tonguing.

Systematic practice for triple tonguing should proceed the same way as it did for double tonguing: Set the metronome at a comfortable triple-tonguing tempo and play the following exercise with it:

Now set the metronome one notch faster and repeat the exercise.

Continue setting the metronome one notch faster and repeating the exercise until you cannot triple-tongue any faster.

After reaching the upper limit, set the metronome one notch *slower* and repeat the exercise.

Continue setting the metronome one notch slower and repeating the exercise. Soon you will return to your original starting point; however, *continue* setting the metronome slower and slower until the *lower* limit of practicable triple tonguing is reached.

Also extend your new triple tonguing to other pieces of clarinet literature wherever there are fast-tongued triplets. *Change* the printed articulation to suit your purpose. For example, No. 18 in the Jeanjean *25 Etudes* begins with slurred, rapid triplets. Try removing the slurs, mentally, and triple-tongue this melody.

When this sort of thing happens in music:

you must put the tongue "in gear" by beginning the passage with "Tuttle" on E and F, and then triple-tongue the G–A–B with the usual "Tuttle-tuh."

PART VI:
How to Practice Multiple Tonguing
in Asymmetrical Meters

After feeling comfortable with your development of double and triple tonguing, you may begin *combining* them in such meters as 5/8, 7/8 etc. Let us look at the Kell Study No. 11 as an example.

The first decision which must be made about this 5/8 piece is whether it is in "3 plus 2" or in "2 plus 3." Let us say it is "2 plus 3." The multiple tonguing syllables would then come out: "Tuttle-tuttle-tuh." First *slur* the piece, then single-tongue all of it, then speed it up and multiple-tongue it in "2 plus 3" style.

You might try reversing it next, and, calling it "3 plus 2," tongue it as "Tuttle-tuh-tuttle," etc. However, this particular piece seems better as "2 plus 3."

Extend this principle to other pieces, and other meters. 7/8, for example, could be "3 plus 2 plus 2," tongued as "Tuttle-tuh-tuttle-tuttle," etc.

Kell Study No. 13 is a special case, mixing double and triple tonguing in a new way. In the first measure, the first beat is:

tongued as "Tuttle-tuh-tuttle-tuh." The second beat is:

tongued as "Tuttle-uttle-uttle."

CHAPTER

8

Musicianship

A player's musicianship can be measured by his ability to play a piece of music in a way that aesthetically satisfies the listener. Some players plod into a performance as though they were heading into a swamp wearing hip boots with the sole purpose of coming out on the other end high and dry. For such people the printed page of music does represent a sort of swamp, or perhaps a map of a swamp, and when they reach the other end they say to themselves, "There! I made it through the swamp! What more could anyone have asked of me?" An expert naturalist would be able to tell them about some of the incalculably beautiful things, organic and inorganic, that they had completely missed, trodden upon, or destroyed in their single-minded push toward dry land.

And just as there is more to marshland than its superficial aspects may indicate to the uninitiated, so is there much more to a piece of music than can ever appear on a printed page.

There is another kind of player, one who knows enough to observe, identify, and make use of the more obvious elements in a piece of music; the artistic subtleties elude him, but he does what a good friend of mine calls "a very workmanlike job."

Those artistic subtleties, however, remain. They exist, not in black and white on the page, but somewhere within the player himself. If you play the Mozart Clarinet Concerto by putting into it only what you see on the page, you may very well do a "workmanlike job," but you have missed those spirit-lifting extra dimensions Mozart implied in the music. He implied them because there is no way that he could have communicated them directly with pen and ink. The irony is that a player must infer these extra dimensions through what the composer *does* put directly on the paper, and so the player who reads that page has the task of bringing to life all the musical dimensions of the music, both the implied ones and the literal ones. The player should do this, of course, by calling upon and judiciously using every musical resource at his command. Together, the breadth of his resources and his ability to draw upon them make up what is known as his musicianship.

Since musicianship really is a combination of things, we must approach a discussion of it from several different angles.

THE PARAMOUNT IMPORTANCE
OF RHYTHM

The clarinetist's approach to rhythm is as important to his musicianship as his airflow is to his playing. At least from the standpoint of performance, rhythm may well be the most important element of music. Rhythm exists on several different levels in a piece of music, and it is the clarinetist's job to be aware of those levels.

Students too often think that "musicianship" means to indulge in some sort of ethereal, syrupy, meter-bending process. That is, they think that they are being "mechanical" if they adhere to the naturally flowing pulse in music, and they believe that in order for their performance to be considered "musical" they must constantly slow down and speed up. The truth is that nothing will kill an otherwise good performance sooner than a listener's unsuccessful search for a performer's rhythmic pulse. And if the performer *has* no discernible rhythmic pulse, there is no chance that the listener will hear one.

In short, the musical value of *ritardandi* and *accelerandi* has been blown all out of proportion in the minds of many musicians. Obviously there are styles of music, particularly the more romantic ones, that would indeed sound too mechanical if they were performed with clocklike strictness of pulse, or if the performance exhibited no rhythmic subtletly. The true artist, however, knows that his richest musical resources lie between the two extremes. He neither disorients his listeners with an excessive use of ritards, nor fails to please or thrill them with an occasional well-placed and well-executed one.

Music must never lose its flow and direction. Even in the music of the Romantic era, the basic metric flow must be maintained throughout. Otherwise the beautiful, added subtleties that *should* be put into a performance at strategic points lose all potential effectiveness. Think of it this way: If you look out from the shore upon a great expanse of ocean, you may become very quickly bored. If, however, the ocean is enlivened by the sudden appearance of an interesting ship, the view is more likely to hold your attention. Similarly, if your view is suddenly filled with hundreds of ships, not any single one of them will hold your interest for very long. The same principle holds for the performance of music: If the listener perceives no subtleties he becomes bored; if he detects nothing *but* subtleties he becomes disoriented *and* bored. Actually a good step in the right direction is to remember that the most basic, most important element in any piece of music is its rhythmic flow.

One other tremendously important aspect of rhythm is what goes on *inside* each beat. Are you, the performer, accurately executing the subdivisions of the beats? Some music flows in such a way that a careful listener can discern two, four, or eight distinct and equal subdivisions within each beat. Some other music is characterized by beats that subdivide naturally into groups of threes, sixes, nines, or twelves. Whatever type of subdivision is prevalent in any piece of music, the player must be certain that he is accurately conveying that subtlety to the listener. This is a tall order for some young and inexperienced players, but all musicians, regardless of age or experience, must strive for rhythmic accuracy and excellence above all the other aspects of music. Otherwise the character of the music will be cut off at its source, and the player will have nothing to *depart from* as the music proceeds.

PHRASING AND FORM

Try to become familiar with the shape or *form* of a piece. It is not necessary laboriously to analyze each minute detail contained in each measure of the music, but it is essential to recognize the beginnings, endings, and the relative lengths of the sections within each movement. For example, your performance of a clarinet sonata, first movement, will be immeasurably enhanced if you are aware of the exact points of division between the sections known as Exposition, Development, Recapitulation, and Coda. (Simpler terms for Exposition and Recapitulation are Statement and Restatement.) In sonatas of the Classic and Romantic eras the second and third movements can generally be analyzed as A–B–A, while the last movements are usually in what is known as rondo form, or A–B–A–C–A. If a final movement is not a rondo, it is usually a theme with variations. An awareness of even these seemingly superficial features of the music will give you, the player, insight into the piece that will greatly enhance your performance of it. However a piece's form can be analyzed, allow your knowledge of that form to enable your performance to "take shape."

Just as important, though on another level, is the idea embodied in the term "phrasing." Phrasing is *not* the same as articulation! Far too often I have heard students confuse the two terms, both in word and in deed. In Chapter 7, "Tonguing and Articulation," I said that articulation is the result of the combined efforts of the tongue and the airflow; as such, articulation is merely a part of, or a device to use in support of, the greater musical idea of phrasing.

Phrasing, then, refers to the manner in which a player shapes and contours a phrase of music. Or perhaps I could go farther, and come closer to the truth, by saying that phrases already have shape; in that case, phrasing must be the manner in which the player *enhances* a phrase for the listener. The musical importance of phrasing is very great, because the player's use of it will determine the effect the performance will have on the listener. As the performance proceeds, the listener grasps the form of the music by what the player does within phrases and between interrelated phrases.

Each phrase must be presented for what it is: a musical "thought." A phrase can be compared to a sentence in spoken or written language, or perhaps it can be compared even more accurately to a phrase or clause within a sentence. Phrases have often been called "musical thoughts," and that is a good description of them as long as you understand that it is an oversimplification. The musical thoughts expressed by phrases are hardly ever complete in themselves; they require additional, related thoughts to clarify them. In practical terms, this means, very simply, that musical phrases depend upon each other to get their idea across to the listener. One phrase must lead into another, out of another, or both, depending upon its position in the form of the music.

The clarinetist's resources, to be drawn upon during the process of effective phrasing, are few and simple: dynamic variety and articulation. (Variety of tone color can be another resource; I will come to that in a moment.) The simplest, most direct, and sometimes most effective approach to phrasing is for you, the player, to match your dynamic levels with the pitch levels of the phrase, bringing out the highest tone more loudly than the lower ones, and so forth. Or bring out the notes more at the points of especially dramatic harmonic movement. At all times have the phrase lead to its high point and fall gracefully away from it to the end of the phrase. Be on guard, however, not to carry that approach to an extreme; too much of a good thing is, in this case, just as undesirable as would be playing with no dynamic variety at all.

Longer tones, the ones lasting more than one beat, let us say, should never just "sit" at one dynamic level. A long tone held out at the same, unchanging dynamic level is no more musical than is the annoying "hum" that issues from an improperly grounded electronic amplifier. Do something dynamically to give longer tones a sense of direction; that direction can be up or down (louder or softer) depending on where the tone occurs in its phrase. Very long tones, ones that are held for a whole measure or more, can usually grow louder to their midpoint and then softer again to the end.

This brings to mind a very common problem: Students can usually make crescendos very gradually and properly, but diminuendos are more troublesome. Most inexperienced players tend to drop the dynamic level far too suddenly during a diminuendo, so that the effect is more sudden than gradual. Be sure that you can grow softer just as well and just as gradually as you can grow louder during single tones or during entire phrases.

If two notes in a row are at the same pitch, it is often very effective to have a slight diminuendo during the first one, and full continuous volume on the second one. For a perfect example of this, look at the high A-naturals in the very first phrase of the slow

movement of the Mozart Concerto, and at the high C-naturals in
the second phrase.

Breathing can easily upset your phrasing if you take a breath in
the "wrong" place. Breathing should be used, like articulation, as a
help, not a hindrance, toward beautiful phrasing. Wherever it is
possible, breathing should take place between phrases rather than
during them. For a guide to breathing-spot selection, look at the
how-to-practice section of Chapter 6, "Technique."

TONE COLOR

The clarinet is capable of reproducing a whole spectrum of tonal
colors. This fact is overlooked by players who think that they
should strive for only one "clarinet tone quality." Those players
refer to "my tone," or "his tone," as though each player were only
capable of producing a single type of tone on his clarinet. Dynamic
levels should vary during playing, and so should tonal color. A
thoughtful clarinetist will realize that his instrument is capable of
producing tone colors that range from a rich, mellow, and
"woody" darkness to a clear, brilliantly penetrating brightness.
The player who has command of that tonal spectrum, and who
knows how to use it in combination with the clarinet's incredible
dynamic range, is a clarinetist who possesses an absolutely formidable reservoir of phrasing resources!

Tonal color, on clarinet, varies through the use of the airflow
(inevitably) and the embouchure. It is a very difficult subject to
discuss but, generally speaking, it is fairly safe to say that the
darker colors can be achieved through relaxing the embouchure
muscles, while the brighter colors can be brought out through the
use of a more alert, more "pointed" embouchure. The degree to
which any of this will be effective is determined by how well the
airflow is cooperating with the embouchure's efforts, whatever
those may be at any given moment. At first glance, it may seem to
be a disadvantage that the airflow must simultaneously see to the
dynamic level and the tonal color. But on further inspection, it
turns out to be a real advantage, because the dynamic level will
enhance the tone color, and the tone color can be used to enhance
the dynamic level. The two aspects of tone in question can, therefore, be considered dependent upon each other in many ways, and
the clarinetist can use that situation to his immense advantage.
The player can try for an "edgier" sound at the height of some

crescendos (not all of them, of course) and for a dark, rich sound at some of the softer spots. This principle is the key to much of artistic phrasing, a key too often overlooked by many players.

DOES VIBRATO HAVE A PLACE
IN CLARINET PLAYING?

The use of vibrato, as a part of tonal quality on clarinet, does not create a desirable effect. Do not reject that declaration (or even agree with it!) before you read on. Nothing related to music is ever quite that simple.

Vibrato on wind instruments, where it is an appropriate part of tone quality, is achieved by the player through slight pulsations in any one of three parts of his body: (1) the airflow-supporting muscles, called "diaphragm vibrato"; (2) the embouchure muscles, called "lip vibrato"; and (3) the hand, an example of which would be the trombonists' "slide vibrato." Necessarily rejecting the third alternative out of hand, the clarinetist who wishes to consider the use of vibrato is left with a choice of the first two alternatives: diaphragm or lip vibrato. The former type tends to pulsate the tone's intensity, whereas the latter tends to pulsate the tone's pitch. Assuming that vibrato is to be used by a player on clarinet, there would be some musical situations in which one type would be more appropriate than the other. The player would have to make his own musical judgment in each case as to which type would be the more appropriate.

But, everything considered, any appropriate use of vibrato on clarinet is, at best, a very rare thing. I have often heard other clarinetists ask, "If the other instruments use vibrato, why don't *we* use it?" It seems a logical question and it deserves an answer. There *is* an answer, one that cannot be ignored.

Remember, first, that the clarinet has a unique harmonic series (see Chapter 3, "The Clarinet Itself and Barrel Joints"). The general absence of even-numbered partials in the clarinet's harmonic series means that clarinet tone is much more sparsely populated with overtones than are the harmonic series of other instruments. Vibrato necessarily alters that sparse tonal spectrum in too great a way for the player to maintain his full, beautiful tone.

Some musical confirmation of that argument is found in the case of the horn. (That instrument is now generally known simply as "the horn"; its older name, "French horn," has fallen into disuse.) Horn players make use of vibrato to a much more limited extent than do the players of other brass instruments, simply because they realize that vibrato does not enhance the horn sound very much. And again, the reason for that lies in the fact that the horn, like the clarinet, does not use the entire harmonic series. The horn's tonal spectrum possesses both odd- and even-numbered partials in abundance, but the horn plays almost entirely upon its *upper* partials. The lower partials are almost inaccessible, for reasons that I will not go into here. The point is that both the clarinet and the horn do not have complete harmonic series available to them (although for vastly different reasons), and the use of vibrato on either of these instruments is, therefore, less effective than it is on other instruments. Vibrato on clarinet always causes the sound to fall flat in quality, and sometimes in pitch. Who needs *that?*

Some players think that vibrato can be used as a means of artistic expression. Such an idea tends to lure the clarinetist away from his most fertile field of resources, the clarinet's tremendous range of dynamics and tone color. In fact, the reason tonal variety on clarinet is so immediate and effective lies in that sparse harmonic series; it allows the player's slightest change in intensity to be noticeable to the listener. Vibrato changes tone color too constantly, and blurs the effect. I will go further, and say that the clarinetists who use a vibrato often are probably doing so to cover up a basically thin tone quality, or partially to compensate for a weakness in phrasing. It is far too easy to "quiver" a phrase ending into oblivion; it is more difficult for players to do it right, by gradually decreasing the controlled airflow in a beautiful diminuendo and final release. In short, clarinet vibrato is too often a "cheap way out.".

I said earlier, however, that nothing in music is ever quite that simple, and there are rare times, perhaps, when some vibrato would not be out of place. The clarinet concerto of Aaron Copland, for example, was not only written for Benny Goodman, who uses a sort of jazz-oriented vibrato in his playing, but the concerto was also written in a jazz-oriented style. If only because of the piece's history, a "tasteful" vibrato may be in order for anyone performing it, particularly during the beautiful opening section.

Very occasionally, too, there is in woodwind quintet playing an especially "close" voicing of the five instruments during which it is the clarinetist's job to blend so completely into the total ensemble sound that he must intentionally obscure his instrument's individuality. A straight tone might, in this case, draw undue attention to the clarinet, and the player should try, rather, to "hide" inside the ensemble by matching, say, the oboist's vibrato with his own. Such moments, even in woodwind quintet playing, are fleeting and rare, and immediately afterward the clarinetist should return to his more usual approach to reassert his instrument's individuality.

Unless a clarinetist finds himself in a situation similar to the two examples given, vibrato is best avoided. Seek artistic expression instead through dynamic range, tone color, and a commanding *control* of the airflow, the embouchure, and the clarinet.

INTONATION

The term intonation, as used by instrumentalists, refers to the tuning of an instrument. If someone speaks of a player's own intonation, he refers to the player's ability to play his instrument in tune.

Clarinets, like other wind instruments, are impossible to play perfectly in tune at all times and in all registers of the instrument. Today's highly developed system of pitches makes such exacting demands (fortunately for our ears!) that it is impossible for clarinet manufacturers to build a clarinet that plays perfectly in tune. It is possible to build a clarinet so that its fundamental tones (those of the chalumeau, or lower register) would play perfectly in tune, but such construction would result in musical disaster, due to the natural discrepancies of the harmonic series. Such a clarinet would have a beautifully pitched low register, but the middle and high registers would be out of tune because they are based on the use of the upper partials of the harmonic series, each one of which has its own cantankerous tendency to go sharp or flat. (The study of acoustics is fascinating.) This scientific problem means that the manufacturers have had to build normal clarinets in such a way that each tone, in some way or other, represents a compromise. Today's clarinets, then, do play nearly in tune, but their intonation is at best approximate. The tone-holes have to be drilled into the wood in some place or other, and the manufacturers have chosen the places as best they could.

It is the player's task, therefore, to play in tune almost in spite of the instrument itself. If a particular tone has been slightly compromised toward the flat side of the pitch, the player has to "lip it up," or slightly firm the embouchure; if another tone tends toward sharpness, the player must call upon his embouchure to "lip it down." Good clarinetists know that they must go through that process to some extent on almost every tone they play. Players must constantly listen to themselves and to the other musicians in the ensemble in order to match the prevailing pitch levels on each tone.

The necessity of "lipping" or "favoring" pitches one way or the other would not present too great a problem to clarinetists if each tone had the same tendencies every time it was played but, here again, life is not that simple! The wooden bodies of clarinets constantly warm up and cool down during a playing session; when a clarinet is cold it will play flat, as a rule, and when it is warmed up by playing it will tend to be much sharper in pitch. A further problem arises from musical causes; let us take the example of the note G. If that G belongs to an E-flat major chord sounded by the ensemble, the clarinetist will want to play the G on its high, or sharp, side. If that same G belongs to an E minor chord, however, it will *sound* more in tune if the player slightly lowers its pitch. The reasons for that phenomenon are too extensive and theoretical to get into here; suffice it to say that any given tone, put into two different musical contexts, will in both cases ideally have different pitches. String players, in fact, will tell you that a G-sharp will almost always be a higher note than A-flat is, even though those two notes are identical on a piano's keyboard. In any case, playing a clarinet in tune is a complicated and delicate business.

From all of this one obvious fact emerges: There is no substitute for a "good ear." The player must listen intently to his pitch during each tone he plays so that he will be able instantly to adjust the tone's pitch to a level pleasing to the listener. I believe that the ability to hear pitches well is one that a player must be born with, and that a "good ear" cannot be taught; hastily, however, I will add that *anyone's* musical ear can be improved through careful listening and study. Clarinetists must continually strive for greater accuracy of pitch, and the key tool for that task is a thorough training of the ear.

You may have noticed that I have discussed intonation, so far, in some detail without even mentioning "tuning up." There is a reason for that; baldly stated, I don't believe that "tuning up," as most players understand the term, does much good on clarinet. Obviously a clarinetist must begin his playing in an ensemble by being sure that his instrument is generally and approximately at the same pitch level as the rest of the group, but to do more than that at the outset is a waste of time. Why? Because not only will the clarinet warm up and grow sharper as the playing proceeds, but the other instruments will also warm up. And unfortunately they do not warm up at the same rate or to the same extent. A prime example is the classic case of the principal oboist sounding "his A" for the rest of the symphony orchestra for tuning purposes. That process may be very good for the strings, but it helps the winds far less and perhaps it helps the clarinets, with their peculiar acoustical properties, least of all. (That isn't quite accurate; trombonists must tune to a B-flat or not at all!) The point is that when the oboist plays that A the clarinet, if cold, will be flat to it and, if warm, will be sharp to it. So, because of the constant fluctuation of the pitch of all the instruments during a rehearsal or performance, sounding that A will never do the clarinets much good. It may even be a pedagogically dangerous practice among student players, because this "tuning up" with only one tone, while most of the instruments are still cool, merely causes the student to think that he has completed all the tuning he will ever need to do for that playing session. He stops listening to his pitch as he plays.

It is often true, of course, that a clarinet may be entirely too sharp or too flat at the very beginning of a rehearsal. If it is flat, the player should make sure that the instrument is as short as possible by checking to see that all the joints are completely assembled. Then he should silently blow air into the clarinet to warm it sufficiently to bring it up nearer to the ensemble's pitch level. If the clarinet is entirely too sharp, the player should lengthen the instrument by partially disassembling the barrel from the upper joint. Sometimes it is also necessary to bring down the pitch of the lowest tones by slightly "pulling" at the very middle of the clarinet, between its upper and lower joints. But that situation can change at any time if, say, the conductor gets busy rehearsing some other section of the ensemble, leaving the clarinets quietly growing rapidly colder and flatter. In such a case, the alert clarinetist knows that he will probably have to push those joints back in again. The process is never-ending.

I mentioned pulling at the barrel and sometimes in the middle to correct sharpness. Some players carry the process further by pulling at the bell or even at the mouthpiece. If your clarinet is generally so sharp that you need to lengthen the instrument at the mouthpiece, you probably need to begin a search for a new barrel joint, one that will bring down the pitch and alleviate the need for such excessive pulling. Such a barrel need not be a longer one, either (see Chapter 3, "The Clarinet Itself and Barrel Joints.")

One common problem with intonation is that, after the clarinet is warm, the tones in the lowest register tend to go sharper than the tones of the higher registers. Assuming that the barrel has already been somewhat pulled out, it is appropriate in such a case to pull the clarinet slightly at the middle, as I mentioned earlier.

Be careful not to pull the middle too far out, however, or there may be two undesirable results: The bridge-key mechanism between the two main joints can fail to operate properly; and the notes of the higher registers can go flat.

To sum up: If you must "pull" to correct sharpness, do so primarily at the barrel and secondarily at the middle; try *not* to pull at the mouthpiece, for reasons relating to acoustics and to the contour of the clarinet's bore. Pulling at the bell will only lower the pitch of the lowest E and the middle B, and it is of questionable value to any clarinetist who does not have pitch problems with those two tones.

Above all, remember that none of these physical "tuning" adjustments made upon the instrument itself will ever substitute for alert, constant, and intelligent listening by the player while he plays. I strongly recommend that any wind ensemble begin its rehearsal without sounding any tuning tone. After playing together for ten or fifteen minutes, a prevailing ensemble pitch will have been established. Group attention can be called to it by the conductor, and any players who still need to make basic adjustments can make them with far greater assurance.

A FINAL WORD

While trying for great expression, remember that the chief means of expressing your musicianship lies in your control of the airflow. The ever-sensitive, ever-changing airflow remains your main musical tool and life line. The embouchure, the tongue, and the fingers merely lend some helpful and necessary assistance.

CHAPTER

9

Musical

Interpretation

Musical interpretation, as I am using the term here, is the manner in which the performer's own ideas are substantively fused with the composer's obvious ones to achieve the greatest musical result. There is nothing magical or secretive about any particular interpretation of a piece of music. Two equally great performances may be very different from each other. This fact, in itself, proves that there is *never only one right way* to play a piece of music.

AVOID LITERAL-MINDEDNESS

I have encountered many musicians who proudly claim that they take great pains to play music according to all the printed markings on the page, with no exceptions, right down to the last detail.

This attitude is what I call literal-mindedness; it is characterized by an almost belligerent adherence to the idea that if the composer had intended anything more, he would have written it in. Or, that if the composer had intended anything less, he would have written it differently or would have entirely omitted it. When listening to a performer who works from that philosophy I am always struck again by the fact that he is yet another player who is "doing a workmanlike job," but who is definitely not an artist. He has missed the point: Musical notation, even today, is imperfect at best and, at worst, inadequate.

There is no way for a composer to put *your performance* of his work on paper. Indeed, your performance must be, by definition, different from any other. When a painter puts a picture on canvas he fulfills the roles of both "composer" and "performer," so that he does not have to rely on a middleman to put his work across to the public. The composer of music also puts his work down on paper, but he knows *as he writes it* that a performing middleman will have to be present to put his work across to the public. The performer's job cannot be one of merely reproducing what he sees on the paper; a computer could probably be programmed to do that. Remember that performing is an art in itself, and all good composers write their music in the full realization of that fact. Performers, in order to be worthy of that name, must *truly* reproduce the "composer's intentions" by being as creative as they can be at all times. In short, put yourself into it; do not settle for being a sort of "rubber stamp."

Too often we are taught to observe blindly (surely a performer should do more than observe!) every little mark on the printed page. Experience has taught me that many of those marks should never have been put there in the first place! From time to time certain music publishers become notorious for the type of "editions" they put on the market; often such music, usually by the great master composers, is marked up by an editor at a desk and not by anyone who has actually performed that music recently. Even if the editor attempts to be as historically correct as possible, the fact is that musical taste changes. Not only do today's performers play instruments differently from the way those instruments were played in the past, but today's audiences *hear* music within an entirely different frame of reference. Anyone pedantic enough to insist upon performances of older music done only according to the "performance practice" of its age is *not* a person clinging to a sense of history; instead, he is one who has definitely *lost* that sense. History has a flow; it moves. Great music from the past, if only because of its greatness, will easily withstand the flow of history.

The aspects of printed editions that are among the worst offenders are the markings for articulation and dynamics. Old method books are especially bad from this standpoint. The Klose, Baermann, and Lazarus books are full of articulation marks that bewilder us today, because they are out of date. When those books were written during the 1800s, wind instrument players were trying to imitate the various string-instrument bowing marks, an attempt that seems almost comical as we look back upon it now. In order to convey on paper an array of various tonguing styles, the composers then resorted to all sorts of strange-looking tonguing marks. Today musicians have realized that wind instruments have an identity of their own; it is folly (and insulting to both winds *and* strings) for wind players to waste effort imitating a violin. Trying to play such artificially accented and pointed notes today is in very bad taste. For students, in fact, it is harmful, because their attempts to play such markings will only result in great tenseness in the tongue, which then will spread to the rest of the body. Avoid hard and tense tonguing at all costs.

Printed dynamic markings present just as great a problem, and this problem is not confined to old method books; it pervades the entire body of clarinet literature. A player's interpretation of dynamic markings must go far beyond what appears on the page! Often, for example, a "p" is marked at the beginning of a phrase to show that it is to be played in a generally soft way. But does this mean that the entire phrase must be uniformly soft, from beginning to end? Of course not. Phrases, *all* phrases, must have shape, contour, and form; dynamic variation and fluctuation must play a role in conveying that to the listener.

Sometimes, indeed, the dynamics as printed in music are obviously wrong. If you come across an example of this, go ahead and *change* the dynamic level or contour, as long as you are absolutely certain that you have made a definite improvement.

Finally, there is an additional problem concerning dynamics that cannot be blamed on the printed page. I refer to the player's lack of awareness of his own musical context. Too many players seem to feel that dynamic levels are *set* or *fixed*. Nothing could be further from the truth! Many famous orchestral clarinet solos are marked to be played softly, but the clarinet soloist playing them must remember that his sound must carry above the rest of the orchestra to be heard by the audience all the way to the back of a large concert hall. On another occasion, however, that same clarinetist may be playing chamber music; the same, soft dynamic marking in such a case may have to be played so softly that it is just barely audible a few feet away.

Dynamics, then, are not universally fixed, but must vary with the context. Even the entire dynamic range can vary in its extremes from ensemble playing to solo playing. In solo playing, contrary to what many may think, it is not necessary to have a very large dynamic range simply because any change at all is noticeable to the listeners. In ensemble playing, however, a large clarinet section must have a correspondingly large dynamic range so that any changes will be noticed. If a clarinet section of a concert band needs to play softly, each player in the section must play almost inaudibly so that the whole section will sound soft enough. On the other hand, if a clarinet section needs to play loudly, each player must play loudly so that the whole section will sound loud enough.

EDITIONS OF MUSIC: MAKE YOUR OWN

Music is so expensive today! Why not buy the least expensive edition and apply your own professional knowledge to it? If you feel you are creative, and if you have a sense of musical style, you can probably do at least as well as the editor who helped in the publishing of that particular piece. Naturally it is not a good idea for inexperienced students to attempt this, but even for students, a private teacher can edit the music so that definite improvements can be made. The teacher will be doing the student's musical education a great service, too, if he leaves some (but not all) of the choices to the student himself. Nothing will teach independent musicianship better or more quickly than having to make choices through trial and error. This can be a wonderful experience if the student is guided throughout the process by a good and understanding teacher who will be patient with the student when he makes mistakes.

Any person who claims that he has knowledge of "the authentic interpretation" of a famous, early clarinet solo work is being intellectually dishonest. I have always been highly amused by one particular edition of the Mozart Clarinet Concerto; inside the front cover of that edition is the claim that it represents the authentic, original interpretation of the piece, and that it is authentic because the editor had it from his famous teacher, who had it from his famous teacher, who had it from *his* famous teacher, and so forth,

all the way back (apparently) to Anton Stadler who first performed the concerto. This claim is, on the face of it, pure poppycock. Mozart wrote almost no articulation marks in the piece himself, and he put in very few dynamic markings. Stadler played the
piece as he felt like playing it, as was the custom at the time, and
he almost certainly never wrote down his own markings. Even if
he did write them down, and his edition survived, we may find
that his ideas no longer appeal to us because of the intervening
200 years of change in musical taste.

The fact is that no one knows how the works of Mozart, Weber,
and the like were originally performed by early clarinetists. This is
especially true of the articulation; it is true to a lesser extent of the
dynamic markings, and sometimes it even applies to the notes and
rhythms themselves. You cannot, and should not, remake a piece
of music in your own image, so to speak, disregarding the
composer's intentions, but you can usefully modify what is written
by following your own (or your teacher's) artistic sense.

One example is a sudden dynamic change printed in the music,
perhaps in an unexpected spot. Such sudden changes are often
very effective; equally often, however, they can be offensive, especially if they are overdone. Decide whether to play the sudden
change literally, subtly, or not at all.

Suggested tempos are another example. I have the distinct impression that sometimes even the best composers write an excellent piece of music, hearing it in their minds a certain way, and
then are just a bit too hasty in adding metronome markings as
an afterthought. Judge for yourself whether you can play what
the composer wrote more successfully by following the printed
metronome markings or by taking a different tempo. Furthermore, there is no question that such markings as *"andante"* and
"allegro" can have vastly different meanings in different contexts, and I could mention several other examples of this sort
of variability.

If you decide to make some change in your performance of a
piece, naturally you must be able to justify it. You should verbal-
ize your reasoning to yourself and to anyone else who may question it. Another musician may disagree with you, but he must
never be given the chance to say that your action was not very
carefully thought out.

Any departure you take from what the printed page says should
be held up in the light of these questions: Does it serve some
musical purpose? And can you verbally justify the change you
have made? Finally, and most important, can you demonstrate by

playing it on your instrument that your version is superior to the printed one?

To be a performing interpreter of what a composer has put on paper is to take on a tremendous responsibility. In carrying out this responsibility, it is your duty to be as sensitive and as imaginative as you possibly can be at all times. You may know another player whose performance you admire, but merely to imitate him would be to deny your own talent and musical independence.

CHAPTER

10

Teaching
Other
Clarinetists

Many professional clarinetists avoid teaching at all costs; they are bored by it, they do not find it rewarding, and they consider it a waste of time. Others teach only from economic necessity. Still others teach and enjoy it. Such differences reflect the natural differences among individuals, whether clarinetists or not. However, I believe that many more clarinetists would enjoy teaching if they had a better idea of how to go about it. Performers generally have had no formal training in the art of teaching, and their efforts are the mixed result of their own personality and the teaching methods used by their former teachers. They have learned by example and they try to teach by example.

Learning and teaching by example can be wonderful in some contexts, but generally speaking, the "example" approach is limited at best. No teacher can teach the "why" aspects of clarinet playing if he relies entirely upon teaching by example. No teacher is doing his job if he cannot cope with students' intelligent questions. Verbal explanations are absolutely indispensable to good teaching. A teacher cannot go through daily lessons simply saying, in effect, "Do it like this." He owes it to the student (and to that student's future students) to explain exactly what he means, and exactly why it is important enough to talk about.

In fact, I believe it can be argued that a professional clarinetist is not worth much if he is not also a good teacher. A remarkably fine symphony player has something to offer if only to his listeners, but think how much more valuable he is to society if he can pass on his artistry to a younger generation. Fine clarinet playing will outlive us all, but if the best players bottle themselves up, jealously guarding their "playing secrets," the art will suffer to the extent that such information is withheld.

The teacher himself must be a mature person, secure in his abilities, and aware of his weaknesses. He shouldn't be ashamed to admit his weaknesses to students; the students will then reciprocate by admitting their own weaknesses, which is the first step toward solving their playing problems.

Teaching has been called an art, and so it is, as regards verbal explanation, musical demonstration, and the formation of abstract concepts. But teaching is also a *science,* however inexact in some respects. I have found that one's success in teaching depends largely upon one's knowledge and application of psychology. Unfortunately, most music teachers lack psychological training. Psychology can be used to get results from two directions, one desirable and the other not. I will deal first with the undesirable application of psychological techniques, and then I will explain the one that I recommend.

This *undesirable* use of psychology in teaching is, fortunately, being applied less and less. I refer to the direct, frontal, dictatorial assault by the teacher upon the supposed ignorant depravity of the student. Psychology is used, here, as a conditioning agent in the worst sense of that term. The teacher assumes that he himself knows "The Way," and that if the student only follows instructions, progress will result. The teacher insists on absolute obedience in all respects. If a student has not followed instructions to the last detail, the teacher gets angry, and the lesson ends in weeping, wailing, and gnashing of teeth. Sometimes the student who is bewildered by this treatment is conveniently dismissed by the teacher as an inept young fool with no talent.

One could call this teaching method the Psychology of Fear.

Occasionally it is successful in the short run; we have all heard of teachers who are known as tyrants, some of whose students win high ratings at solo and ensemble contests. But in the end the Psychology of Fear defeats the purpose of music education. The students involved rarely enjoy going on with music in college; they have been completely "burned out." Some have great potential, but for them music has become the battlefield of a love–hate relationship. In the end, hate wins out.

A too-stern private teacher can have this devastating effect on a student at any stage of his development. I have taught entering college freshmen who had been thoroughly disheartened in high school; they didn't even want to bring their clarinet to college, but did so only because their parents had paid for all those earlier lessons. When I get such a student I can't start teaching right away. I sometimes have to spend weeks in psychologically deprogramming and reprogramming the student.

The first difficulty with reorienting a student is the fact that he has been forced to become totally *dependent,* musically, upon the tyrant in his past. He does not dare to think for himself, and has lost all musical self-opinion. That is to say, he does not think "I am learning to be a musician," but rather "How do *you,* Teacher, want me to play *this?*" Such students are terrified if I tell them to begin playing at whatever tempo they think best, or even at the tempo at which they have practiced that music for a week or more, so great is their fear of displeasing me with their choice. They are loaded down with inhibiting fears: that I will be just another in a series of tyrants, that they have not "observed" something in the music, that they should have put on a new reed for their lesson, that their dynamic range was not *extreme* enough, and so on. It is tragic to see fine, talented young people with their *natural, musical independence* so thoroughly thwarted.

When I finally get one of these students going on a piece of music in more or less his own way, he invariably stops, even *then,* at the end of just a phrase or so, to ask me nervously, "Was that all right?" And the poor creature hasn't really played anything yet! A total lack of trust in himself as a musician bedevils him, even though he is already a fine player as long as he is told exactly what to do and when to do it. His problem, then, is not related to his clarinet playing, but to his state of mind. Only when the Psychology of Fear is conquered can he hope to begin genuine work on his clarinet playing.

NO-FAULT TEACHING

I therefore advocate a way that gets results by fostering the student's own natural abilities, by avoiding any crushing of the ego, by strengthening self-confidence, and by encouraging musical experimentation. Later in this chapter, I will describe what I mean both generally and more specifically, but for now I will point out that this "no-fault" approach to teaching is *not* directed at ensemble conductors, but at private, one-to-one teacher–student relations. It remains true that directors of ensembles must exert their will upon the group to a large extent, or chaos would result. So, let me repeat: What I am about to describe concerns private-lesson teachers, not conductors. (Conductors, by the way, do not have to behave like frustrated Fascist dictators, either, but that is another matter.)

We try to allow for social immaturity among young people, and to lessen it through guidance. Why not treat musical immaturity the same way? Musical independence and maturity come with experience and through patient guidance; they can never be force-fed to a student. If the student's musical ideas make little sense, try to understand how he reached them and, without overtly criticizing him, explain why an alternative idea is better. Don't bother to tell him why his own idea was *not* as good; if you thoroughly explain the alternative idea, he will see the light. A teacher who slices a student's original idea to shreds merely hurts the student's feelings. The private lesson is in itself a creative situation, and should remain so, for both teacher and student. The basic principle here is not to knock anything down directly, but rather to replace it with an obviously superior alternative.

Be proud of your own ideas about a certain piece of music, tell the student about them, and urge him to try them for himself. Do not absolutely *insist* on this, however; encourage him to evolve his own musical ideas if they are well-grounded. Encourage his independence! If a student asks "How fast do you want this?" try to let him figure out what the most appropriate tempo would be. If you simply *tell* him, you are not helping him develop any kind of musical independence. This also applies to the question "How does that rhythm go?" Guide the student toward figuring out rhythmic patterns for himself. The whole point is that you should teach him a *process,* not just some isolated rhythmic pattern. Later, he will need to know how to figure such things out for himself in all contexts without a teacher at his elbow. Bluntly stated, avoid singing him the "right answer."

A student's intelligence must never be insulted. Speak to them so that they understand that you *want* them to succeed, but do it in a manner that does not put them under the pressure of a *direct order*. This is psychology at its best: The student gets the idea that you are calmly, patiently, and confidently expecting progress from him, and that you will remain friendly and helpful throughout the process.

This approach is tremendously effective because the student ends up by fervently wanting to prove you right. He becomes far more motivated than he was. He will be grateful to you for not having lectured him every time he didn't practice enough, and for not blaming him when he makes a technical mistake while playing a difficult passage. In fact, *don't* blame him; instead, help him by suggesting a friendly way out of the problem. Even with apparently lazy students, this approach is the most effective one in the long run. It will take the lazy student longer to become motivated, but this motivation through encouragement will have a long-lasting effect. Attempts to overcome laziness through the Psychology of Fear will indeed work more quickly, but the long-term effect will be, most likely, that the student simply drops out. I can think of several rather lazy students I have had, for four years of college each; almost without exception they took longer to catch on than did some of their classmates, but nearly every one of them who had musical ability eventually gave excellent solo clarinet recitals during the senior year.

It is well known that teenagers like to be treated as adults. If you teach them while bearing that in mind, they will respect you as a *person* and give you the desired results.

I have called this no-fault teaching, and why not? Is it the student's fault he is not perfect? Obviously his weaknesses must be worked on, he must know what they are, and he must be expected to work to improve them. If the teacher leads him to believe that having problems is abnormal, however, and if the teacher attacks him as a *person* for having problems, the only possible result is a student who will be overly discouraged for the wrong reasons. Accept the student as a person first; then you will be able to discuss his playing problems with him more abstractly, and he will be able to face them much more objectively. Intentionally separate his personality from his playing problems, and you will see him become far more ready to tackle such problems in the practice room. He will approach his own problems almost with the air of a scientist working in a laboratory.

Discuss with the student what his problems are, tell him that progress is not possible at a snap of the fingers, tell him that it is *normal* to have playing problems, and tell him that he must be patient with himself. Then, set an example by being patient with him yourself. Treat him, indeed, like an experimental scientist who works by himself all week in the laboratory, and who then comes to you once a week for consultation. Rejoice with him in his discoveries (for he *will* make some) and encourage him when he feels that he has accomplished nothing. Interest and motivation can be rekindled by the mere suggestion of a new approach to an old problem.

None of this, by the way, means that a no-fault teacher must expect lower standards. Quite the reverse! The very fact that this approach is relatively long-range means that you can aim for, and achieve, greater heights; often, in fact, this achievement may occur sooner than it would otherwise, simply because the student has been able to have the goal clearly in mind from the start, and because he knows, throughout, that you are "on his side." Indeed, it could be that no-fault teaching is the only way realistically to expect an immature student to understand and aim for (let alone achieve) true artistic standards while still feeling good about himself!

I was fortunate enough to study clarinet with Keith Stein for fifteen years, longer than any other student he had during his half-century of teaching. He *never once* raised his voice at me during those fifteen years, although I gave him plenty of just cause. The point is that he remained a constant in my life, not a variable. The result, for me, was long-term musical progress and, I think, steady growth as a person. Although he never called this no-fault teaching (an admittedly oversimplified catchphrase of my own invention), Keith Stein left an indelible stamp on me by using this teaching method. And, though there will never be another Keith Stein, I firmly believe that all clarinet teachers and their students would benefit by adopting this excellent method.

I do have one word of caution. I believe that the "no-fault" approach is the best way to inspire confidence, motivation, and progress. *But*, there is no approach to teaching and/or learning to which all teachers and students can respond equally well. Further, there is no teacher who can teach all students equally well. Occasionally, there is a student who does not respond to no-fault teaching; fortunately, this situation is extremely rare, and, where it does occur, it is usually caused by some deep-seated emotional problem. In such a case it is essential for the clarinet teacher to remember that he is not a psychiatrist and that he cannot offer such a student what he really needs. Serious emotional problems should be dealt with, in any case, by those who are qualified to do so. Emotionally unstable students should not be relied upon for long-range creative work, so the no-fault teacher should not blame himself for a lack of progress in the disturbed student. Instead he should try to do whatever he can to help the student obtain the required assistance.

TEACHING RELAXATION

In Chapter 4, "The Two Basics in Clarinet Playing" (the two basics being airflow and relaxation), I mentioned those two subjects in that order because the reader had to know what, related to the airflow, had to be relaxed and what had to be alerted. In discussing teaching, however, I'll assume that the teacher understands what I mean about the airflow, and start at the *very* beginning: basic relaxation, and the teaching of it.

First, no student is going to be truly relaxed at the outset, not only because of inexperience but also because students seem to suffer a certain amount of unavoidable nervousness during lessons. So, the teacher must put the student as much at ease as possible, and then begin work by presenting basic relaxation as it applies to playing a wind instrument.

The concept that he really should try to relax his body to the point where it is, in the words of Keith Stein, "just a degree or so above the point of collapse," must be thoroughly impressed upon the student. To some this may seem an exaggeration; I assure you that it is not. Tension must be totally absent. The only qualifying factor here is that there are four places in the body (listed in Chapter 4, "The Two Basics in Clarinet Playing") that must take on a certain amount of "muscular alertness" in order to accomplish the task of clarinet playing. If any amount of alertness, let alone tension, creeps into the body at any other point, the player will soon be tense all over and therefore severely restricted in his ability to function as a clarinet player.

The hardest thing about teaching relaxation is that it must be thought of constantly, even while working on *other* aspects of clarinet playing. The teacher must resist the temptation to ignore tension while working, say, on airflow, embouchure, technique, or tonguing. With a beginner, relaxation should be taught (after its initial introduction) in conjunction with the airflow, so that the student not only grasps those two most basic things, but so that he also gets used to trying to think of more than one aspect of his playing at a time. A teacher must remind the student to relax each time the student's relaxation disappears. The student will see that the teacher is really serious about the overriding importance of relaxation, even if the immediate subject at hand is the airflow, or whatever else may be under discussion.

Even advanced students will, from time to time, make superficial breakthroughs in other areas of their playing while not actually being in a proper state of relaxation. (The human mind and body seem capable of overcoming tremendous obstacles.) Such breakthroughs should be hailed as such by the teacher, the student should be highly complimented and encouraged by the teacher because of the breakthrough, but the teacher must also point out that the breakthrough, whatever it was, would be even more effective if the student would use his new-found knowledge *while he is relaxed!* Immediately, with the loss of no time whatsoever, and in the glowing atmosphere of a new achievement, the teacher must have the student repeat what he has just done in a more relaxed way. The new breakthrough will be reinforced, and the student will see that when he remembers to relax at the same time, his new achievement is even more effective. It is moments like this, of course, that make teaching so gratifying.

The best approach, then, is to view all aspects of clarinet playing as pointless when tension is present. The teacher who is able to impress that fact upon a student has given that student the greatest gift a teacher can give a future clarinetist.

TEACHING THE USE OF THE AIRFLOW

Assuming that relaxation is already established (to whatever extent that is possible with any particular student), the airflow must always remain most important among the "active" aspects of clarinet playing. Relaxation must come before (and be concurrent with) the airflow, but the embouchure must come *after* the airflow in relative importance.

See Chapter 4, "The Two Basics in Clarinet Playing," for a discussion of what the airflow is and what it does, and explain its overriding importance to the student. A comparison of a clarinetist's use of the airflow with the mechanical operation of a church pipe organ is an excellent illustration: The student can easily see that, until a "blower in the basement" is switched on, no amount of key pressing at the organ's console will do any good. No pipe organ will make a sound until the proper amount of air pressure is present in the wind chests. It is easy to understand that if a pipe organ's wind chests *are* filled with the proper amount of air pressure, a very light touch upon the keys will bring forth a beautiful, instantaneous, and full tone. In fact, a clarinet is, in a way, a whole rank (or series) of organ pipes all in one, since its length is variable depending upon how many tone-holes are covered. The clarinet student can be shown, then, that if he activates his muscles at the waistline in the manner of a pipe organ's "blower in the basement," his fingers on the tone-holes will bring forth whatever pitch he needs at any given moment simply because the proper air pressure is available in his "wind chest."

Another visual image to conjure up for the student is that of a spring that flows above ground because of underground pressure. Once above ground the flowing water does not stop; it continues to flow until it pools in some basinlike low spot. The clarinetist's airflow can be said to flow upward in a similar manner due to inner muscular pressure; it continues to flow unimpeded through the clarinet and out into the room in the form of sound, finally pooling, perhaps, over in a far corner of the room. This analogy can help the teacher convey to the student the way in which he should pressurize his airflow, and it can also help the teacher illustrate to the student the way the airflow should flow unimpeded through his instrument, out of that instrument, and into the ears of listeners *beyond* the immediate area.

A visual image along these same lines, but one that directly includes relaxation, is the comparison of the player's airflow to pressurized water flowing from the end of a garden hose. It is obvious to the student that if someone comes along and steps on the garden hose, the flowing water will be restricted even though the basic pressure remains the same. This can be compared to the player who uses plenty of good muscular pressure at the waistline only to choke it off in a tense throat area or in a biting embouchure. The teacher can make the point, then, that while muscular support of the airflow is tremendously important, it will not do the student enough good if he plays with a tense, restricting throat or embouchure.

Incidentally, here is a problem for the teacher to watch for in each student who has trouble keeping the throat relaxed while maintaining good muscular support: Often, when such a student is consciously thinking of relaxing his throat while playing, he loses control of the muscles at the waistline. When this happens, he usually begins "bouncing" the stomach muscles in an effort to "find" that control. Point out to him that he doesn't have to do anything magical to correct this problem; all he needs to do is firm up those muscles and *keep* them firm, while he relaxes his throat. This is really a problem in coordination that takes much time and skill to master.

In certain cases students may have a lot of trouble with that coordination. These students find it very difficult to maintain firm waistline muscles simultaneously with a relaxed throat. I tell such people to firm up the waistline and keep it that way while they are *talking* with me about the problem; the light dawns on them almost at once. The reason for the success of this device is quite simple: One cannot talk with a tense throat without sounding strangled! At the same time, one *can* talk with a firm set of waistline muscles. In this way the student gets the idea that, yes, he *can* play the clarinet with firm muscular support *and* with a relaxed throat.

If you want your student to "support," by the way, you *must* get him to use a reed that will *take* it. There will be more about this in Chapter 11, "Reeds," of course, but the point must be made here, too. No "soft" reed will properly respond to a correctly supported airflow over the entire range of the clarinet; overall, the tone quality will be a thin one, but the high notes will especially suffer. They will not come out at all or they will, at best, sound not only thin but also very flat in pitch. Let the student discover the *reason* for this truth for himself; when he is unhappy with the sound or the pitch of his high notes, point out to him that the trouble lies with his reed and not with himself. Then, help him fix up a firmer, more responsive reed. When he has tried this "new idea," he will be forever in your debt, and will realize that a soft reed may be "easier to *blow*," but is actually "harder to *play*." A too-soft reed simply will not stand up to a good, strong airflow. Such reeds therefore encourage throat tightening and embouchure biting in a desperate attempt by the player to gain control of the instrument. I have seen students whose playing improved vastly, seemingly overnight, after they realized this basic, if paradoxical, fact.

To sum up, there are three basic principles involved in teaching the use of the airflow: Relaxation must always be present first or concurrently; the airflow is more important and more basic than are any of the remaining aspects of playing; and the clarinet, the mouthpiece, and especially the reed must be able to receive a strong airflow.

TEACHING CLARINET EMBOUCHURE

It seems obvious, and even needless to say, that a teacher must know his subject matter before trying to teach it to someone else. The trouble with teaching clarinet embouchure, however, is that many fine clarinetists who have excellent embouchures themselves have a terrible time putting the *process* of embouchure *formation* into words. I have found that clarinet embouchure is, indeed, the most difficult woodwind instrument embouchure to describe. Other teachers have had the same problem, and many of them have "solved" that problem by making it seem even more elusive than it is. Fine clarinet embouchures can be described in countless ways, and I have given my version of the process in Chapter 5, "The Embouchure." In the absence of a better approach, and unless you disagree with it for some reason, I recommend describing clarinet embouchure to students just as I have described it in that chapter.

At this point, then, we must be concerned with embouchure *problems* and how to solve them.

Perhaps the chief embouchure problem is that tension creeps back in while the student is concentrating on forming his embouchure. After that, too, the airflow is usually forgotten. Relaxation and airflow must be reestablished or no embouchure, good or bad, will be of any use. Remind the student that the embouchure is only the doorway through which the air must properly travel to achieve a beautiful sound, and that doorways are useless unless there is something to go through them.

Once relaxation and airflow are reestablished, perhaps the most common embouchure problem is *non*embouchure. That is, the student tends to "bunch up" the chin skin under the reed, neglecting what the teacher has told him about the downward stretch that should exist in that part of the embouchure. The chin skin tends to travel upwards mainly because the student is seeking physical security around the mouthpiece and reed, the same urge that sometimes leads to "jaw bite." Assure the student that his embouchure will be secure enough if he remembers to stay "open" with the jaw *and* if he remembers to compensate for that openness by drawing the muscles *inward* at the *sides* of the mouthpiece. The corners of the mouth and the cheek muscles as well should draw in toward the sides of the mouthpiece, to give all the physical security and control necessary for a good embouchure, especially when this is coupled with *inward roundness* in all the muscles of the lips. Remind the student to think of his embouchure goal as the achievement of a *vertical oval* shape. If his embouchure feels as if he has formed a vertical oval, he will have achieved his goal: a beautiful roundness.

Remind the student also at this point that his upper and lower teeth should be vertically in line with each other; many students tend to forget that subtlety, and they allow their lower teeth and jaw to creep gradually back to a position behind the upper teeth.

Another embouchure problem occurs when the student has formed a beautiful embouchure just prior to playing, only to have it disintegrate the minute he begins to play. This is caused, of course, by a lack of concentration and coordination on the part of the inexperienced student, and the situation calls for great patience on the part of the teacher. By all means tell the student that his embouchure is falling apart due to his temporary lack of concentration and coordination, but be sure to tell him according to the basic principles of the no-fault teaching method. That is, assure him in a very sympathetic manner that it is normal to have trouble maintaining the embouchure while trying to remember all the other aspects of playing a wind instrument. Convey to him your willingness (not in words, of course, but by your manner) to see him through the difficulty in a friendly, helpful way. Don't blame the student personally, but explain that he, like everyone else, has muscles that are reluctant to do what he wants them to and that concentration will gradually train the muscles. This again places the blame where it belongs: on the untrained muscles, and *not* on the student's ego.

It may be necessary to mention again how important the cheeks are in forming the clarinet embouchure; be sure that the student's cheeks never puff outward. Instead they should draw in against the teeth and in toward the sides of the mouthpiece, contributing to that beautiful, active, inward roundness of the lip muscles.

A special embouchure problem sometimes occurs with college students who are brass instrument majors, especially if their major instrument is one of the lower brasses. Often such students learn to play some clarinet in woodwind "methods" classes if they plan to become high-school band directors after they graduate. Even though these students know that their upper teeth should actually touch the top of the clarinet mouthpiece, their upper lip is so strong from the training it received while playing a lower brass instrument that it tends to raise the teeth right off the clarinet mouthpiece! This creates great instability in clarinet embouchure, needless to say, but some of those upper lips are so strong that this problem can occur with a student who doesn't even realize that it has happened. The clarinet teacher needs to watch for this.

A legitimate "double-lip" embouchure can, of course, be taught to any clarinetist who needs it, particularly one who has trouble with "jaw bite." The double-lip embouchure on clarinet is exactly the same as the normal single-lip embouchure except that some of the upper lip is tucked in between the upper teeth and the mouthpiece in much the same way that oboists and bassoonists do it. The double-lip embouchure is an excellent way to open up a tight, biting embouchure, even if it is used as a temporary, remedial measure.

In summing up these ideas on teaching clarinet embouchure, I cannot possibly emphasize enough that embouchure is nothing but a doorway for the airflow. In fact, the only reason for working on embouchure is to improve it as the airflow's doorway into the clarinet. Relaxation and airflow must come first in importance, but embouchure is a close second.

TEACHING CLARINET TECHNIQUE

This is where, perhaps, *most* teaching troubles lie. The problem of a student's temporary inability to play a certain "technical" passage is fraught with peril for teacher and student alike. The no-fault approach to this problem is an absolute necessity. It is, of course, up to the teacher to be sure that the student is not trying to play something that *actually is* beyond his technical skill even if the student is familiar with the piece. Never assign any piece of music that will upset the student's relaxation, airflow, and embouchure. To do so would be to defeat your own teaching purposes.

First, remember that technique is not synonymous with *speed,* but rather, with *coordination.* The student must back off and have a completely fresh look at the passage in order to avoid mental blocks. Look at the passage with the student and point out the musical *patterns* in it, according to what he has learned about music theory. Being able to "label" certain patterns can be a tremendous help. Is the passage, for instance, some form of diatonic scale or arpeggio, or is it at least partly that? Show the student that his playing of the passage depends upon his analytical knowledge of it, and *not* upon mindless drilling. Back off, reestablish relaxation, and look for patterns. This process should bring about the student's latent ability to play the passage.

If tenseness is not the problem and the student is already aware of the patterns in the passage but *still* can't play it, be extremely cautious at this point, because he may be very close to establishing a mental block against it. Instead, point out that his fingers are leading his brain, a process that is precisely backwards. *Rhythm* is now the key to success. Usually the fault lies in a lack of rhythmic steadiness and evenness *within* the beat groups. In sixteenth notes, make sure there are four even notes within each beat when the student plays the passage. Or, in compound meters, make sure that he is playing the groups of threes or sixes as evenly as possible. He will be delighted to discover the old truth: Evenly played notes sound faster than they really are!

Mental blocks and feelings of helplessness can usually be avoided if technical passages are approached through relaxation and rhythmic accuracy, rather than through mindless, time-consuming, and exhausting drilling. Keep this fact uppermost in your mind, so that you can convey that principle to the student. If a mental block and a feeling of despair do creep in, what can the teacher do about this seeming impasse? Slow practice is usually recommended at this point, and it has some value as long as it is slow, *even* practice, and as long as it does not degenerate into that state of mindless, boring drilling that I keep railing against. Of far more value is to play the offending passage in *varying rhythmic patterns*. Too few players of wind instruments use this practice technique, although it is apparently well-known among pianists. If the passage in question involves, for instance, an unbroken run of sixteenth notes, the most obvious application of this idea is to change the rhythmic pattern, mentally, to one of alternating dotted sixteenths and thirty-seconds. After playing the passage that way a couple of times, the student should then reverse the pattern, and play it a couple of times with alternating thirty-seconds and dotted sixteenths. Next, he might play the passage in triplets, still in evenly spaced sixteenths, but misplacing the beats. The possibilities are endless. The success of this technique tells us much about how the mental block arose in the first place: If we consider the brain to be a sort of computer that runs the rest of the clarinet-playing mechanism, the mental block problem must be the result of what can be called "faulty programming." Playing the problem passage in a series of "wrong rhythms" can have the beneficial effect of "scrambling" the brain's computer program. After scrambling the faulty program, the student's brain is ready to be "reprogrammed" through the usual techniques of relaxation and rhythmic accuracy. The student never fails to be delighted by his success, and it is easy for him to remember that technique in the future.

This is another example of no-fault teaching, since it blames some sort of impersonal "brain program" (which really is the true culprit) rather than the player's own ego. Students need confidence in their clarinet technique, for that is where their ego is most easily damaged if the teacher is not careful.

I like to tell students that almost anyone can learn to type very rapidly, but that typewriters are not known for the music they produce. The point is, of course, that "fast fingers" do not make a musician. The key to fine clarinet playing lies in what the brain is thinking about musically, whether those musical thoughts include finger action or some other area of musical production on the clarinet. In short, good technique *and* good clarinet playing require a lot of thought, both before and during practice or performance.

TEACHING THE HANDS, FINGERS, AND HOLDING POSITIONS

Perhaps the simplest approach to this is to tie it in with comfort and relaxation. Anything that distorts relaxation is, as always, to be avoided. Make sure the student's head and neck are relaxed, as well as his shoulders, elbows, wrists, and fingers. Make sure the clarinet is held at about 35 or 40 degrees out from the body, while the head is still approximately erect. At this point, remember once again that great phrase of Keith Stein's, that the whole body should be relaxed to "just a degree or so above the point of collapse."

After that, concentrate on the fingers. There should be a little roundness in every knuckle, and the pressure of the finger ends on the tone-holes should never bend the knuckles backwards. Nearly all beginning students press very hard upon the tone-holes in an effort to keep them covered; the result, of course, is just the opposite. Firmly pressing fingers tend to "slide" or "climb" right off the tone-holes they are trying desperately to keep covered, which in turn results in more feverish pressing. Stop the student when this occurs, and show him the *very small springs* that keep other tone-holes covered with key pads. Show him how little pressure is required to close those key pads, and that those tiny springs, small as they are, are strong enough to keep the holes covered. Then show him that the round, fleshy part of his fingertips must also act as "key pads" on the tone-holes, and that they are big and strong enough to do the job without extra muscular pressure. Recall another of Keith Stein's fine phrases, that the tone-holes are best covered when the fingers "fall of their own weight." Anything more than that, in the way of finger pressure, is counterproductive.

In young students, I have found that two particular fingers are more likely than the others to "climb off" the tone-holes due to excessive pressure: the middle finger of the left hand and the ring finger of the right hand. (Or, the fingers for low D and low G.) Teachers should especially watch for this tendency.

Finally, there is one more big problem that afflicts nearly all beginning students: Subconsciously, they call upon the other nine fingers to help the right thumb hold the clarinet. Perhaps this is, indeed, the root of all other finger problems, especially with beginners. They are seeking security; they are afraid they will *drop* the clarinet. The teacher must point out that, when this happens, the right thumb is shirking its duties. The right thumb, and the right thumb alone (steadied by the embouchure), holds the clarinet, and it is the only finger that should have any part of this job. The other nine fingers will not be able to do their own duties if they distort their positions to help hang on to the instrument.

Very often, beginners help brace the instrument by placing both "little" fingers stiffly *below* the body of the clarinet. Needless to say, this will prevent the little-finger extension keys from being operated at the proper time, simply because the poor little fingers have too far to go in order to *find* those keys!

I have found a "magic word" to say to students who have perennial problems with stiff, tense fingers. For a long time I tried to get at the problem directly by urging the students to relax the fingers; alas, I did not meet with much success. When I hit upon the idea of relaxing the *palm* of the *hand*, I had much more success; it seems that one cannot relax that part of the hand without also relaxing the fingers. Furthermore, this particular relaxation also seems to relax the wrists, an added benefit.

TEACHING A STUDENT
HOW TO PRACTICE

Students are often psychologically held back and discouraged in advance by the assumption that the teacher will have tyrannical ideas about practicing.

Make the point that you do not particularly care how long a

student practices, as long as it is at least a little, six days a week, and as long as progress is evident. It should also be understood that he should work at least a little on all parts of his weekly assignment each time he does practice. "Partial practice" is just that, and it will not get the job done. The results of one practice should carry over to the next session, as well as gain value from the preceding one. Beyond this, I do not believe that hard and fast rules about practicing should be laid down. The student's own series of practice sessions should be, for him in his own way, a creative experience. Let him experiment. Between weekly lessons, many students are often struck by an idea, or by a particular piece of music that their teacher did not assign. Time spent by a student in this manner, assuming that he has not neglected his studies, should be encouraged, and the student should *know* that his teacher encourages such creative thought. In fact, if you as the teacher discourage such activity, fruitful communication between you and your student will be cut off; both of you will be the losers, too, because you will remain less aware of just what sort of thing tends to motivate that particular student. Make him feel free to discuss his ideas with you.

Perhaps the teacher's greatest problem about practice sessions is knowing whether or not the student has actually practiced, or at least whether he has adequately practiced. Sometimes a student will sincerely maintain that he has practiced a long time every day, and he cannot understand why he is not doing well on his music or on his instrument. The teacher has to assume that such a student is *telling the truth* because (1) he can't prove otherwise; (2) if it is not the truth, but the student sees that you believe him anyway, he will probably be shamed into *making* it the truth the next week; (3) he will see that you are treating him like a rational being instead of like a lying cheat; (4) he will see that he fooled *himself,* by not practicing, much more than he fooled the teacher; and (5) this latter point will be brought home all the more when the teacher assigns the same material for another week, wanting more progress. For these reasons, then, the teacher should assume that it is *true* the student both practiced, and is genuinely bewildered by his lack of progress during the week. A discussion of how to practice is needed, not an angry lecture. Indeed, another point to consider is that if the student really did practice and still made no progress, your angry lecture on the subject of laziness will frustrate him. He will not be helped; he will be discouraged, and he will lose respect for you.

Keeping in mind what was said in the section on how to practice, found in Chapter 6, "Technique," the teacher should first ascertain whether the student thinks he is tense when he practices. If he is, then that is his major problem. Tense practicing, for however long, will teach only finger memory at best and, at worst, will help build mental blocks. Therefore, if the student drilled and drilled and still can't play the piece (or passage), he probably practiced too feverishly and tensely. Point out to him that he is not Pavlov's dog, and that learning to play well is a *thinking* experience. Have him look for the patterns in the music, and relate them to what he knows of music theory; have him play the passage in alternative rhythmic patterns; have him go on to something else and leave it for another day when he will be fresher.

See also Chapter 12, "Public Performance," especially the discussion on pacing oneself. These basic principles also apply to normal, everyday practice sessions.

TEACHING TONGUING

The teaching of tonguing can be fun, simply because good results are likely to occur very quickly if you use the following approach. These good results never fail to brighten the day for both teacher and student; the student, in fact, is always amazed.

I have already said (see Chapter 7, "Tonguing and Articulation") that tonguing is at the bottom of the list of priorities. You know, then, that relaxation, airflow, embouchure, and the rest of it must be ready *before* a tone is begun. So, from the standpoint of tonal preparation, you know that the *last* thing that happens to a tone is that the tongue releases the reed to vibrate freely in the airflow. Unfortunately, students usually have the opposite idea—that the tongue is the *first* thing that happens to a tone. They forget that no amount of tonguing will produce a tone unless all those other aspects of wind instrument playing are already active. Even then, of course, it still isn't the tongue that *produces* the tone; the tongue merely *allows* the other aspects of clarinet playing to have the proper effect on tone production.

So, explain to the student who says he "can't tongue fast enough to play it" that his priorities need realignment. Get those in order, then tongue a tone remembering that, because of the priorities, good tonguing begins with good *slurring*. On numerous occasions I have been amused to guide a student through the following sequence of events, knowing in advance just what the good result will be. I say something like "So you are having trouble tonguing that passage. Well, I suppose you can *slur* it?" The student says (as though on cue, as part of a prepared script), "Oh, sure, there is no trouble about *that* at *all*," and of course he proceeds to play the passage beautifully, all slurred. Then, he looks at me and says, "Anybody can play that slurred, but I just can't *tongue* it." At this point I tell him to play it again, bearing two things in mind: First, he must play it just as he already did while slurring, with that fine, continuously moving airflow, the good embouchure, and all the rest of it. Second, he must try to tongue the notes in such a way that his tongue will seem lazy and late-acting. His tongue should feel like it is so far behind that there is no way that it will keep up with the notes. Doubting that anything will come of this, the student tries it. Surprise, shock, delight! It works! He proves to himself, then and there, that his tongue was *not* too slow, but rather it was far too fast, early, and tense. The student will not forget such a pleasant and dramatic experience, and you will have taught him a valuable lesson.

If it does happen that he can't play the passage even while slurring, of course, you have taught a different, but equally valuable lesson: There is no point in trying to blame the tongue when finger coordination is at fault. In this situation the student needs to forget all about the tongue in order to learn to play the passage all slurred, and *then* he needs to apply the late and lazy tongue to achieve proper articulation of the passage.

Another way of putting this idea to the student is to say that his airflow and his fingers must *lead* the tongue; they should never *follow* it. Conversely, the student must be certain that his tongue never tries to lead his airflow and fingers.

You may, someday, actually come across a student who, while tonguing correctly, cannot come up with enough rapid motion in his tongue. On-the-reed multiple tonguing may be an answer, or a partial answer, for such a student. See Chapter 7, "Tonguing and Articulation," for an explanation of this technique.

On-the-reed double tonguing is also a tremendous diagnostic aid in discovering and solving problems with tongue *placement*. The mere attempt at this type of double tonguing forces the tongue to articulate upon the reed tip rather than upon some other, lower portion of the reed. Many students tongue too low on the reed without knowing it, and this technique uncovers that fact in a hurry. Of course, once this on-the-reed double-tonguing technique has served its diagnostic purpose, the student can dispense with it entirely and use his new knowledge about tongue placement as it is applied to his normal, single tonguing.

TEACHING INDEPENDENT MUSICIANSHIP
AND PHRASING

Here the teacher must request a student to "think like a professional" about the music. The whole thrust of this chapter on teaching is, of course, aimed at an approach that will foster independent musicianship in the student, but some amplification is perhaps needed.

A new student inevitably asks, "How fast do you want it?" *Resist* the temptation to tell him. Instead, answer "Whatever tempo you prefer, or at whatever tempo you have practiced it." Then wait to see what happens. If he plays it at an extreme tempo that is non-sensical, ask him what made him decide on that tempo. If he says "It's marked *vivace*," or some such thing, tell him that all tempo markings are *relative* and that, no matter what they are, they must be musically pleasing. They must be within reason; they must be played in such a way that the student, if he were the listener rather than the player, would enjoy hearing them.

At this point, too, the teacher must bear in mind that there is probably another, and less obvious, reason why the student tried playing at too fast a tempo. The student is probably worried that you, the teacher, will be upset with him if he plays music marked *vivace* at anything less than breakneck speed. This fear is unfounded (I hope) but it is very real nonetheless.

Another point: How often I have heard fine players say that they prefer slightly different tempos for a piece of music every time they play it; yet, they don't want their own students to experiment with tempos! If the professional teacher is proud of his own continued search for new musical ideas, is he right to prevent his students' musical experiments? Obviously not.

"Where to take a breath" provides one of the easiest and most essential opportunities to "teach" good phrasing. Have the student try to decide where to breathe on the basis of "musical thoughts." This will usually make good breathing spots easy to identify in traditionally styled music. There are, however, two musical styles in which it is not usually so easy to identify good places to breathe: In Baroque music (the style epitomized by Bach) and in Impressionistic music (the style usually identified with Debussy), phrasing is often an open question. In music of these two styles (although for vastly different reasons), the beginnings and endings of phrases can be vague, overlapping, and obscure. The student faces an additional challenge that leaves much room for experimentation and for differences of opinion. The teacher's role in this decision-making process must be, then, one of intelligent, flexible guidance toward the student's final selection of places to breathe. These breathing places must be chosen on the basis of two criteria: phrasing and the player's need for air.

Breathing spots must never be allowed to foul up phrasing or rhythm. Some pieces of music have long passages containing no rests at all; this is particularly apt to be true in study material and in Baroque transcriptions of string music. In such cases it is preferable to have the student leave *notes* out, here and there, rather than to have him call a halt to the rhythmic flow of the music while he takes a breath. There are bound to be some implied phrase breaks in those long passages, where a note or two in a weak part of a weak beat can be dispensed with. This approach will ensure that the rhythmic or metric flow, music's most basic element, will not suffer. Look at it this way: Why should important aspects of a piece of music suffer just because the music is played by a wind instrument rather than by a string instrument? The intelligent omission of certain notes can solve the breathing problem very nicely.

Students should be made aware of a basic approach to what may be called "phrase shaping." The dynamic shaping of a phrase will vary with each new context, but there are several general principles. Be sure the student knows, first, that higher notes will seem naturally louder than lower ones. Phrase shaping can make use of this fact by accentuating it (bringing out the higher notes even more) or, less often, by *obscuring* it (that is, by intentionally softening the volume level of higher notes, creating a sort of artistic surprise).

Some students tend to overdo this in an attempt to "be more musical." They seem to think that if a little dynamic variety in a phrase is a good thing, a whole lot of dynamic fluctuation, up and down, will be better yet. This of course is not true; too much of a good thing is too much, and in this case it will ruin the natural contour of the phrase. Natural phrase contour is, in fact, the key. Have the student look at a phrase as an artistic unit and try to visualize its line of contour. If he plays that phrase, simply following its general contour with a corresponding general dynamic contour, he won't go too far wrong.

It is very rare that a phrase will end on its loudest note; usually the most prominent note in a phrase will be somewhere nearer the middle. This means that the student is already well on the road toward good phrasing ideas if he consciously "tapers" the end of the phrase dynamically, something that the clarinet can do better, perhaps, than any other wind instrument. This technique is even more effective, of course, at the end of whole sections.

At the beginning of phrases, too, there are often "pick-up notes." These notes, by definition, lift up a phrase from nothing in order to land it squarely on a strong beat, which in turn offers a more established beginning to the phrase. As a rule, these pick-up notes should be played more lightly than some of the later notes in the phrase, the ones that lead to the phrase's climax point. The most important point to remember, however, is simply that all phrases should be shaped dynamically to represent beautiful, aesthetic units, so that they fit into the context of the music in the proper relationships with all the other phrases.

Sequences can present a phrasing problem. A sequence refers to the repetition of a certain rhythmic and melodic pattern; there are usually three or more such repetitions in a sequence. Something must be done, dynamically, to prevent the repetitions in a sequence from becoming dull and boring to the listener. It is usually more effective to grow louder during a sequence, but sometimes, of course, the player needs to soften gradually. If the sequence is long enough, some fitting combination of the two general dynamic directions must be found.

Finally, concerning the teaching of independent musicianship, it is vital that the teacher tell the student in words, and demonstrate to him by actions, that musicianship represents the ability to create, and that the student himself is free to create.

TEACHING THE USE OF TONE COLOR

The varying of tone colors is an important factor in phrasing and should be an integral part of "expression," almost inseparable from dynamic variation. Hastily, however, I must add that this is true only at an advanced level, and it should be introduced only after the student's basic tone quality is well established.

The clarinet is capable of producing a wide range of tone color, as wide as the clarinet's dynamic range, which is tremendous. It is marvelously effective to approach phrasing with a knowledge of how to employ both the dynamic and tone color ranges of the clarinet.

The simplest example of this is to intensify passages by using a little brighter, edgier sound, and to mellow the sound during quiet passages. To brighten the sound, ask the student to use slightly greater lip pressure than normal, and to mellow the sound have him *very slightly* relax the sides of the embouchure. Neither action, of course, should affect the tone's pitch, which is the main reason why this technique should be used only by clarinetists who are fairly advanced both in the command of the instrument and in musical maturity.

Still another prerequisite to the use of this technique is the presence of a reed with "heart" in it. If the reed is too thin, all attempts to change the color of its thin sound will be pointless.

Changes in tone color can also be effected by adding fingers or keys (either to open or to close them, as in "venting") to a repeated pitch, in different combinations on each note. A good example of this would be to add, and subsequently to subtract in varying combinations, the fingers of the right hand during immediate repetitions of second-space A-natural. Subtly done, this can be very beautiful, and it can be an additional way to keep the phrase alive during such a series of repeated pitches. Overdone, of course, it can become tasteless, but this is true of any artistic technique. All of the "throat tones," from open G up through B-flat on the middle line, are especially open to the use of this technique (and sometimes they need fingers added to them anyway for reasons of pitch); and a good, creative clarinet student can probably think of other applications of this idea elsewhere in the clarinet's range.

TEACHING THE COORDINATION
OF PROMINENT BASICS

Often students fail to achieve progress, even during private lessons, because their coordination of the basics has fallen apart. Usually the student either has trouble with high notes, or he has trouble tonguing. In either case, his problem is most likely *not* what he thinks it is.

In the case of high notes, the student complains that his embouchure is inadequate, and he tries to compensate through greater pressure, or jaw bite. Almost invariably, he has merely created a *second* problem. When this occurs, have him do two things: First, play the high notes with the *same embouchure* as for the low notes (to avoid jaw bite) and then greatly increase the air speed (which will take care of his original problem).

In the case of tonguing problems, the student tries to speed up the tongue through tenseness. Again, he now has *two* problems instead of one. Have him *relax* and *slur* the passage (which takes care of the tenseness). Then solve his original problem by having him tongue the passage in such a way that he thinks his tongue will be *lazy* and *late*. This will show him that his tongue was rushing before, rather than dragging.

When students try to solve a problem, they often cause a second and simultaneous problem. The second one does not solve the first but, rather, makes it worse. It is the teacher's job to recognize what has happened, and then to solve both problems. Fortunately, this is usually not too difficult if the teacher points out to the student exactly what has happened and capitalizes on the humor of the situation. A good laugh together goes a long way.

Finally, the teacher should point out that such problems do not arise when the student's priorities are in line. See Chapter 13, "The Clarinetist's Order of Priorities."

TEACHING MUSICAL INTERPRETATION

This is a difficult task. Many teachers take the easy way out, by insisting, note by note and phrase by phrase, on a certain "correct" way to play a piece. I vehemently oppose this approach because it robs the student of the development of his own creative decision making. You as a teacher make musical decisions in a systematic way; someday your student will be as experienced and knowledge-able as you are, so he must begin developing his approach to music before his musical growth is stunted. Remember, teaching by example is good but limited. Who will set an example when you are no longer teaching him? If you develop his own thought processes, *you* will still be teaching him *yourself, in absentia!* He will fall back on the creative ideas you helped foster, and not on the dictatorial, narrow-minded ones that someone *else* may have given him.

Teach him to avoid literal-mindedness in music (see Chapter 9, "Musical Interpretation") so that he will not become a slave to the printed page. Encourage him to use his own head and his own ear to decide how that printed page should really be played or "interpreted." Be sure to mention historical contingencies that may cast doubt on a printed marking and that may argue in favor of an alternative approach. Be sure also to relate what the music is doing to what the student already knows of music theory to broaden his concept of what the music involves.

Finally, remember that when you are teaching musical interpretation, you are not merely teaching "the clarinet"; you are teaching a young musician to think for himself. That is the real reason, of course, why it is not an easy task.

TEACHING AN APPROACH TO REEDS

I have found that, more often than not, a student's disappointment in his own playing can be traced to a source unrelated to his playing capability: his reed.

Students have so many misconceptions about reeds. They do not, as a result, make good reeds last long enough, and they do not know when to give up on a reed that will probably never be satisfactory.

Today, no new reed is a finished product. Actually, there probably never was a day when even the best commercially made reeds could have been considered finished products, but certainly they were more readily playable in the days when the cane was properly seasoned and dried before going to the Paris reed factories. A reed today, no matter what its brand name, must be considered as an unfinished product by all clarinetists, including students. Students must be taught that it is actually *wrong* to grab a new reed out of a box and play it without doing anything to it first. It is true that many reeds will play more or less satisfactorily right out of the box, but even those reeds will be improved, and will last much longer, if they are properly treated before playing on them is attempted.

The flat, back side of each new reed must first be leveled. *All* new reeds are warped; hence they must all be returned to their level, flat condition. Response and freedom of vibration are, by implication and in fact, *always* improved by flattening the back of the reed. See Chapter 11, "Reeds," for the process to follow for doing this.

The top half of the front side of the reed should also be briefly sanded with a piece of sandpaper (or Dutch rush) wrapped around an index finger while the reed is flat on a piece of glass. This closes off the pores of the cross section of the reed, fixing it so that the reed will last longer.

Only after these two sanding jobs are complete can a reed be considered ready to wet up and blow on, even in a preliminary fashion. Impress this fact firmly upon the mind of the student, and he will be amazed at the increase in the percentage of his new reeds that become really good ones.

However, students must bear in mind that after a short while, that new, green reed will warp again. The flattening and leveling process must be repeated at that point, and the reed will probably need to be sanded level again on three or four successive occasions before it "settles in." The glass and sandpaper combination must be kept handy at all times.

If the reed becomes too soft at some point during this process, the tip must be clipped with a high-quality reed clipper. After clipping, it is a good idea to sand the front side of the reed another time to help close off the newly exposed pore ends at the tip of the reed. And if the thin tip area of the reed becomes too short through clipping, the student should know how to scrape the reed tip with a good reed knife to restore order.

The student's reed will be a much better one and it will last much longer if he remembers the judicious use of these three reed-repairing devices: sanding, clipping, and scraping.

No reed should ever be thrown away unless it has been physically damaged beyond repair. I mean that literally. Just because a reed will not immediately respond to any of the above treatments is not cause enough to throw it away. It may be the wrong time of year for that reed to play properly. Be sure that the student saves his reeds, old and new alike, and that he periodically goes through his "collection" to see what *time* has done to them. On numerous occasions I have had students appear at their lessons in an absolutely jubilant mood, having discovered an old box of reeds, long ago put aside, and saying that *most* of those reeds, newly sanded and clipped, play very well.

The presence of long cracks in a reed is probably the only good justification for throwing a reed away. Even chipped tips can often be repaired through clipping and scraping. So, except under very rare circumstances, instruct your students never to throw a reed away, but to *store* it away for the future.

So far I have dealt only with commercially made reeds, for therein lies the bulk of what most students need to know about reeds. For students interested in making their own reeds, the teacher has several options. He can (and probably should) first have the student read up on the making of reeds, and follow this with instructions on how to obtain the equipment needed.

No student should attempt making reeds, of course, until he is fairly good at playing on, and adjusting, the commercially made reeds; otherwise he really does not have the experience necessary to know what he wants in a reed. Assuming this level of achievement, and assuming the acquisition of the necessary equipment, the teacher can then incorporate reed-making discussions and demonstrations in the private lesson. Or, he can set up special reed-making sessions that meet outside of class. This can often be set up on college campuses by the clarinet teacher as a noncredit course, or credit for it can be offered through one of the chamber ensemble course numbers.

PREPARING A STUDENT
FOR PUBLIC PERFORMANCE

I am convinced that *no* one is more frightened by the idea of public performance than I was as a young student. Jittery nerves are a tremendous problem in performance, and I will discuss this problem thoroughly in Chapter 12, "Public Performance."

First, proper work must be done in leading up to the playing situation. It should go without saying that the music to be performed should be well and thoroughly practiced. Any mistakes made should only be momentary lapses: They must not arise from any lack of knowledge of the music.

If the music is accompanied, the teacher should not worry too much about the student's dynamic levels since they will be adjusted later in relation to the various dynamic levels of the piano part. Above all, however, while the student is working on his own part and before he has played it with piano in rehearsal, do not allow him to play too softly. If he practices his part too softly, particularly in the low register passages, the piano will be sure to drown him out later. Constantly remind him, in fact, that he *will* have to balance dynamically with the piano later, even in his low and softly played passages.

Be sure to listen in on at least one rehearsal session between the clarinetist and the pianist. Either or both of them may be having severe problems. Particularly if either one of the players is an inexperienced performer, it may take the forceful weight of you, the teacher, to straighten out an ensemble problem they may be having. You must be careful not to say anything to the pianist that he may construe as an insult either to him or to his teacher (leave his "technique" alone, for example) but, at the same time, do not spare any musical advice you may have to impart to either player, if only for the general musical good of your own student.

For a discussion on how to help the student approach his performance with a healthy attitude and without undue fears, see Chapter 12, "Public Peformance." Especially note the concept of *playacting a role* as a means toward removing the *self,* or one's self-consciousness, as much as possible from the player's mind.

A key point here is that if the student is aware of his problems and knows their solutions, you can, in good conscience, send him out on the stage with confidence that he will do his best. His best is all you can ask of him.

ALIGNING THE STUDENT'S PRIORITIES

Any reader of this book already knows that I am continually returning to the idea that every clarinetist should be well aware of a proper order of priorities concerning his approach to his instrument. It follows that the clarinet teacher's duty is to see that his students are aware of these priorities. I list them, of course, and discuss them, in Chapter 13, "The Clarinetist's Order of Priorities."

When I speak of passing on your knowledge of the clarinetist's priorities to a student, what I am really saying is that you need to share your own approaches to problems. You must bring your own teaching methods out into the open where the student can see them, consider them, and make intelligent use of them.

Let's say that your student is having trouble with the opening few measures of the Poulenc Clarinet Sonata, a passage delightful to hear but one that is loaded with technical problems. Those particular measures are characterized by short but awkward groups of sixteenths that tend to alternate between the extreme ranges of the various registers of the clarinet. In short, the passage cannot be played without a proper order of priorities in the player's mind.

If the student has trouble with that passage, he will probably assume that his trouble stems from faulty finger technique. Well, now, he *may* be entirely correct in making that assumption, but the whole point is that finger technique is never the *first* place to look for trouble. Without going into undue detail at this point, let's just say that you must approach his problem with three things in mind. You must tell the student that you have three things in mind, and that they must be thought of in the *following order:* relaxation, airflow, and embouchure.

Is he relaxed enough while he is trying to play that passage? Finger technique, which the student is likely to dwell on, is worthless if he is not relaxed. Is the student's airflow firm, continuous, and intense enough to operate the clarinet in the most desirable way? Finally, is the embouchure properly rounded, open, and un-pinching, so that it does not squeeze off the airflow and the reed? A pinching, biting embouchure will, of course, restrict the airflow, and it will almost ensure enough loss of control that the reed will then squeak rather than play.

You have now done the student a great service. You have prob-ably solved his problem, and you have also taught him how to solve his own problems by knowing where to look. Even if his problem with playing those opening measures of the Poulenc piece persists, you can assure him that he has made great progress toward the solution merely by having *eliminated* the items at the top of his list of priorities. Only after settling those main questions can he reasonably suspect his finger technique, a faulty reed, a faulty key, or pad adjustment, or any number of other secondary problems. I say again that this is a most valuable lesson, because I have seen too many students whose progress is at a standstill merely because they have no idea how to search for the solutions to their problems.

To align the student's priorities, then, you simply show him, step by step, what your *own* priorities are in your search for solu-tions to playing problems. He sees that the same priorities apply to professionals and students alike, and when he sees that, you have taught him how to be his own teacher, later in life. You have even taught him how to teach *others* later in life, although he will not realize this until he begins teaching his own students.

CHAPTER

11

Reeds

What is a clarinet reed? Many clarinetists would readily answer, "It's a little wooden piece of *trouble; that's* what it is!"

Actually, while clarinetists often envy flutists and brass players for not having to spend time on reeds, the clarinet's reed is the vibrating, pulsating generator of that beautiful sound for which the clarinet is noted. The reed determines the difference in tone from one player to the next. The reed, if improperly fit to the instrument and the player, can make that player feel miserable; if it is properly fit, it can excite the player, and affect his playing.

When the player's firm airflow makes contact with the thin, responsive tip of the reed, the reed begins to vibrate. These vibrations travel through the reed from the tip to the increasingly thicker parts of the reed, and cause the air contained in the clarinet's bore to vibrate. It is the vibration of the air column contained within the clarinet that we hear in the form of clarinet tone, but the *reed*, with its own vibrations, is the element that will determine the *manner in which* the clarinet's air column will vibrate; this means that the reed, as mentioned earlier, carries much of the responsibility concerning the *quality* of sound reaching us when the clarinet is played.

Incidentally, many people are surprised to learn that a clarinet reed vibrates only *toward* the mouthpiece (and back to its original position); it does not vibrate in the *outward* direction, away from the mouthpiece.

In the earliest days of the clarinet, even though it may seem incredible to us today, there *was* no separate reed; the reed and mouthpiece were carved from a *single piece* of wood that remained joined together. Whenever the reed and mouthpiece combination was worn out, an instrument maker had to carve a new one. Imagine how hard such reeds must have been to blow on! It is no wonder that those early clarinets sounded like "clarion" trumpets from a distance; up close, they must have been deafening and completely lacking in refinement or subtlety.

Fortunately it was not long before someone began making reeds separate from the mouthpiece, and the reed became replaceable. This meant that mouthpieces could be made of more durable material than wood, and that reeds could be made from a wood that is more flexible and porous than most hardwoods. It was finally established that the best reeds are made from a type of cane, a bamboolike material.

Reed cane today comes from the plant known as *Arundo donax*. Most of it is grown in the Fréjus and Cannes areas of France, some of it is grown in northern Spain, and some of the cane that is used for reeds in America comes from mountainous areas of central Mexico.

Today, clarinet reeds are generally about 68 mm. long. Their shape is not quite that of an even rectangle because, while they are usually about 13 mm. wide at the tip (or upper) end, the long sides taper down to the lower end of the reed at an angle that makes the width of that end of the reed only 11 mm. At its thickest point, near the middle, the reed is usually a little more than 1 mm. thick, and at the tip, where the vibrations begin, the reed may be as thin as 1/200 of an inch, though it is usually 1/100 of an inch thick.

The bottom half of a reed is left untouched on its front side and remains covered with bark. The top half of the front of the reed is the part that is artfully sculptured and tapered from the tip to the center of the reed's length. The back side of the reed, the side that rests against the flat table on the mouthpiece, is entirely level and flat.

This is, of course, a description of the ideal reed. Most reeds are less than ideal, and that's where the trouble starts.

THE TROUBLE WITH REEDS

Very simply, the trouble with reeds is twofold: First, much about them remains a mystery, and second, reed manufacturers no longer process them as they should. We can't do any more about the mysteries except to keep searching for answers, but we can at least partially compensate for manufacturers' failures and short-cuts by treating any new, commercially made reed as an *unfinished product*.

In former days, particularly during the earliest decade of the 1900s, reed cane was grown to maturity (which really means only that it was grown to a diameter appropriate for cutting reeds from it); it was then cut and laid out on huge racks in the fields to dry and age in the sunshine for two years. Only then was it considered ready to send to Paris so that the manufacturers could transform those aged, hardened, and browned "fishing-pole-type" pieces of cane into reeds.

At the reed factory, inspectors selected only the very best cane for making reeds. An inferior cane would be discarded. The inspectors looked for straightness and closeness of grain, a rich yellow or golden-brown color in the bark of the cane, and for the presence of bad spots and worm holes.

When the highest-quality cane had been selected, it was cut by carefully adjusted machines into reeds of varying thicknesses. Since there is much variation in clarinet mouthpieces, there had to be a corresponding variation in the thickness of the tips and "hearts" of reeds. Mouthpieces that are generally very "open" (that is, the ones with facings that curve farther away from the reed than average) needed reeds that were relatively thin and less resistant to the player's airflow. Mouthpieces that were rather "closed," without much curving away from the reed, needed reeds that were relatively firm and more resistant. Because reeds also had to be provided for mouthpiece facings that did not represent either of those extremes, the reed manufacturers came up with reeds of several varying thicknesses.

The Paris reedmakers standardized these thicknesses and marketed them according to a numbering system, from 1 to 5. No. 1

reeds were the thinnest and least resistant; No. 5 reeds were the thickest and most resistant. Half sizes were also available. All this meant to the clarinetist was that he had to determine, through experimentation, just which strength or thickness he needed in his reeds, by number, and purchase his reeds accordingly. A good mouthpiece with a medium facing usually took a 2½, 3, or 3½ reed, and the player could buy a box of twenty-five reeds in his favorite strength number confident that at least fifteen or twenty of those reeds would serve him very well in his particular clarinet and mouthpiece combination. Ironically, players complained that they could only play on fifteen or twenty of those twenty-five reeds bought in each box, and I suppose they had a point.

But, alas! Life in the world of clarinet reeds today makes those earlier years look like a clarinetist's paradise. The price of a clarinet reed has more than tripled in my own lifetime, and a box of reeds today contains only ten, not twenty-five.

Far worse, of course, has been the tremendous drop in quality. Commercially made clarinet reeds today are so inconsistent that a player is very lucky to be able to play without extensive adjustment on two or three reeds out of his new box of ten. That same inconsistency is also manifest in the fact that the strength of the ten reeds, all out of the same box, will vary greatly. Finally, even the *average* reed strength has *softened* so drastically that No. 4 reeds generally have about the same playing qualities that No. 3 reeds had. Sometimes I think even that is a conservative guess; it may be that No. 4½ reeds are now required to do the same job that used to be done by the No. 3s.

What accounts for this puzzling, frustrating drop in reed reliability and consistency? There is one simple cause, a basic economic fact: Demand for top-quality reeds has exceeded the supply.

The people who raise cane and the people who manufacture clarinet reeds from that cane have been terribly hard-pressed to meet the demand for their products. They have had to resort to using cane that is not properly aged and that is of inferior quality to start with. Cane is no longer aged on field racks for two years; it is so green even when delivered to the consumer that there is much room for doubt that it was aged at all. The coarseness of grain of much of the cane, aged or not, used today is the chief evidence that some of it is of very low quality indeed.

The result of all this presents clarinetists with a deteriorating situation. No. 5 reeds may be cut in just the same way that they used to be, but since they are cut green they shrink in thickness during the few months they are stored in the box. This means that your new No. 5 reeds are not nearly as thick as the old No. 5s were; the old ones were cut after having been aged, so they generally maintained their original thickness and strength.

Not only do these new green reeds shrink; they also warp. Good "response" in a clarinet reed depends in large measure upon the level flatness of the back of the reed. No carpenter would ever think of attempting to achieve permanent flatness on a piece of green wood, but reed manufacturers do exactly that. It is safe to say, then, that every new reed you buy today has warped since it was turned out on a machine. A common joke among clarinetists, one in which there may be some truth, is that reeds are so green now that they may sprout and take root in the mouthpiece.

When this shrinkage and warping is combined with coarseness of grain, the clarinetist is faced with reeds that do not respond properly, that are of insufficient and inconsistent strength, and that make it increasingly difficult for the player to achieve a full, beautiful sound with his clarinet. The player himself, then, if he expects to continue aiming for high standards in his art, must learn to cope with this situation and to compensate for it.

WHAT TO DO ABOUT REEDS

My personal solution to the reed problem has been to make my own reeds from "reed blanks" that I have aged myself, and I urge others to do the same. It is true, however, that the lifestyle of many players, particularly of those who are busy and rather unsettled students, tend to thwart any attempt at learning this skill. Before you completely reject the idea, though, I urge you to read the section of this chapter that deals with reed making. Making your own reeds by hand really is the best solution, but for now we will discuss what to do in order to make the best of commercially made reeds.

Begin by purchasing a high-numbered reed strength. Remember, even if No. 4½ or 5 reeds do turn out to be too stiff for your mouthpiece and clarinet combination, you can always take wood off the reeds. The trouble is that the softer reed strengths no longer have enough "heart" in them to do the job for you, and it is the heart of the reed that will determine to a tremendous extent the quality of your tone.

Next, remember always to view these new reeds as unfinished

products. Assume that *none* of them will play well enough to suit you and proceed to work on them.

Ideally, the first thing you should do to your new, green, commercially made reeds is to age them yourself. The older they are, the less green they will be. See if you can buy some extra reeds and store them away; after a few years they will have aged enough that they will "change" less while you use them. In a moment, I will discuss this problem of "changing" reeds more fully.

Meanwhile, whether you have aged these reeds or not, they will be warped. So the first thing you should do to the reeds you are getting ready to use is to return their backsides to the flat, level condition they were in when they left the factory. I cannot stress this enough! Until the backs of the reeds are flat, level, and shiny, almost like a glassy surface, your reeds will not even be ready to test in the most preliminary fashion. Instead they will remain "unfinished products," and will continually give you trouble.

To flatten the back of a reed, simply put it, flat side down, on a piece of the finest sandpaper you can buy, placed on a piece of glass or similar shiny, flat surface, such as a laminated plastic (like Formica) tabletop. The sandpaper *must* be fine. That it is possible to do the job with a plain piece of typing paper indicates the degree of fineness required. Sandpaper is probably better than typing paper in the long run, but, no matter how fine it is, you will have to break it in at first by sanding it on old reeds that are no longer usable. Only after some sanding has been done on that particular piece of sandpaper will it be suitable for your good reeds.

Sand the back of the reed by placing four fingers on the top of the reed, equally spaced, and moving the reed back and forth across the sandpaper only in the direction of the wood's grain. Sanding "cross-grained" will tear wood off that reed in a hurry. You may find it helpful, also, to turn the reed around the other way (end-to-end) and sand it that way, to insure even more uniform sanding. Do not bother with trying to shine the back of the tip of the reed; apparently it is perfectly normal for the tip of the reed to pull away from the sandpaper during this process, and if you attempt to sand the back of the reed tip it will only unduly thin the tip. Make sure, however, that the rest of the back of the reed is sanded until it really shines.

Through all this, remember that your only purpose in sanding the back of the reed is to correct its inherent warpage; you do not want to *thin* the reed. Therefore, it should be obvious that you will not sand very much, or for a very long time, on each reed.

Much has been said in the past about holding a reed up to the light to look for a "V" or "U" shape in the heart of the reed. This was a good idea when reeds were being properly manufactured, but reed cane varies so much today that reed selection by "looks" has become *completely futile*.

After your sanding has produced a reed back that is uniformly shiny (except at the very tip), wet the entire reed in your mouth. You may find that the tip then will become wavy or very warped all the way across. This is nothing to be alarmed about; all it means is that you need to soak it a little longer in your mouth. When the tip straightens out, and the entire reed is wet, you should put the reed on the clarinet for a brief playing test.

During this initial playing test be sure to play notes and short runs in all registers of the clarinet, and do all this with mixed articulations, combining tongued passages with slurred ones. This will give you an initial impression of the potential qualities of that reed's response and tone. The test should take no longer than one minute. Remember that this reed is still essentially a new piece of wood.

If you feel that the reed is in general too unresponsive, or "too hard," you should shave wood off the tip by scraping, with a good bassoon-type reed scraping knife, toward each of the tip corners of the reed by turns. Take off only a few grains of sawdust at each corner! Then, test it again.

But, suppose this unresponsiveness is confined to only one or two registers of the clarinet range. If the trouble is in the low notes only, scrape wood off the lower portion of the cut part of the reed. If the throat tones and/or the middle range is unresponsive, shave wood off the edges of the middle of the cut portion (avoiding the heart of the reed). If the high notes are unresponsive, shave wood off the tip. It seems, in short, that there is a direct relationship between the low, middle, and high notes and the low, middle, and high portions on the face of the reed.

If, on the other hand, you decided during your playing test that the reed is too soft, which would have been indicated by a weakness or thinness of sound, you will need to clip just a hair's breadth of wood off the tip of the reed with a good reed clipper. Now, test it again. It may need more clipping still. Do not be afraid of clipping any reed that seems to need it. If quite a bit has to be clipped off the tip, you may then have to take the scraping knife and thin the lower portion of the tip area so that it blends into the heart of the reed properly again.

Whatever the results are, however, of this initial playing test and adjustment, be sure not to play that reed any more that day. It needs a rest.

Another day, test the reed again. It will probably need another back sanding, which can be done whether the reed is wet or dry. It will probably need this additional sanding because your first playing of it will have caused further warpage. Remember that it is still a new, green reed. If this second sanding causes any difference in its playing qualities, adjust accordingly, either by clipping or sanding or both. Again, play it only for a few minutes on this second occasion.

On a third occasion the reed will probably again need sanding on its back, and this may well be the last time that it needs such treatment for quite a while. It is now beginning to "break in," and it can be played for perhaps as long as twenty or thirty minutes, but no longer than that. On subsequent occasions, the reed can be played for longer periods of time without damage.

This brings us to one of my favorite subjects: What do you do when a reed shows signs of age? That is, what should be done with a reed whose tone quality is getting thinner by the day, and one that responds in an increasingly soggy manner? First, what *not* to do: *Don't throw it away!* Instead, what you should do is *store* it, perhaps in a box in some little-used drawer. Several months, or even years, later, try it again, and that same "old" reed may work brilliantly once more. The reason behind this possibility is that when you return to that reed, it will most likely be a different time of year, with different conditions of atmospheric pressure and humidity. Periodically take out the old reeds that you have stored away, give their backs another sanding, and test them out. You may well be pleasantly surprised.

That really is all there is to it. I say that not to imply that your reed troubles will be over if you follow these simple guidelines: reeds will probably never be problem-free. I do mean that the reeds you buy will give you their fullest measure of service. At the very least, you will have learned how to finish these unfinished products, and the money you spend for the reeds will have become money more wisely invested.

This approach to reeds can be summarized as follows.

A SUMMARY OF COMMERCIAL REED ADJUSTMENT

1.   Age the reed through storage if possible.
2.   Sand the back on sandpaper-and-glass until the back is uniformly shiny except possibly at the very tip.

3. Do not bother with trying to select a reed by its looks.

4. Wet the entire reed in your mouth, only until the tip is no longer "wavy" or warped.

5. Test the reed by using it briefly on your clarinet.

6. If it is too "hard" in general, thin the tip by scraping toward the corners with a scraping knife.

    a. If only the low notes are unresponsive, shave some wood off at the bottom of the cut portion of the reed.

    b. If only the throat tones and middle (clarion) register are unresponsive, shave wood off the edges of the middle of the cut portion.

    c. If only the high notes are unresponsive, thin the tip area of the reed.

7. If the reed is too "soft," or seems to have a thin heart and a weak or thin tone, clip the reed tip with a good reed clipper.

    a. If the reed needs a lot of clipping, thin its tip again with the scraping knife for better response.

8. In any case, do not play the new reed more than a *very few* minutes that first day!

9. Another day, the back of the reed will need flattening again, because its greenness will have caused it to warp again.

    a. If this second sanding makes any playing difference in the reed from its first trial, make the appropriate minor adjustments with either the clipper or the knife, or both.

    b. Again, play the reed only a *few minutes* this second time.

10. On a third day, sand the back again; this will probably be the last time for many days that such sanding may be needed.

    a. On this third day, play the reed for only twenty or thirty minutes.

11. The reed is now almost "broken in." On subsequent days it can be played for increasingly longer periods of time.

    a. Whenever unresponsiveness creeps in, sand the back again and make whatever minor adjustments are necessary.

12. When the reed's playing qualities show signs of age, sand the back, and (most likely) it will need clipping. This should give it new life.

13. When the reed can no longer by played satisfactorily, *store* it; *do not throw* it away!

14. A year or so later that reed may surprise you all over again, and you will be glad you saved it.

One final hint: Reeds can be made to last longer if you sometimes "polish" the front side of the reed with a piece of paper wrapped around the end of your index finger. Place the reed flat on the glass and polish it in that position. If you are careful your paper-covered fingertip can move back and forth on and off the reed tip without breaking the tip, and the entire cut portion of the reed can be given a nice polishing. This is desirable because the polishing closes off the open fiber ends found on the front of the reed. This in turn prevents an undue amount of chemicals in the saliva from entering the interior of the reed, where they tend to clog the pores and break down the strength of the fibers.

REED STORAGE

Since it is so important to keep reeds from warping, it is also important to keep your reeds on a flat surface while they are not being played. Many gadgets are sold for reed storage and, sadly, hardly any of them do a proper job. The best reed storer is an item that is not made for musicians at all, but for scientists. It is the plain, old microscope slide. A box of microscope slides can be purchased from almost any university book and supply store, along with a plastic box designed for their safekeeping. Wrap a rubber band around a few of the rectangular, glass microscope slides (one rubber band for each slide, of course), and you will find that a reed will fit beautifully onto one side of the slide. The rubber band holds it in place. Another reed will fit onto the other side of the slide in the same manner. There is room in the plastic storage box for twelve reed-filled glass slides, which means that you can have twenty-four reeds at a time, ideally stored. I owe this discovery to my student Gary Meyer who, several years ago, hit upon this idea in our local university bookstore. He showed me the result of his creative thinking, and, twenty minutes later, I had my own set of microscope slides.

Do not bother with the plastic or cardboard containers reeds are individually sold in, because such containers promote warping. Storing the reed on the mouthpiece will also warp it.

The widely marketed metal reed containers are an improvement over most everything else, but I do not like the way they tend to pinch the heart of the reed, not allowing it to "breathe" and dry out at the same rate that the rest of the reed does. The metal bar, or flange, used to hold the reed in place has even been known to make an indentation in the heart of the reed.

In short, I have seen nothing to compare with the rubber-band-wrapped microscope slide as the ideal storage place for reeds. Place such an item in the plastic box designed for that purpose, and you have a really superior method for keeping your reeds safe and in good shape.

WHY YOU SHOULD MAKE
YOUR OWN REEDS

The foregoing sections dealt with commercially made reeds which, expensive though they are, remain unfinished products. A better answer in the long run is to make your own reeds from reed blanks.

Following are reasons why your own handmade reeds are better for you to use than are the commercially made reeds:

1.   Since they are custom-made by you for your own embouchure – clarinet – mouthpiece outfit, your own reeds will play with ease of response and good tone quality.

2.   A reed blank costs approximately 20 to 25 percent less than a store-bought reed. While you may waste or ruin some of those blanks and will have to buy some reed-making tools, this cost is more than compensated for by two factors: (a) A clarinetist can never use all of the ready-made reeds he buys, either; and (b) the average handmade reed will last *many times* longer than the ones that come out of a box. Overall cost of making your own reeds is therefore much less.

3.   Reed blanks may be aged as long as you like *before* they are made into reeds. There is almost never an excuse for having to play on green wood. Because your handmade reeds are not green, they will last longer and their playing qualities will not *change* over a period of time. Such predictability and stability is sadly lacking in the machine-made reeds, of course.

4.   Even when they have been properly aged before use (a condition very rare in itself), ready-made reeds never seem to have enough heart for fine tone quality. Your own reeds can have as much heart as you like.

5.   Handmade reeds, because of their "customized" aspects, will vibrate under conditions of much less stress on the

wood than will commercially made reeds. Therefore they will last *much longer*. I have used only sixty reeds over the last eleven years, each of them handmade. That is an average of fewer than six reeds a year!

6.   Handmade reeds can last so long that they may actually *save time*. Of course it takes longer to handmake a reed than it does to readjust a commercially made one, but the latter will have to be replaced soon anyway. Clarinetists can spend so much time going through boxes of reeds looking for something good that this time can be far better spent making reeds from blanks.

7.   Even after a handmade reed has seemed to outlive its usefulness, it very often can be brought out after a year or two in storage, whereupon it will play with renewed vigor. I have one handmade reed that I used not only during two long solo recording sessions and for a solo recital but also during countless hours of practicing and rehearsals. The same reed, after a two-year rest, has recently been brought out again for use during another solo recital, two different woodwind quintet concerts, and the usual practicing and rehearsals!

HOW TO MAKE YOUR OWN REEDS

Reed making may not be for everyone, but neither is the continual frustration of "looking for a good reed." If you are tired of such frustration, reed making is probably for you. Here is how you go about it.

Reed blanks are not sold in most areas of the country, so they must be ordered through the mail. Order your reed blanks *first;* then start gathering your tools. All the tools can be purchased locally, but the postal service cannot be relied on to be as quick as you are, so order your reed blanks in plenty of time.

They can be ordered from one of the addresses given in Appendix III, "Some Mailing Addresses Useful to Clarinetists." I recommend ordering at least two dozen to start with, unless your source sells them not by the dozen but in lots of twenty-five, fifty, or one hundred. Write first for a price list. That is a good way to "shop" for the best price, and it also means that when you actually order the reed blanks you can send a check for the proper amount in advance. Sending money with your order usually speeds up the service.

It may even be a good idea to order twenty-five blanks from one source and twenty-five from another; you may find one outlet to be much more efficient than the other. Specify that you want *clari-net* reed blanks, since reed blanks are also made for saxophone. Needless to say, the latter are too large to do you any good. (I have observed that saxophone reeds are *much more difficult* to make than are clarinet reeds because they are so much wider. This makes the cutting and scraping much harder to gauge and the whole process is slower and less certain of success. My encouragement toward making your own reeds applies to clarinet only, and not to the saxophone.)

Once your reed blanks have been ordered, you can set about gathering the tools you will need. These tools are, fortunately, less expensive, fewer, and simpler than those required to make either oboe or bassoon reeds. Here is what you will need.

Two Special Knives

Two knives are needed because one of them will be used for the rough work, or the "chipping," and the other one will be used for the finer, more delicate "scraping." The easiest way to obtain these knives is to buy *one* Exacto (brand) knife, the type with the large plastic handle, for which you can purchase two styles of removable blades. What you actually will buy, then, is just the knife handle; the blades are bought separately. Be sure you don't buy the smaller, metal Exacto knife handle, because that type of handle is designed for a completely different set of blades, none of them suited for reed work. With your larger, plastic Exacto knife handle, buy No. 22 blades for chipping and No. 26 blades for scraping.

You may prefer to use the Exacto knife with its No. 22 blade for the rough chipping work, and then use a bassoon scraping knife instead of the other Exacto blade for scraping. A fine bassoon knife is really better for scraping, but it is much more expensive and it requires the frequent use of a good sharpening stone. If you do get a bassoon knife (which is better for clarinet reeds than is the standard oboe knife), be sure to get the heavy bevel-edged type, and specify whether you want the right-handed or the left-handed form of it. You may feel that as long as you need the Exacto knife for chipping anyway, you might as well get two types of blades for it and use it for both purposes.

Two Pieces of Glass

You will need one small piece of glass to support the reed blank in your hand while you are working, and one larger piece of glass for entirely different purposes while it lies flat on a table or desk top.

The glass should be, in both cases, safety plate glass ¼ inch thick. The glass company where you purchase it should grind or polish all cut edges and corners to reduce the danger of cutting your fingers or hands.

The smaller, working piece of glass must be 4 inches long and only ½ inch wide. The people at the glass company will probably think you are crazy when you tell them you want a nice, cut and polished piece of glass only ½ inch wide, but you must be insistent and tell them what you will be using it for. If the glass is any wider than ½ inch, it will be so much wider than the reed blank that your knife blade will continually bump into the edge of the glass, very quickly dulling the blade. The reason it should be 4 inches long (much longer than the reed blank) is that the extra length makes the glass easier to handle.

The larger piece of glass should be approximately 9 by 5 inches in size, or large enough to hold comfortably a half sheet of sandpaper.

A Reed Clipper

If you are advanced enough in your clarinet playing to want to try reed making, you probably already own a good French-made Cordier reed clipper. If you don't, now is the time to buy one. Since reed blanks arrive square-ended at the tip, you will find such a reed clipper an absolute necessity.

Two Wood Files

You will need one 4-inch and one 6-inch wood file. Both can be purchased at a hardware store. The official name of the files you want is "flat bastard" files. It is possible to make do with only the 6-inch size if the rarer 4-inch size is unavailable, but the smaller one is handy if you can get it. The 6-inch flat bastard file is a necessity.

Fine Sandpaper

Do not buy just any old package of assorted pieces of sandpaper; such packages are made up for amateur carpenters, and you will be lucky if one or two sheets in the package will be usable in reed making. Instead, go to the hardware store and buy several sheets of *absolutely the finest* sandpaper the store has in stock. Sandpaper of even a slight coarseness will put grooves in the back of your reeds and will tear wood off the reed blank so fast that you will very likely ruin the blank in a few seconds.

A Metric-System Ruler

Nearly any metric-system ruler will do, but the ideal one is short and made of transparent plastic.

A Reed-Making Toolbox

There are several carrying cases on the market, and any one of them will do as long as it has enough room in it to carry all of your reed supplies, including the 5-by-9 piece of glass. Perhaps the best box for this purpose is an ordinary fishing-tackle or small toolbox, made of metal with a handle on its lid. Avoid the type of box that contains folding shelves and drawers; such features merely take up usable space inside the box.

A Lap Rag

You probably will not have to purchase a lap rag; simply use some old, large handkerchief for the purpose. Use it for wiping sawdust off your scraping knife.

A Large Wastebasket

The size of the wastebasket makes it easier to aim while you are whittling or chipping the reed blank; if the top of the wastebasket is large enough, you will not have too many wood chips to sweep up later.

A Model Reed

You may think that you already know what a clarinet reed looks like, and that you will have no trouble carving one from a reed blank. While it is not too difficult, your first look at a reed blank may well dismay you. You should have a ready-made reed handy at all times so that you can compare your progress on the reed blank with the appearance of the (more or less) finished product.

A Reed-Thickness Measuring Gauge (Optional)

I made several good reeds back when I was first experimenting with reed making with no more equipment than the items mentioned in the foregoing list, but after I got a reed-thickness measuring gauge I was able to avoid much of the guesswork involved. I consider such a gauge a real advantage, but I have listed it here as optional for two reasons. First, reeds can be made perfectly well without a gauge, and second, the cost of a good gauge is ridiculously high. The best gauge I have seen so far is the one called PerfectaReed, and I have given the address of its manufacturer in Appendix III, "Some Mailing Addresses Useful to Clarinetists."

If you become serious about reed making, you probably should spend the money for a PerfectaReed. This gauge is a fine piece of equipment. The last time I looked the price was in the neighborhood of fifty dollars. A PerfectaReed measures the thickness of any clarinet (or saxophone) reed at any or all of sixty-four different points of contact, which can be most useful in determining whether your reed is properly "balanced." The reed thicknesses are expressed by this gauge in thousandths of an inch, a circumstance that allows for the discovery of the most minute discrepancies in the reed's dimensions.

THE PROCEDURE FOR MAKING REEDS

Thinking of how to make a clarinet reed reminds me of a paraphrase of an old joke: "Simply take a clarinet reed blank and shave off everything that doesn't look like a reed." Well, it obviously isn't that simple, but there is a grain of truth in the quotation. Here is a step-by-step procedure:

1.   Before you start, you must season the reed blank. When a beginning reed maker is anxious to begin, the seasoning process can represent a most annoying delay; but it must be done, and it must be done with every reed blank that you are going to work on. It is good to season four or five reed blanks at a time, so that the delay need not occur again.

Put the larger piece of glass (the one that is about 9 by 5 inches) on your worktable. Then thoroughly wet each reed blank, one at a time, in your mouth. Wet the reed blank so thoroughly that saliva is left standing uniformly all over the flat side of the blank. Place the soaked blank *flat side up* (curved side down) on the piece of glass, and let it sit there for a few hours. All this is rather messy, but clarinetists can't afford to be squeamish about a few wet reeds.

A few hours later, repeat the process of thoroughly wetting the

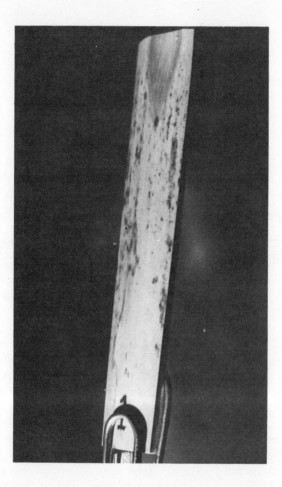

blank in your mouth and allowing it to stand, flat side up, for a few more hours.

Believe it or not, you should alternate these periodic wettings and dryings for a total of about twenty times! You can wet the blanks four times a day for five days, or five times a day for four days, or perhaps three times a day for a week. In any case it is important to wet the blanks about twenty times; anything less than that does not seem to do the job. What job? Well, the more the chemicals in your saliva are given a chance to act upon the fibers of the blank *before* it is made into a reed, the less those chemicals will break down the fibers *after* you have completed the reed. Furthermore, the less the fiber breakdown while you are playing on your reed, the less the reed's behavior will change over a period of time. This means that your future reed will be more reliable, day after day—one of the chief advantages of making your own reeds.

Figure 1 shows a reed blank as it originally comes to you. If your blank arrives with a chip out of it near the tip, as the one shown here has, disregard it. The chip is of no significance to you at all. It was put there by the person who sells the reed blanks so that his walk-in customers could see what the wood looks like under the bark. As I said earlier, however, the appearance of the wood in a reed blank means absolutely nothing. Wonderful reeds have been made from blanks that have uneven grain and that even seem to be the wrong color.

2.   When your reed blank has been seasoned, turn your attention to its dimensions. Its overall length does not matter too much, as long as the blank is in the neighborhood of 68 or 70 mm. long. The width is more important: The blank should be very close to 11 mm. wide at its bottom end, and should be equally close to 13 mm. wide at the top end. It does not matter too much if it is slightly wider than 13 mm. at the top, because you will eventually clip the corners off.

The thickness of the blank can be significant, too. If you have a PerfectaReed measuring gauge, set its contact arm down on the approximate dead center of the reed blank. The dial reading will probably show a thickness of anywhere from about 95 to 125 thousandths of an inch. Anything under 100 is probably a little thin, although this should not deter you from attempting to make a reed from that blank. Anything over 120, however, is entirely too thick. Bring the thickness of the blank down to something between 100 and 120 by sanding it on a relatively little-used piece of your fine sandpaper. Simply sand the flat back of the blank until it reaches the desired thickness; the ideal may be about 110 thousandths of an inch, but remember that each reed is an individual. Use your eye to judge whether a reed blank that is, say, 116 thousandths of an inch thick really needs to be thinned any further.

If you don't have a PerfectaReed, you can judge the relative thickness of your blank by comparing its bottom end with the bottom end of your model reed. That will give you a good approximation.

3.   This next step is one of the most important in the whole process: the shining or polishing of the flat back of the reed blank. This, too, is done by "sanding" on your finest sandpaper, but this time your objective is not to take any more significant amounts of wood off the blank; all you want to do is shine or polish. Settle for nothing less than a completely uniform and brilliantly polished appearance covering the entire flat back of the reed blank.

This is not done for the sake of appearance, however. Such polishing will ensure, as nothing else will, that the back of your future reed is indeed level and flat. Until the blank has been put in that condition, you will never be sure that your future reed will possess the quality of reliable response, no matter what else you do to it. Polish the back of the blank until it reflects light almost as brilliantly as would a piece of glass.

4. Now put your smaller piece of glass (the one measuring 4 by ½ inches) down on the worktable. At this time, also, insert a No. 22 blade in the Exacto knife handle. Place your reed blank on the small glass, and measure from the bottom end of the blank up 34 or 35 mm., or up to whatever point is exactly halfway up the blank's length. Then, at midpoint along the blank's length, "score" a groove all the way across the width of the blank with the knife. Cut no deeper than it takes to go all the way through the bark on the curved side of the blank. From this scored groove to the top end of the blank is where the cut portion of your future reed will be.

5. Position the top end of the blank evenly with one end of the small piece of glass, and hold it that way in one hand. With the knife in your other hand, carve or "whittle" all the bark off the top half of the blank's length from the scored groove to the top end. Use long strokes with a "follow-through" that carries the blade from the scored groove all the way out *past* the top end of the blank. Shorter strokes will only make the job more tedious and will unnecessarily chop up the newly exposed surface of the blank. Figure 2 shows a reed blank with its bark properly removed.

6. Figure 3 shows terraced levels of thickness in the cut portion of the future reed. Notice that there are four such terraced levels, all equally spaced along the cut portion of the blank. We will count them from the scored groove to the top end of the blank; so, the first terrace (Terrace No. 1) is the one that is right next to the scored groove. Terrace No. 1 requires no further work because it is already there; you have already established it simply by removing the bark.

Terrace No. 2 is a relatively shallow cut, as you can see. Achieve this by taking two or three long strokes (beginning about a quarter of the way up toward the top end of the blank) all the way out past the end of the blank.

Next, Terrace No. 3 needs to be cut; for that purpose, use long strokes that go from about halfway up the cut portion of the blank,

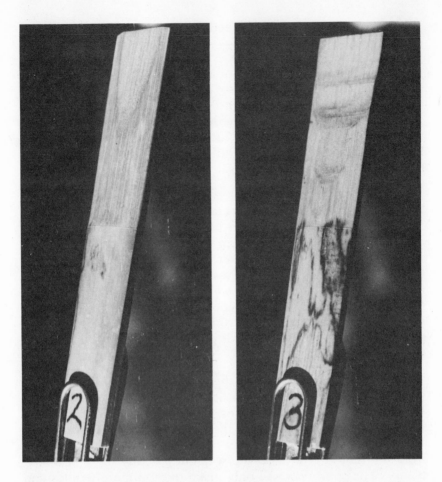

all the way out past the top end again. Furthermore, Terrace No. 3 represents a much deeper cut than No. 2 did, so you will have to use several strokes to achieve it. As you carve, keep comparing your work with the picture in Figure 3.

Terrace No. 4, the final one, begins three-quarters of the way up the blank from the scored groove to the top end of the blank. You need to cut deeply enough into the wood at this point so that Terrace No. 4 will be noticeably thinner than No. 3, but be careful that you don't overdo this thinness or you will have problems later.

Making these terraces is called "chipping" the blank. This is a very important process because it represents the formation of a rough contour for your future reed. Remember these key points: Terrace No. 1 is already on your reed blank, and has been there ever since you removed the bark from the blank; No. 2 represents a very shallow cut; No. 3 represents a much deeper cut; and No. 4

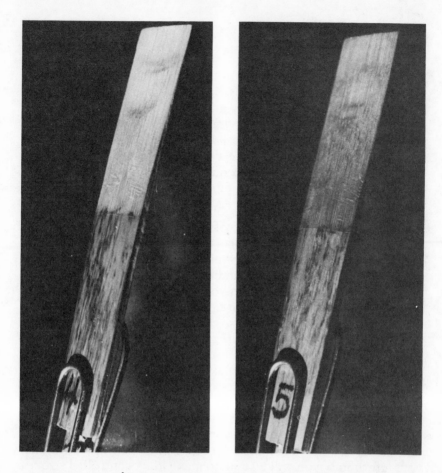

represents a cut deep enough to result in a fairly thin blank tip, but not so thin that you will be in danger of breaking it off as you continue your work.

Remember also that throughout this whole process you should work with the blank mounted on your 4-by-½-inch piece of glass, with the squared-off top end of the blank positioned evenly with a square end of the glass. This positioning is important for the protection of the blank and also for the protection of the knife blade; one good crunch of the blade against the piece of glass can easily put a very large nick in the blade.

7. Now you need to file the rough edges off those terraces, and fix it so that the terraces blend in with each other a little more. If you look at Figure 4, you can still see the terraces, but they have become decidedly less obvious. Do this job with your 6-inch file. The more you do with the file now, the less you will have to do

later with the scraping knife. On the other hand, you have to be very careful with the file because it will remove wood in a terrific hurry. In other words, don't overdo it with the file.

While working with the file, you may save time later by giving the side edges of the blank a slight taper; this taper goes, of course, from the scored groove downward (in thickness) toward the top end of the blank. This requires skillful file work, however, so you may prefer to make that taper later with the scraping knife.

8.   Now put in the No. 26 blade (or take up your scraping knife) and smooth the surface of the blank even more, until it looks like a reed with a square-cornered tip, as shown in Figure 5.

A word here about scraping-knife technique: If you are right-handed, you hold the knife handle in that hand, while you have the reed blank and the glass in your left hand. Your left thumb, presumably, is resting on the bark of the blank. Point your thumbnail up into the air just enough so that you will be able to brace the top of the knife blade against the end of your thumb. The cutting edge of the blade maintains almost constant contact with the reed blank during the scraping process, scraping back and forth on the surface of the wood, so it is a tremendous advantage to brace the other edge of the blade against your left thumb, which then serves as a controlling guide for the blade.

By rolling the knife handle forward and backward with your right hand, and by leaving the top edge of the blade braced against your left thumb, you will be able to make long, controlled strokes with the blade. As sawdust shavings accumulate on the cutting edge, wipe them off on your lap rag so that they are not in your line of vision.

Avoid continuous scraping in one small area of the wood. There is no quicker way to scrape a hole right through your reed blank. Instead, as you scrape, keep the blade continually moving over an area large enough that you will not "dig" a hole or gouge the wood. One of the most common problems with beginning reed makers is, in fact, that they don't keep the scraping blade going over a sufficiently broad surface.

It is now more important than ever to compare continually what you are doing to the reed blank with your model reed's appearance.

9.   When the "reed" has taken shape (that is, like the model reed, but with square corners and, probably, a thicker heart), you need to thin the tip to a "clipping" thickness. Scrape with long strokes *diagonally,* first toward one corner and then the other from the center of the reed blank about ½ inch back from the tip. A few strokes straight up and off the center of the tip will do no

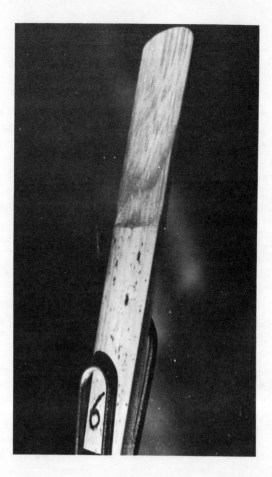

harm, either, but when your reed is finished, the center of its tip should be a few thousandths of an inch thicker than the tip corners.

If you have a PerfectaReed, measure the thickness of the tip as you work. You should get the two corners of the blank down to about 10 or 11 thousandths of an inch, and the center of the tip down to about 14 or 15 thousandths before clipping the tip with your reed clipper. Without a measuring gauge, you can tell when to clip the tip just by flexing the tip with your finger from the back side of the blank; it should flex about the same amount as would a ready-made reed of a rather heavy strength. Remember: Let the *feel* of the tip be your guide; do not bother to try to determine when to clip by holding the blank up to the light to *look* at it. The look will not tell you anything of any significance.

Go ahead and clip the tip of your new reed when you think the tip is thin enough to do so. You now have a reed, but it is probably still too hard or "stiff" to blow on. Its appearance should be very much like that of the reed shown in Figure 6.

10.   You will notice that, until now, we have gone through each step by moving generally from the bottom of the cut (at the scored groove) to the top end of the blank. But now that the tip of the new reed has been clipped, we must move generally from the tip *back* toward the scored groove while putting the finishing touches on the new reed.

Since that is the case, you should now measure the newly clipped reed tip to determine how much farther you have to go to complete that very important part of the reed. The corners of the reed should be, ideally, approximately 6 to 8 thousandths of an inch thick, and the center of the tip should be about 10 or 12 thousandths. Whatever the thickness of the corners, the center should be about 4 thousandths thicker than that. And, whether you have a PerfectaReed or not, constantly compare the feel of the new tip with the feel of the model reed's tip. Scrape diagonally toward the corners from a point about ½ inch back from the center of the tip, as mentioned earlier. This time, however, your reed has rounded corners and not square ones, so you will have to set the tip of the reed out *past* the end of your small piece of glass to avoid hitting the glass with your scraping knife. Continue to compare your new reed with the model reed, and obtain a complete set of PerfectaReed measurements on your new reed to find any discrepancies in "balance."

11.   After the tip seems right, compare the reed with your model again, this time from a *side view*. Does the new reed's heart look too thick? Is there enough slope or taper from the scored groove to the tip? Experience has shown that the back part of a handmade reed can be somewhat thicker than that of a commercially made one, but you must try to make the top half of the cut section (where Terraces 3 and 4 used to be) look as much like a commercially made reed as possible.

When you have achieved this state of affairs, you can forget all about the model reed. Your new reed may still have problems (it may not even vibrate yet), but the model reed will be of no further help. From here on your new reed will express its individuality, and it may do so maddeningly, but be patient with it.

Wet the reed in your mouth just as you have always done with commercially made reeds, but be sure to get the *entire reed* wet, not just the top half of it. Put it on your clarinet and try blowing a note or two.

12.   It is always fun to watch someone who is trying to blow on a brand-new homemade reed. The musical result is disgustingly

unpredictable. The only thing that can be predicted is that there will be a very strong verbal reaction on the part of the player, either of frustration or of delight, hope, and pride. This will depend, of course, on whether his new reed made a sound or not. Ironically, it is really too early to tell, at this point, how good the new reed will be when it is finished.

So instead of delivering orations or feeling a premature pride, go ahead and figure out what next needs to be done to your reed. If the reed will not vibrate *at all,* there can be no question that the tip is far too thick for any kind of response. No matter what its measurements are, thin the tip some more, mostly toward the corners as before.

When the reed's tip will vibrate for you, adjust the rest of the cut portion of the reed just as you would a commercially made reed. If you are in doubt about this, go back and read the section of this chapter that deals with reed adjustment.

While adjusting your new reed, pay particular attention to the relationship I mentioned earlier between the tonal ranges of the clarinet and the ranges on the face of the reed. That is: If your stuffiness is in the low notes only, scrape the lower one-third of the cut portion of the reed, down by the scored groove; if stuffiness (or lack of response) is in the middle range only, scrape the middle third of your reed's face; if stuffy high notes are the only problem, scrape the upper third of the reed's face. Reeds that are too soft can be clipped again, and so forth. The point is that once you have made a basic reed, you can adjust it in the same way you would adjust any other.

13.   When the reed plays fairly well, but you still aren't completely satisfied with it, *set it aside* until the next day. It is a big mistake to try to make a reed all in one sitting anyway. Often, as though by magic, reeds that don't seem "quite right yet" tend to "settle in" overnight.

14.   When you are fairly satisfied with the reed, play it only for a few minutes. The next day play it for only ten or fifteen minutes; next, for fifteen or twenty minutes; next, for no more than thirty. Thereafter, you can play your new reed for as long as you wish. Polish its front side to promote greater longevity.

You are now playing on a reed you made all by yourself. By giving it periodic rests you may be able to play on it for several months or even for a few years. What a sense of accomplishment that can give you!

MARKING YOUR REEDS
FOR IDENTIFICATION

After you have made four or five good reeds, and are playing on them alternately or in rotation, put some sort of identifying mark on each of them; otherwise, you soon will be unable to tell them apart. Being sure of the individual qualities of each reed helps you make intelligent choices. Some reeds tend to have brighter tone than others; some may be characterized by a dark sound, or by mellowness. Some may respond a little better than others. Whatever their various strengths and weaknesses may be, it is nice to get to know your individual reeds and to be able to fit the reed to the occasion.

For this purpose I recommend obtaining a small soldering iron with a pointed tip. A wood burner from a child's wood-burning craft set is suitable, too. With such a soldering iron you can make any kind of mark on the bark of the reed. (Don't make any marks anywhere on a reed *except* on the bark.) You can put your name on the reed (well, that's its brand name, isn't it?), or a serial number, or both. Perhaps you would prefer marking a small shape or design on the bark of the reed. Any "sign" you want to use is fine as long as it is only on the bark of the reed, where it will never cause any trouble.

CHAPTER

12

Public
Performance

The clarinet's versatility is evidenced by its use in symphony orchestras, bands, chamber groups, jazz groups, and other ensembles, but its place of glory is in the solo recital. There is an art to
giving recitals, as all astute audiences know, and when musicians
plan to play a recital they usually worry about the music as individual pieces. This is fine, and obviously necessary; but much more
attention should be given to the recital as a whole.

PLANNING FOR A RECITAL

The first preparation for a recital is to be sure that your performance will bring pleasure and satisfaction to you. Are you ashamed
of your playing abilities or are you reasonably sure you will not
feel disgraced by your performance?

If you are a student, remember that no good teacher will send you out on stage until he thinks you are ready. If your teacher says you are ready to perform, have confidence, because very often the teacher knows when the student should perform, even though the student has no confidence in himself and continues to shake in his boots. Take your teacher's word for it if he says you are ready, and plunge in bravely.

On the other hand, I admit that I know of teachers who say, in effect, "You are not really fully prepared yet on this piece of music, but the experience of performing will do you good." I believe this to be an awful piece of advice: How can any performing experience be beneficial if the performer is not fully prepared for it? Perhaps an unprepared student whose teacher wants him to perform "because the experience will do him good" should ask that teacher whether *he* would go out on stage unprepared!

Having decided that you can go ahead with recital plans, the next thing to do is choose the music you want to perform. Pick a varied and interesting program made up of nothing but high-quality music. Good programs may well include music that is "heavy" and music that is "light," but all of it must be of high quality from the standpoint of composition. Set yourself a high standard so that you will never be in danger of insulting the audience's intellectual or cultural sensibilities. Pick out enough music to make your recital last about an hour or so. A recital no longer than fifty minutes may leave the audience unsatisfied. An ideal length for a solo clarinet recital may be around an hour and five, ten, or fifteen minutes, depending on what music is to be performed. No clarinet recital, however, should ever be any longer than an hour and twenty or thirty minutes; if you want to perform more music than that, spread it out over two recitals given on separate occasions. Overlong recitals only bore an audience.

Especially if you are not an experienced recitalist, you should allow three or four months or more for preparation and practice time. By the time you play the recital, the music should seem as unproblematic as possible. Three or four months will also give you enough time to work on music other than your recital pieces; do not confine yourself to the recital music only, or you will be bored with it even before you have thoroughly practiced it. The recital music should stay fresh in your mind and fresh in your ear at all times so that your interpretation of it can creatively develop.

Choosing a pianist who will play the recital with you is often not an easy task. Not too many pianists are willing, able, and available, and the pianist you play with must be all three. Refrain from referring to this person as your "accompanist," by the way. If singers want to speak of their accompanists, that is one thing; however, if a clarinetist refers to his colleague at the keyboard as his accompanist, he is, in my opinion, a Clarinetist Chauvinist Pig. Music for clarinet and piano is chamber music, and recitals given jointly by clarinetist and pianist are chamber music concerts. Or perhaps you could think of the program as a duo recital. In any case, you will perform as musical equals, just as Richard Muehlfeld and Johannes Brahms did when they presented the two Brahms sonatas for the first time. Surely Muehlfeld didn't refer to Brahms as his "accompanist."

You may also have other musicians join you for the performance of larger chamber works. These players will also perform as your musical equals; however, if the recital is your idea, and if you are not already in an organized professional chamber group with these players and/or the pianist, be prepared to pay all of them for their services. Then treat them as respected colleagues, not as mercenary hirelings.

PRACTICING FOR A RECITAL

You must approach practicing for a recital on two levels: as an individual player, and as a chamber ensemble.

Your individual practice must go on all the time, between rehearsals with the pianist. I discussed techniques of practicing in Chapter 6, "Technique," but preparing a recital is a special case. It involves *pacing* yourself.

Ideally you should have many rehearsals with the pianist, or at least several. These sessions must be wisely used. You and the pianist should be familiar enough with your parts in all your recital music, *before* your first rehearsal, to keep from wasting time at the rehearsal through not understanding the music. This should be the case even though you will not be playing the music up to tempo at the first rehearsal. Have any basic rhythmic or technical problems worked out in advance.

It is nice to rehearse together for an hour or so at a time, twice a week, starting about eight or ten weeks before the recital. For the first two or three weeks of that time, probably one rehearsal a week is enough. During the last week before the recital, you should rehearse at least three times, and at least two of those sessions should be held right in the recital hall itself, especially if you have never performed in that hall before. If the acoustics of the hall seem strange to you, or if you feel that there may be a "balance" problem there between the clarinet and the piano, do not hesitate to have a third person come in and listen to your rehearsal from out in the auditorium somewhere. This person should be musically knowledgeable enough to be able to recommend to you whether the piano lid should be raised to the height of the long stick, the short stick, or not raised at all. When there is no special problem, the usual position of a grand piano lid during a recital with clarinet is that of resting on its short stick.

Concerning your rehearsals with the pianist, both of you should approach the music together, democratically. You should not create an adversary situation. Make musical decisions through intelligent consensus, not through demanding your own way. If a musical disagreement arises, discuss your positions pleasantly and unemotionally, aiming toward understanding the other's viewpoint. This seems basic, but beautiful music has often been ruined through acrimonious rehearsing. If you cannot convert the other to your way of thinking, reach a compromise. Sometimes it helps to agree to think over the problem separately, and to discuss it again at the *next* rehearsal. But never try to impose your will on other players; they too must make music to the best of their own abilities, and you cannot afford to make enemies of them at the very time you need to count on them. I have been fortunate to work with the pianist Frances Mitchum Webb for many years. Her musicianship, flexibility, and pleasantness have made her a perfect example of a first-class chamber music colleague. I would be foolish indeed if I attempted to treat her in a manner unworthy of her amiability. To "make beautiful music" with your pianist, keep the music and its composer uppermost in mind, and your performance will be excellent.

In your individual practice, on the days when you don't rehearse with the pianist, you must wisely pace yourself over each weekly period. There should be days of heavy practice, days of lighter work, and one day a week on which you don't play any clarinet at all. Generally alternate the heavy days with the light ones. If you attempt to practice the same routine every day for the same, set length of time, emotional and psychological fatigue and discouragement will quickly set in. Avoid that, by all means.

When the recital is about two weeks away, however, a set routine should be established to be sure you will have the physical endurance to carry you through the recital. At that time, begin playing straight through your recital music, in recital order, every day. Do not count out rests in your part that are over a measure in

length, and at the end keep right on playing, using *other* music that
you enjoy playing, until you feel you have had a good, solid work-
out. This system will build endurance for the performance, and it
will also build your confidence. However, even *then*, do not practice on all seven days of the week; skip one of them entirely. Adjust the weekly schedule so that the *last* day you *don't* play any
clarinet occurs about three or four days before the recital.

Now comes the important question concerning memorizing the
music to be performed. I am *against* the practice of going out on
stage to perform without the printed page right out there with the
player. Performing without the printed page denies the chamber
music concept; nearly all good chamber groups perform with the
music in front of each player. Consider the pianist from this standpoint: In a solo piano recital, the music is almost never used, and
for a very good reason. The page turns would be a terrible nui-
sance. Each time that same pianist participates in a chamber music
performance, however, he uses both the music and a page turner
to help him, and for a very good reason: He wants the score in
front of him so that he can concentrate on how his part fits in with
the parts of the other player or players. Clarinetists can also benefit from having the printed music in front of them, even if the
entire score is not printed out in the clarinet part. And clarinet
parts very seldom have problems with page turns, since publishers
very considerately adjust the printing so that a rest occurs at the
bottom of right-hand pages.

The memorized recital tradition, furthermore, is a throwback to
the days of the Romantic era when great-personality cults re-
volved around certain famous soloists, mostly violinists, who were
saying to their audiences, in effect, "Look at me! I am the great
soloist who can play better than any of you, even to the point of
not having to look at the music! Never mind my accompanist over
there in the corner; he uses his music because he is not as great as I
am." Surely there is no place in the late twentieth century for this
sort of performance ethic. The moment you go on stage without
your music, you have tried to set yourself above, and apart from,
the pianist. You have also tried to reduce the composers to a position in which they play a merely supportive role in the showing-off
of your playing abilities. Do not present a recital to "show off"; do
so only to present the music of great composers to an appreciative
audience. Imitate the members of the Vienna Octet who walk
modestly out on stage, sit down, smile at each other, and then play
the famous Schubert Octet so beautifully that it is Franz Schubert
who remains in the minds of the audience. This approach to the

music is what makes the Vienna Octet truly one of the finest musical groups in the world today.

Even from the practical standpoint, it makes no sense to me to be without the printed music on stage. Aren't the performers under enough pressure already without having to worry about what the next note is? Anything, within reason, that encourages the performer to relax is all to the good. This does not mean that memorizing music has no purpose; you should know the music well enough before performing it so that it is nearly memorized anyway. But having the music on stage with you can allow you much more relaxation.

Then there is the question whether to sit or stand while playing your recital. Some clarinetists feel that standing up allows the waistline muscles greater freedom, which contributes to better control of the airflow. If they feel that way, and are really more comfortable standing up, fine. Personally I feel much more comfortable sitting on a chair on stage; this also contributes to greater relaxation for me. Those who think that a clarinetist *must* stand during a recital have fallen victim again to the traditions of that same old Romantic era, during which the soloist intentionally set himself apart from the pianist. And even to those who feel that sitting down restricts the airflow, I can only point out that some of the world's finest clarinet playing occurs in symphony orchestras by players who are sitting down.

PLAYING A RECITAL

As the date approaches, be sure that the piano in the recital hall is in tune, and see that your programs are printed well in advance of the recital date. Keep several copies of the program to mail out as publicity for the recital, and, later, to help support your applications for jobs. I need hardly mention that you also must be sure your clarinet is in excellent repair and that you *already have* a good selection of reeds.

Endurance becomes the main factor at this point. The day before the recital I recommend playing very little more than one quick run-through of your recital music. On the day of the recital I recommend that you play only long enough to discover the behavior of your reeds that day. Do *not* attempt to "brush up" on the "hard parts" in your recital music! Such last-minute attempts, like "cramming" for an examination, will be of no real value, and if you make mistakes the experience can be psychologically disastrous.

On the day of a recital I never play the clarinet at all until I am actually getting ready to perform, although I admit that this is a bit extreme. Usually there is some good derived from playing your clarinet briefly sometime during the morning of the day of an evening recital, but never overdo this or you will be wishing for a new lip about halfway through the recital.

Get to the recital hall well in advance of starting time so that you can be leisurely about making sure that the stage is set and playing a few warming-up phrases on the reed you have chosen to use during the performance.

Go out on the stage before anyone in the audience has arrived to check the pitch of your clarinet as it compares to that of the piano. Tune by playing full chords on the piano with the damper pedal depressed; then, while the chord is still sounding, play an arpeggio in that same (concert-pitch) key on your clarinet, carefully listening to each of your tones. Do this in several different keys. When you are satisfied, go backstage again, and don't concern yourself with any further "tuning" until the music is well underway, and only then if you hear, while playing, that the clarinet has gone slightly sharp or slightly flat.

This approach to tuning precludes your having to go out on stage with the pianist, to acknowledge the audience's applause and then to blow a tuning note at everybody! Instead, you can begin the first number immediately. Tuning to only one note is, in the first place, inadequate, as discussed earlier. Blowing one note at a pianist in front of the audience accomplishes nothing, and to me it even seems rude. Remember, you are not a violinist who must be constantly checking the pitch of all four strings. The clarinet is either the right length to begin a recital or it isn't, and this can be determined a half-hour ahead of time just as easily, if not more easily, than it can be determined in front of the audience. After you play a few measures, the clarinet may well warm up to a higher pitch anyway, and you will have to "pull" some more at one joint or another.

You will probably feel very nervous during the last few hours before the recital. Controlling your nerves is a whole subject in itself, so I will deal with it in its own special section later on.

Let's say that the stage has been set to your liking, that your reed is working, and that you have warmed up briefly. You may want to take the music out onto the music stand in advance, so that when you go out to perform, your music will already be there. Whether you do that or not, put a paper towel in with your music. If water gets into a tone-hole during the performance, the corner of the paper towel will draw it out. Have your cleaning swab handy, too.

When the time comes to go out on stage, do so unaffectedly, bow to acknowledge the audience's applause at the same time the pianist bows, have a seat (if you sit to play), be sure you and the pianist can see each other, and begin playing. Enjoy it!

While playing, listen to your intonation (tuning) and adjust the clarinet accordingly during your intermittent rests. Usually more "pulling" has to be done at the barrel than at the middle joint, especially when playing with piano. Listen particularly for sharpness in the throat tones; if this appears, pull the barrel a little farther.

The clarinet almost never plays "flat" to the piano after it is warmed up, so, if while playing you are in doubt about whether you are sharp or flat, assume you are sharp. If you turn out by some rare chance to be wrong, you can always remedy the problem during your next rest.

At the end of the first number, you and the pianist should stand and bow simultaneously, as you did at the opening of the recital. Do not stand alone first and then "acknowledge" the pianist, because that, again, denies the basic principle of player equality in chamber music. Do the same before and after each succeeding number, going offstage between numbers. Being backstage between numbers gives you a good opportunity to completely swab out the clarinet and to do whatever you need to do about your reed, if anything. Of course, if one or two of the numbers are very short, it may be better not to go offstage between them; simply stand, bow, and be reseated.

If you take an "intermission," and I recommend an eight- or ten-minute one if you have an hour of music to play, be sure to swab out the clarinet completely, but change reeds only if you consider it an absolute necessity. You may not be completely happy with the reed you began with, but unless it has developed serious problems you will be far better off to continue with it. It is very difficult to adjust to a different reed while you are under the pressures of a performance.

Throughout, remember that the composer is communicating with the audience through you; you are not merely using the composer's music to communicate with the audience yourself. You should indeed communicate with the audience, but the composer's communication should remain primary.

At the end of the recital, you may be recalled to the stage for additional bows. Make sure your pianist comes back onstage with you; do not leave him behind. Then, backstage, you can put your clarinet away, and joined again by the pianist, you can relax and enjoy the complimentary remarks you will receive from various members of the audience who come back to see you.

CONTROLLING PERFORMANCE NERVES

We get nervous before a performance for one reason: We want to do a good job, but we are afraid that we won't! What we lack at such times is easy to identify: We lack confidence. Any performer who cares at all what he sounds like will always be nervous before a performance, no matter how long he performs, but the more confidence he has, the less he will allow his nervousness to affect his performance.

So how do you gain confidence? How do you reach the point where you are able to command physical and emotional control over the effects of nervousness? Fortunately, there are a variety of ways. None of these ways succeeds alone, but together they can have a significantly beneficial effect.

Many performers claim that nothing but experience will have any effect on the nerves during performance. As in all endeavors, experience will indeed help; the more performing experience you have, the easier will control of the nerves become. This is one reason why it is good for students, quite early in their careers, to play a number occasionally on one of their teacher's studio recitals. Later, two of them may share a joint recital, so that, later yet, a full solo recital will not seem such a formidable undertaking. In the case of joint recitals, it is always nice when a clarinetist shares a recital with a player of some other instrument such as flute, horn or voice. Perhaps the last number on the program could be one that involves both players in a larger chamber ensemble such as a woodwind quintet.

If a teacher tells a beginning recitalist that experience will help him control his nerves, that will be very small consolation to him at the time. There is one other way of controlling nervousness that has more immediacy for all players, regardless of their experience: relaxation. Yes, just as relaxation seems to be the most basic ingredient in good clarinet playing, so is it also in the control of performance nerves. The prospective recitalist should attend the recitals of older, more experienced players, and observe their demeanor on stage. Observe that the "old pro" looks very relaxed; he has worked hard, no doubt, to achieve that level of relaxation, realizing that he will be able to play his instrument well only if he *is* physically relaxed. It is a case of "mind over situation." Somehow a performer must convince his muscles to relax even if it means that he has to put on an *act* to do so; perhaps this could be thought of as *forced relaxation*.

As a college student I always had such a bad case of performance nerves that I finally arrived at a desperate answer to the problem, an answer that is a rather extreme manifestation of the concept of putting on an act with forced relaxation. During one of the semester-end "jury" examinations, I was so nervous that I really did not play my clarinet for the assembled teachers anywhere nearly as well as I knew I could have done, and afterward I was so disgusted by this that I determined then and there to do something about it in the future. After much thought, I decided that I would go into my next "jury" as though I were an actor in a play, an actor who was playing the part of one of the finest clarinetists who ever lived! Not only did I carry out that plan, but it seemed to make a significant difference in the quality of my playing: It was *much better*.

What was really so significant about it was that, by pretending that I was someone else, I lost my *self*-consciousness. By playing the role of a truly great clarinetist (a completely fictitious, nameless one), I could pretend that the teachers listening would *expect greatness*, and that this great clarinetist would have, obviously, no trouble in *giving* it to them! You could say that I was not facing the real world, or that I was merely playing a psychological trick on myself, or that there is no way that I could have played any better than my own ability would allow. If you say any of those things, you are absolutely right; however, we performers need all the help we can get to control our nerves, and this play-acting trick helped me tremendously. All I asked of it in the first place was that it help me play to the best of my own ability under pressure, and it certainly did that.

I applied this technique on future occasions also, and the more I did it, and the more it helped me, I gradually came to realize that if I could play clarinet even that well while pretending that I was someone else, I must be able to play pretty well just being myself. In short, this psychological trick helped me to gain the confidence that I so completely lacked, and as I said earlier, confidence is what we really need to combat nervousness while playing.

That trick worked so well for me that I have often recommended it to my own nervous students. It has had more meaning for some than for others, but I remain sold on it in the long run.

Sometimes just hearing the story, and that it worked for me, has been enough for students to get the idea, so that they haven't actually had to go through with it as I did.

Another confidence builder, a much more obvious one, is simply to be sure that you have adequately prepared your recital music. Someone who has not worked enough yet on his music is going to be much more nervous than someone who is prepared, and for a very good reason. Before you go out on stage to perform, be sure that you have not only prepared your music thoroughly, but that you have also adequately built up your physical endurance. That in itself should remove any *real* reason for a lack of confidence in yourself.

Since all performers become somewhat nervous before a performance, even when that nervousness is under control, it is wise to eat very lightly during the last half day or so before the recital. If your recital is to be played in the evening, eat a very good breakfast and lunch, but eat a supper consisting only of small quantities of foods that are easy to digest. Later, when the "butterflies in the stomach" appear, you will be glad your stomach is quite empty. I am always very hungry after a recital anyway, and enjoy eating a good meal at that time.

Do not combat nervousness with tranquilizers! Even in very small doses, tranquilizers cause muscles to relax, resulting in an actual loss of muscle control. The player can also suffer from a loss of judgment, so that his performance is marked by squeaks and missed notes.

Through self-imposed relaxation, then, and through experience as well, a clarinetist can gain the confidence he needs to control his case of performance nerves. Such an achievement is never easy, but it is well worth undertaking.

CHAPTER
13

The Clarinetist's Order
of
Priorities

Perhaps the most important point to be made in this book is that the clarinetist must set priorities in a definite, identifiable order. I have reiterated these priorities already because they are so essential to any discussion, whether general or specific, of the clarinet. Some aspects of clarinet playing are simply more important than others. Many, perhaps most, clarinetists have been hampered in their development because they either misunderstand the basic priorities or the relationship between them. If a clarinetist understands the priorities, he will be a better player.

A clarinetist is above all a musician, and the only reason we call him a clarinetist is that he has chosen the clarinet as his instrument. Priorities can be assigned to the musician in general and to the clarinetist in particular.

You may look at these lists and argue that I have slighted the importance of articulation, say, as compared with that of the embouchure. In fact, the order in which I have listed the various aspects of clarinet playing and of musicianship is not to be considered an order of *importance*. The order is based on *interdependence*. I have listed technique above articulation, for example, not because I believe articulation to be unimportant, but because articulation depends upon technique for its effectiveness. The embouchure, similarly, is placed on the list below the airflow because the quality of one's embouchure depends upon the quality of one's airflow for its effectiveness. Every aspect of clarinet playing and musicianship that is listed is extremely important. Who can doubt the importance of phrasing as a part of musicianship? The fact that phrasing is listed last on the musician list means that it is pointless to worry about phrasing until the first four things on that list have been established. It could be, then, that this order of priority might also be thought of as a hierarchy of interdependence.

Order of Priorities	*Order of Priorities*
for Musicianship	*for Clarinet Playing*
1. Relaxation	1. Relaxation
2. Rhythm and meter	2. Airflow
3. Tempo	3. Embouchure
4. Intonation	4. Technique
5. Phrasing	5. Articulation

You will notice immediately that relaxation is first on both lists. Relaxation is of primary importance in both areas.

Rhythm and meter, followed by tempo, are the next entries on the musician list. A good tempo, in order to be effective, depends on the accuracy and steadiness of the player's rhythmic flow, and on the accurate placement of subdivisions inside each beat.

Phrasing may seem to be more closely related to rhythm, meter, and tempo than does intonation, but intonation is listed above phrasing because good phrasing will never sound like much if a player attempts it while he is out of tune, either with himself or with the players around him.

The clarinetist list is straightforward. Good articulation depends upon relaxation, airflow, embouchure, and technique; good technique relies on relaxation, airflow, and embouchure. A good embouchure depends upon relaxation and airflow; and a highly developed airflow, the most important physical activity of clarinet playing, cannot be established without relaxation.

If you follow the priorities in these two lists, the way you play, learn, and teach will improve. Other players may have ordered the lists a little differently; still others may have ordered them very differently, perhaps even with additions or deletions. I urge those people to read again the chapters on specific items on the lists, and then to reconsider the lists.

CHAPTER
14

A Look
at the Life Story
of the Clarinet

Today the clarinet seems to be a well-established and permanent member of orchestras, bands, and chamber groups, but its role in the symphonic orchestra is of comparatively recent vintage. Single-reed instruments are not new, but they are among the most recent arrivals in symphony orchestras. The saxophone, today's other well-known single-reed instrument, has not yet found a permanent home in the orchestra, although some symphonic composers have included one or more saxophones in a few orchestral scores. The clarinet is the only permanent member of the modern symphony orchestra to operate on the single-reed principle.

ANCIENT AND MEDIEVAL BEGINNINGS

Nearly 5,000 years ago, in about 2700 B.C., the Egyptians had an instrument known as the *zummára*. The zummára operated on the principle of a single beating reed, as does the modern clarinet, but it was an instrument with a double bore like the early Greek *aulos* (the aulos, however, was a double-reed instrument). The zummára's two pipes were parallel to each other so that each finger the player used covered two holes, one in each pipe. The pipes were out of tune with each other so that the sound produced was dissonant and pulsating.

There was also an ancient "double clarinet" in India known variously as the *pungi* or the *magudi*. It differed from the Egyptian zummára by having its reed enclosed within a wooden chamber, and the left-hand pipe was a drone while the right-hand pipe played melodically. Another variation was a bagpipe with a bag replacing the wooden reed chamber.

In the Orient, the ancient Chinese had a single-piped, single-reed instrument with both ends enclosed in ox horn. One end enclosed the reed and the other end served as the instrument's bell. Its name is not known.

The next development in single-reed instruments seems to have been the medieval European folk instrument known to us by its French name, the *chalumeau*. The most common chalumeau was only 8 or 9 inches long, with six holes on the top and one below for the thumb, and a reed tongue sliced into the upper end of the instrument itself. The chalumeau was the direct ancestor of the modern clarinet.

Meanwhile, however, the double-reed instruments were rapidly developing, and the expertise gained by medieval instrument makers during that era must surely have had as great an effect on the clarinet's later development as did the advent of the single-reed chalumeau. The chalumeau gave the clarinet its single reed, but since it was not used by serious composers until the clarinet itself was developed, we must conclude that when instrument makers finally started making clarinets they applied the technical knowledge learned while making double-reed instruments. The chalumeau was scorned during the Middle Ages as an instrument of the peasants, and no respected instrument maker seems to have wasted time on it. It seems, therefore, that peasants not only played the chalumeau but also made it at home.

The aristocracy favored many medieval double-reed instruments, but the favorite one, the one that most directly gave rise to the oboe, was called the *shawm*. The shawm and other double-reed instruments were perfected during the Middle Ages and the Renaissance. All over Europe at that time, the shawm was given its double reed mounted on a tube, or staple, that was removable

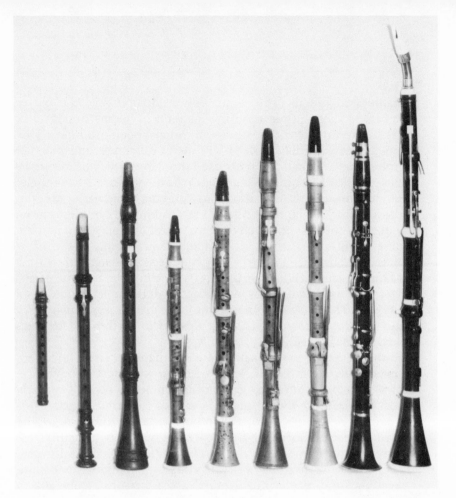

OLD CLARINETS. From left to right: *Chalumeau (reproduction of the type used in the 1700s, made of walnut); Clarinet in C (reproduction of one of the earliest types, c. 1700, made of maple with two square brass keys); Clarinet in C (reproduction of an early J. C. Denner type, c. 1700, made of walnut with two square brass keys); Clarinet in E-flat (a six-keyed model made of ivory-trimmed boxwood by Goulding & Company, 45 Pall Mall, London, c. 1800); Clarinet in C (an eight-keyed model made of ivory-trimmed boxwood in the early 1800s by D'Almaine & Company, Soho Square, London); Clarinet in B-flat (a six-keyed model made of boxwood in Brunswick, Germany, during the late 1700s, and bearing the stamp "H. C. Tolcke, Bronsvig"); Clarinet in A (a five-keyed model made of ivory-trimmed boxwood by A. Bland & Weller, 28 Oxford Street, London, during the late 1700s); Clarinet in B-flat (a thirteen-keyed model of the Ivan Müller type, made of rosewood with keys and trimmings of German silver, by Riviere & Hawkes, 28 Leicester Square, London, c. 1870); Alto Clarinet in F (a thirteen-keyed model of ivory-trimmed boxwood made by Thomas Key of Charing Cross, London, during the early 1800s).* These instruments are part of the Lesley Lindsey Mason Collection of Musical Instruments, Museum of Fine Arts, Boston. Photograph used by permission.

from the instrument. The removable reed tube gave the player much more flexibility in adapting his reed to his instrument.

The reason that chalumeaux seem to have been used mostly by the peasants and folk musicians in medieval times, and that the more serious woodwind players used the shawm, may be the reeds themselves. Amateur musicians may have preferred the single-reed chalumeaux because those instruments were easier to construct at home, while the professionals found the double, removable reed of the shawm much easier to work with in producing the higher quality performances demanded of them. The professionals may have been horrified by the idea of having to rely on a reed tongue cut into the instrument itself, while the folk musicians were probably mystified by the shawm's detachable double reed on its sophisticated tube. In any case the shawm was much more highly developed than the chalumeau was during the Middle Ages and the Renaissance.

In the 1500s, wooden instruments of maple or boxwood were very carefully constructed. Most of them were made in Venice. This was the great era of consorts of instruments; recorders (early flutes), for example, were made in sets of differing sizes corresponding to today's soprano, alto, tenor, and bass, and so were the shawms, the crumhorns, and the cornetts or "zinks." Such instruments were used to double the corresponding voice lines in vocal music, and were used as well in "consorts" of their own kind. There is no indication, however, of a consort of chalumeaux in such august company.

THE BAROQUE ERA

Woodwinds fell into disrepute in the early 1600s for a variety of reasons, such as the extremely high caliber of the Italian violin during that century and the great importance of vocal and brass music in the churches. Voice was paramount inside the church, though in Germany, "tower music" for brass instruments sent its noble sonorities out into the towns from the steeples of the churches. By the middle of the 1600s, however, double-reed instruments were beginning to be fairly common members of instrumental ensembles.

In Jean-Baptiste Lully's time (1632–1687), two oboes were added to the homogeneous sound of the strings (to play mostly in thirds); the players often doubled on recorders. Bassoons, which are really a form of bass oboe, were sometimes added to the bass line. Lully found a small group of Parisian woodwind makers who were turning out some of the finest instruments of the time, and the greatest of these was Jean Hotteterre.

Hotteterre and others in Paris made jointed instruments designed to be taken apart and put back together for the sake of convenience. In the past these instruments had been made, as much as possible, in one piece. One holdover from the Renaissance, however, was the fact that the Parisian instruments of the 1600s were thick-bodied and ornately decorated. The bores of Hotteterre's instruments had broken, uneven profiles; sometimes within the same instrument one joint would have a large, cylindrical bore while the next joint would have a small, conical one. Hotteterre is credited with "inventing" the oboe as Henry Purcell and George Frederick Handel were to know it by combining the ideas of the old shawm, the newer bagpipe chanters, and the recorder. He and a colleague performed on the new oboes, in fact, in Lully's orchestra.

The French also made very fine woodwinds in the 1700s, and because of their expertise the pitch at which they built these instruments (about A-422, more than a half step lower than today's A-440) became more or less standardized throughout all of Europe during the early part of the 1700s. Later on in the century the pitch was raised to a point closer to modern pitch, but discrepancies in pitch persisted all over the Western world until the early 1900s.

As mentioned earlier, it is now generally accepted that the clarinet developed from the earlier instrument known as the chalumeau. Musical scores written around the year 1700, give or take two or three decades, occasionally call on oboists to pick up chalumeaux. At no time before that, apparently, was the chalumeau considered worthy of being included in ensemble musical performance.

There is much confusion surrounding chalumeaux, and the term itself seems to have been used for a number of different purposes. In the 1600s the term "chalumeau" was applied to any type of musical pipe in general, or more specifically to the chanter on a bagpipe, as well as to the chalumeau itself. Later, even during the latter part of the 1700s, when, as we shall see, the clarinet was becoming well established, composers sometimes wrote the term "chalumeau" into the woodwind parts, leaving in doubt whether they meant: (1) the chalumeau itself (very doubtful at that late date); (2) the clarinet; or (3) that a clarinetist should play the written notes in the low register.

THE CLARINET AND J. C. DENNER

The man credited with the development of the clarinet was Johann Christoph Denner (1655–1707), of Nuremberg, Germany. Denner was an instrument maker who was already well known and respected for the high quality of his woodwind instruments. He seems to have had an inquiring and creative mind, and the clarinet was the result of apparent experimentation with the chalumeau. There is no proof that Denner developed the clarinet, however; two of his contemporaries, Klenig and Oberlender, also made clarinets, and there is no indisputable documentation to prove which one of them first made the clarinet.

Originally it was thought that Denner developed the clarinet around 1690, but research has led scholars to believe that it was some years later, perhaps around 1701–1704. It is possible, however, that the earliest known clarinets were called "mock trumpets." The scholar Thurston Dart has discovered a music book published for the "mock trumpet" in 1698 that was followed by three similar volumes throughout the next decade. Doubt remains, therefore, as to the exact date of the development of the clarinet and even as to exactly who the maker was, but the best guess is that Denner made it and that he did so sometime around the year 1700. J. G. Doppelmayr, a contemporary of Denner, wrote a *Report on the Mathematicians and Artists of Nuremberg* in 1730, twenty-three years after Denner's death. The report states that Denner invented the clarinet shortly after the year 1700. Before Doppelmayr's writing was discovered, researchers in clarinet history had no source except one written in 1778, much later and probably less reliable, by C. G. Murr, who wrote a *Description of the Distinguished Features of Nuremberg,* in which he claimed that Denner had invented the clarinet in 1690.

No matter when he developed the clarinet, we do know for certain that Denner greatly improved the old chalumeau. He made chalumeaux of boxwood with replaceable reeds tied on with string. To create the clarinet from a chalumeau he caused the instrument to "overblow," that is, to play upon its higher harmonics, thus creating a whole new and higher register for the instrument. He also provided it with a bell; he enlarged the bore; he made the mouthpiece and barrel joint one piece; and after he lengthened the instrument, he added two keys to make the original two-keyed clarinet.

One of the improvements mentioned in the preceding section is of greater historical importance than is generally realized. The chalumeau, as noted earlier, was only 8 or 9 inches long; a clarinet could not possibly be developed from such a small instrument. The clarinet, then, must have been developed from a *larger* chalumeau, perhaps one that had been used in its own right as an alto or tenor chalumeau. The regular soprano version of the chalumeau would have been too small, in any case, and Denner made his clarinet much longer. (It is interesting to note here that Hector Berlioz, who wrote his *Treatise on Instrumentation* about 1840, refers to *four* registers of the clarinet instead of the usual three; he enumerates the "lowest" register, *then* the "chalumeau" for what we now call the "throat tones," then the "clarion," and finally the "altissimo" register. It could be that Berlioz was acquainted with the fact that most common chalumeaux were very small and short, and could only play in the clarinet's "throat" range. Today, of course, the most common description of clarinet registers involves three terms: chalumeau, clarion, and altissimo.)

The Bavarian National Museum in Munich has one of Denner's original clarinets, No. 136, perfectly preserved. In addition to the two keys, it has twin half-step holes for the right-hand little finger, just as recorders do. Denner's two-keyed clarinet had a register key and an "A" key, but it turns out that the respective roles played by those two keys were quite different from those of the same keys found on modern clarinets. The thumb key, below, is the "A" key on Denner's clarinet, and the key above gives the neighboring B-flat all by itself. The two keys together give B-natural, higher still. But, just as with today's clarinets, the thumb key also served as a register or "speaker" key.

It is the presence of that register key (indeed, it is the mere concept of it) that marks the most historically and musically important difference between the old chalumeau and Denner's new instrument. The register key made it possible to play and to control overtones in addition to the fundamental pitches of the lower register already present in the basic chalumeau. (For a discussion of fundamentals and their overtones, see Chapter 3, "The Clarinet Itself and Barrel Joints.") The clarinet had two registers now; the lower one, for reasons already seen, became known as the "chalumeau" register of the instrument. This was, and still is, the "fundamental" range of the clarinet or, in other words, it is the register in which the clarinet sounds its first partials. Then, with the addition of Denner's register key, the clarinet could play in its range of third partials (we are still referring to its second register, however), thus practically doubling the full extent of the instrument's range. The second key Denner added was one that helped to fill in the natural gap between those two registers.

This new and higher second register of the clarinet became known as the "clarion register" because it was described as sounding like a clarion trumpet when it was heard from a distance. There is no doubt that the clarion register is the source of the name "clarinet" (frequent English spelling was "clarionet"), and the terms "clarion" and "clarino" seem to have caused confusion between the clarinet and the clarion trumpet until well into the second half of the 1700s.

Very exciting to early clarinetists, however, must have been the discovery that yet another, and even higher, register was available to the player by the simple act of removing the left-hand index finger from its place on the uppermost tone-hole of the instrument. By combining the use of the clarion register key with the uncovering of that particular tone-hole the "altissimo" register appeared; this highest register plays upon the clarinet's fifth-, seventh-, and ninth-partials through the use of what are sometimes very complicated "harmonic" fingerings. Thus, the presence of just one register key opened the way to new possibilities in single-reed instruments, and the chalumeau was immediately rendered obsolete.

MOUTHPIECE DEVELOPMENT

A word might be said here about the mouthpieces found on the earliest clarinets. These mouthpieces were open down the entire length of the reed, instead of being open only about halfway down as they are today, and the early mouthpiece's reed rested on an extremely narrow table. The most startling thing about them to the modern observer, however, is the fact that they were only about the size of today's bassoon reed, counting both the mouthpiece and the reed! Mouthpiece materials were experimented with to see if an improvement could be made on the wooden ones originally used since these were not durable: They were vulnerable to warpage caused by moisture and were easily damaged. These experiments involved ivory, metal, glass, china, and even marble, all of which, in those days at least, proved unsuitable. Mouthpieces of hard rubber, the most common modern mouthpiece material, first appeared in the 1870s, and plastic or Plexiglas mouthpieces appeared in the 1930s. The original small size of clarinet mouthpieces increased gradually over the years, but the big, modern mouthpieces did not reach their present size until the 1840s, the decade in which much happened to all woodwind instruments, and a decade about which more will be said later.

THE CLARINET'S EARLIEST YEARS

It is now clearly apparent that Denner's register key created the clarinet and rendered the old chalumeau obsolete, but the significance of that historic breakthrough was not at all obvious to the musical society of Denner's day. There is no mention of the term "clarinet" at all, in fact, until 1712, probably more than a decade after its maker first produced a playable clarinet. In 1712, four clarinets made of boxwood were bought by the Nuremberg Town Band (or "Ratsmusik"). Since Denner worked in Nuremberg, it could be that he was the one who gave the instrument its name.

Most of the earliest clarinets seem to have been pitched in D, but it was not long before they were being built in various keys, especially in C and B-flat and occasionally in A. Constructing clarinets in various sizes, pitched in various fundamental keys, was done to facilitate playing music in closely related keys. The early clarinet's lack of keys made that desirable.

The clarinet possessed only those two original keys during the first few decades of the 1700s. In about 1740, a third key was added, one that extended the range of the clarinet downward a half step from its low F to its low E. Since the tone-hole controlled by this new key was near the bottom of the instrument, the overall length of the clarinet had to be increased once again. No one knows what instrument maker was responsible for the addition of the low E key. That key also afforded a new fingering for the B-natural an octave and a half up from low E, and so is known as the E-B key; it was operated by the right thumb, and *not* by the left-hand little finger as it is today. In fact, it appears that the player had the option either to use the left or the right hand uppermost while playing these early clarinets. The low F hole was put in two different spots, one on one side of the clarinet and one on the other, and the player put wax into whichever of those holes he chose not to use.

The oldest picture of a clarinetist playing the instrument dates from about 1740 and is captioned by a poetic inscription comparing the clarinet to the trumpet.

Sometime during the 1740s, probably during the latter part of the decade, Johann M. Molter wrote four clarinet concertos. Discussion of those concertos actually belongs in the chapter on the clarinet's literature, but I mention them here since they represent a historical milestone. Molter's concertos seem to be the first such works written for the clarinet, and they are the oldest solo clarinet music in existence.

THE CLARINET IN THE LATE 1700s

The wind sections of most orchestras continued to grow throughout the 1700s. Specialist flute players were added to the normal orchestra of that day, and, for loud passages and for music written to be played outdoors, extra oboists and bassoonists were added. Johann Sebastian Bach (1685–1750) apparently never called for clarinets to participate in any of his music, but the time of his death coincides with two important developments in the use of the clarinet: Jean-Philippe Rameau introduced the clarinet to the sophisticated people of Paris in 1749 by including the instrument in the score of his opera *Zoroastre,* and one of Bach's sons, Johann Christian Bach, introduced the clarinet in London in 1751 by using it in several of his compositions.

During the 1750s, two French horns were added to the normal orchestral wind section, and the clarinet continued to develop mechanically. The A-flat/E-flat key for the right-hand little finger and the F-sharp /C-sharp key for the left-hand little finger appeared at about that time, and by 1770 this instrument had become known as the five-keyed clarinet, played prominently by the then-famous players Franz Tausch and Josef Beer.

By 1759, the clarinet is mentioned as being played in St. Petersburg, Russia, and a few years ago I was astonished to read that Benjamin Franklin wrote in his *Autobiography* (1788) that he had heard clarinets being played in a Moravian church in Bethlehem, Pennsylvania, in 1756. I read about this in Oskar Kroll's book on the clarinet, and it amazed me to think that, even among the musically advanced Moravians, clarinets could be found as early as 1756. If Franklin's report is reliable, it means that these precocious Moravians were using clarinets in America almost simultaneously with the instrument's first appearance in Paris and London! Being interested in the American history of the clarinet, I looked up Franklin's *Autobiography* to find the passage for myself. Franklin does indeed claim to have heard "the Organ being accompanied with Violins, Hautboys, Flutes, Clarinets, &c," in 1756. Just as I was thinking that, in the absence of any evidence to the contrary, perhaps we should take Franklin at his word, I came across the doctoral dissertation written by Donald M. McCorkle at Indiana University. He is obviously a most thorough researcher, and a clarinetist to boot. McCorkle was able to look through the entire Moravian Archives. He also mentions Franklin's statement about Moravian clarinets in 1756, surmises that Franklin may have confused music he heard in Paris at about that same time with that which he heard in Bethlehem, Pennsylvania, since he was writing thirty years after the fact, and finally states that "Certainly, no other evidence has turned up to indicate that the clarinet was known in Bethlehem as early as 1756."

In Paris in 1757, the Italian composer Ruggi (and possibly others) is said to have included clarinets in one of his symphonies. If that is so, it would be the first reported instance of clarinets being used in symphonic music. The Mannheim orchestra had two clarinets from about 1758 onward, and this was the first time a court orchestra anywhere listed clarinetists as regular orchestra members. It was once thought that the orchestra at Regensburg included full-time clarinetists in 1755, but this has been proven incorrect; Mannheim was the first. It was a momentous development, too, for an orchestra to include full-time clarinetists because earlier, on the few occasions when clarinets had been called for, they had been played by oboists. Throughout the 1700s, in fact, the practice of using oboes and clarinets somewhat interchangeably seems to have persisted in many areas.

Also by about 1760, wind chamber groups consisting of an octet of pairs of oboes, clarinets, horns, and bassoons were fairly widespread. In later years, through the first quarter of the 1800s, nearly all the great composers, most notably Wolfgang Amadeus Mozart and Ludwig van Beethoven, wrote music for those woodwind octets. That particular octet instrumentation also formed the basis for the wind section of the normal classical orchestra. In 1762, the Royal Artillery Band was founded in England, and it consisted of exactly that wind octet and nothing more. Also in 1762, Louis XV established several French army bands made up entirely of oboes, clarinets, horns, and bassoons, but in this case they were double octets with four players on each of the four instruments.

In these earliest days of the clarinet's life its Germanic origins continued to wield a significant influence. Even in France up through the time of Berlioz, the best clarinetists were Germans; most French clarinetists could not compete with them.

In the 1760s, Christoph Willibald Gluck used the clarinet in operas, but he did so in a very cautious manner; he even called for the old chalumeau along with the other woodwinds, which may show a lack of confidence in the clarinet even at that comparatively late date. Franz Joseph Haydn had clarinets available to him at the court of Duke Morzin during the years 1759 to 1761, but he apparently wrote no solo works for clarinet. Much later Haydn included clarinets in a few of his very last symphonies. Clarinets are found in his Symphonies Nos. 99, 100, and 103 and they were later added to No. 101.

Even though the clarinet was not yet fully accepted as a legitimate orchestral instrument by the 1760s, the fact is that it was already widespread throughout Europe and had found its way to the major cities of America. Treatises written on instrumentation at that time contained articles concerning the clarinet. As the instrument was used more and more, it was inevitable that makers of woodwinds would become interested in enlarging the clarinet family. The bass clarinet and the basset horn (another member of the family) were both introduced around the year 1770. The bass clarinet was produced by G. Lot of Paris, and the first basset horn was produced by a German maker whose name is not known today. The basset horn, usually pitched in F (a perfect fourth below the B-flat clarinet and a perfect fifth above the B-flat bass clarinet), used the same mouthpiece and had the same bore size as the clarinets in B-flat and in A. The key mechanism was basically the same as that of the clarinet, but the basset horn's bore was extended enough so that it could play all the way down to a low C, not having to stop at low E as the clarinet did, and still does. In order to cover the lower tone-holes added to the basset horn, the makers installed extra keys for the little fingers and the right-hand thumb to operate. This instrument became fairly common in chamber music of the Classical era, but its popularity declined early in the 1800s to the point where the instrument itself practically died out. The bass clarinet, on the other hand, did not enjoy much popularity during the Classical era, but came into its own when symphonic and operatic composers of the later Romantic period, Richard Wagner especially, began to use it extensively.

It is safe to say that by 1780, which was a full eighty years after the clarinet first appeared, most orchestras included a pair of clarinets in their regular membership. It was at this period that orchestral second clarinet parts were often written an octave higher than they were supposed to sound; such parts were marked "Chal." so that the player would know that he should play the music in his chalumeau register. Later on the music would be marked "Clar.," telling the player to play the part higher, in his clarion register.

The clarinets of that era were almost always made in C and in B-flat. Occasionally the B-flats were provided with a lower joint that was interchangeable with another one; the alternative lower joint was elongated just enough to cause the clarinet to be pitched in A. The A clarinet was still comparatively rare, however. All the clarinets then seem to have had bore diameters of 13 or 14 mm. The reeds used were very hard, very small, and narrow. Today, most clarinetists would be horrified to see the way those reeds of the late 1700s were played; the player placed the flat table on the mouthpiece (and therefore the reed also) *uppermost* so that his upper lip, not his lower lip, was supporting the vibrating reed. This practice of playing with the reed on top persisted in many areas until the middle of the 1800s. Furthermore, many of these reeds of the late 1700s were not even made of cane; though most of them were of cane, some were made from fir or pine wood.

THE MOZART ERA

The name Anton Stadler may not mean too much to a casual acquaintance of the clarinet, but his significance becomes immediately obvious when we learn that Anton Stadler was the clarinetist for whom Mozart wrote his famous concerto. The Vienna court orchestra hired Stadler and his younger brother Johann as its clarinetists in 1787. This was an event of historic importance of which more will be said in Chapter 15, "The Clarinet Literature." Stadler is interesting from one other standpoint, however; in 1788, he performed a concerto on a specially made clarinet whose range was extended down to its low C in much the same way as the lower basset horn's range was extended. The extra notes, like those of the basset horn, were played with keys for the right-hand thumb on the back of the instrument. Stadler was reported to be a virtuoso on the basset horn as well as on the clarinet, and he had the Viennese instrument maker Lotz make him a clarinet whose range was just as wide as that of the basset horn. Mozart's later concerto and his Quintet for Clarinet and Strings were both written to be played originally on that Stadler-Lotz instrument, in A. Mozart himself became interested in the clarinet sometime in the early 1760s and began composing for it in 1771. More will be said about that in Chapter 15, "The Clarinet Literature," too.

In 1791, the year of Mozart's death, the Parisian clarinet virtuoso J.-X. Lefèvre added a sixth key to the well-established five-keyed clarinet; this was the C-sharp/G-sharp key. Although his may not have been the first six-keyed clarinet, it is the one that was used until the later great reforms of Ivan Müller or, in other words, for about twenty years. The six-keyed clarinet still presented many technical problems, however, and clarinetists still found it difficult to play in keys containing many sharps or flats. To play in complicated keys the clarinet would need a much more highly sophisticated mechanism.

Sometimes the wind bands of this era were augmented with trumpets, serpents (large, low-pitched, curved woodwinds with "cup" mouthpieces like those of brass instruments), and drums. By 1800, the clarinet had replaced the oboe as the most prominent woodwind member of the wind bands.

By the end of the 1700s, in fact, the clarinet had begun to have an identity of its own. Previously it had always been compared only to other instruments such as the trumpet or the oboe. The clarinet began to be described as the best instrument to convey sadness and grief, and as the best imitator of the human voice.

THE EARLY 1800s:
THE CLARINET COMES INTO ITS OWN

This brings us to the 1800s, the century that brought full awareness to musicians and to the general public alike of the instrumental potential not only of the clarinet but of the entire symphony orchestra. As we look over what happened to the clarinet and to clarinetists during the 1800s, it may be useful to bear in mind three distinct periods of development. (1) The first quarter of the century saw the development of what has been referred to as the "simple systems" of woodwind mechanism. These key systems are "simple" as compared to those of woodwind instruments today, but, at the time, they made playing the instruments much easier than playing had been before. (2) The second quarter of the 1800s is probably the most musically significant period of the century; during that period key systems were developed, which, with only minor refinements, are still in use today. (3) Finally, the last half of the 1800s was an era of great technical improvement in the making of woodwind instruments by machine; the so-called industrial revolution made the manufacturing of these instruments an easy feat. As a result, this was also a period of many refinements in the instruments themselves.

Clarinets, during the earliest decade of the 1800s, still physically resembled the ancient instruments. The most common clarinets were ones with six keys, and those six keys were almost the only things on them to distinguish them from the ancient recorders, at least to the casual observer. Many of the tones still had to be produced by strange fingering combinations, strange enough to make clarinet technique a most complicated business.

In about 1806, the clarinetist Ivan Müller embarked upon a plan to improve the clarinet's mechanism. Many clarinetists were attempting the same thing at about that period; composers were placing increasing musical demands upon instrumentalists, and it was only natural that clarinetists would retaliate out of self-defense. Müller made several significant improvements in the clarinet; he seems to have been the one who invented key pads as we know them today. These pads were made of leather or gut, and they were then stuffed with wool to make them pliable and flexible. They were called "elastic balls," and represented a great improvement over the old strips of felt or leather that previously had been glued to the inner side of wide, spatulate keys. These newer, thicker pads were glued inside pad cups in much the same manner that modern ones are today. Later, Müller also came up with the metal thumb-rest and the screw-type ligature, which holds the reed in place on the mouthpiece.

Müller's main purpose was to improve the key mechanism, of course; and, in 1812, after he had been at work on it for six years, he submitted his finished clarinet with its easier-to-play key mechanism to a committee of Paris experts for their approval. This new clarinet had all thirteen keys on it, and it represented a major breakthrough in clarinet design. Müller wanted the committee's approval because only through such approval would his new key system be permitted into the Paris Conservatory, and only through its use at the Conservatory could Müller hope to gain much recognition for his instrument. Even though all were in agreement that the old six-keyed clarinet needed improvement, the committee nevertheless rejected Müller's invention. Conservatism apparently carried the day. All was not lost for Müller, however; some prominent players, notably Friedrich Berr and J. B. Gambaro, used his thirteen-keyed clarinet to good advantage.

The more I learn about early clarinet history, the more curious I become about how those instruments sounded. Contemporary descriptions are rare, and their testimonies conflict. But a startling description of clarinet reeds appeared in 1803 in a clarinet method book written by a clarinetist and flutist named J. H. G. Backofen,

who wrote that the clarinetists of his day used reeds generally of
two different types; one type he described as having a thinned tip
just as today's reeds have. A thin reed tip promotes instantaneous
"response" from the reed, making it easier for the player to get the
reed to vibrate at just the exact split second that he wants it to. But
Backofen says that the other type of reed had a very thick tip,
sometimes almost a whole millimeter thick! How players of such
reeds ever got them to vibrate, and how they must have sounded
while vibrating, remains a mystery to me. Around 1825, Ivan
Müller wrote that thin-tipped reeds were much to be preferred
over thick-tipped ones, and I cannot help thinking that, even as
early as 1790, when Mozart's friend Stadler was flourishing, the
better players must have been using reeds with thin tips. Clean
and clear articulation such as that demanded in Mozart's concerto
would have been almost impossible on reeds that were thick from
one end to the other. Certainly the same observation could be
made concerning the two great concertos of Weber, of 1811,
which were written for the greatest clarinetist of his time,
Heinrich Bärmann. At that time, at least, Bärmann played on a
ten-keyed clarinet.

All of this activity was not isolated or limited to the clarinet.
Neither was it brought on necessarily by increased awareness of
the clarinet. Another very important factor was that the music-
loving public of Europe became more and more caught up in an
appreciation of solo wind music. We can say that there was, in fact,
a sort of "golden age" of virtuoso wind music from about 1790 to
about 1820. It is reported that there were more solo wind players
featured at concerts in Vienna during that period than there were
solo violinists. Even more striking is the report that the Paris Conservatory, in 1795, had twelve clarinet teachers who, between
them, had 104 students; these outnumbered the flute and oboe
teachers and students.

In England, Thomas L. Willman was a clarinetist rated second
only to the great Bärmann. About 1820, Willman adopted the
thirteen-keyed clarinet, the most advanced instrument of his day,
but he still played with the reed on the top of the mouthpiece
instead of on the lower side. The French also, for the most part,
played with the reed above; only the Germans at that time seem to
have played consistently with the reed below, a practice almost
universal today.

Willman was very popular on London concert series, sharing
the limelight with Charles Nicholson, an equally popular flutist.
Nicholson, by the way, played a flute built according to the new

key system developed by Theobald Boehm. He was a tremendous influence on all the woodwind instruments from the mechanical viewpoint, as we will see in a moment.

Interest in wind bands continued, meanwhile. Beethoven wrote his Military March in D in 1816, calling for two piccolos, five clarinets in C, two bassoons, one contrabassoon, eight trumpets, four horns, one bass horn, two trombones, one serpent and several percussionists—a total of thirty-two players.

Around 1820, the pitch levels of orchestras and bands seem to have been quite different. London orchestras were pitched at about A-433; the bands, however, were pitched higher and higher, until around 1850, the band instruments built then were so high that they are unplayable today. What this did to a clarinetist who may have attempted to play in both a band and an orchestra is not reported.

The introduction of "roller keys," in about 1823, is said to have been accomplished by the instrument maker C. Janssen. Roller keys provided smooth passage from one key to an immediately adjoining one by using the same finger; previously it had been very difficult to "slide" a finger from one key to the next.

The French followed the Germans in the practice of playing with the reed downwards when Friedrich Berr, a German, joined the faculty of the Paris Conservatory. The English still played with the reed on the top, but they shortly followed suit.

THE MID-1800s:
THE MODERN CLARINET APPEARS

The 1830s brought two significant mechanical developments that were destined to become part of the far greater developments of the next decade. One of these occurred in 1832; in that year Boehm introduced what he called the "long axle" for his flute keys. The other event happened in 1837, when the Parisian instrument maker Auguste Buffet, whose name later came to be synonymous with clarinet development, introduced the "needle spring," mounted on posts screwed directly into the wooden body of the clarinet. Both of those devices constituted an integral part of the clarinet's mechanical reforms of the 1840s.

The way those reforms were accomplished and how they came about have given rise to some confusion, which is most unfortunate since the result of those reforms was the modern clarinet, nearly identical to the ones in almost worldwide use today. The reforms are no less significant because of the confusion, however, and we should now examine how the modern clarinet evolved.

The man who followed Berr as the clarinet teacher at the Paris Conservatory was H. E. Klose. He was unsatisfied with the clarinet mechanism as it was then and wanted to do something about it. His desire was to create a completely new clarinet key system that would be based upon the principles involved in the earlier Boehm flute. He found an eager ally in the instrument maker Auguste Buffet, and the two of them developed what they called the "clarinet with movable rings." These rings surround the tone-holes; when a finger descends to cover those holes, it also pushes a metal ring down to a level flush with the top of the hole. The ring, in turn, is connected to a "long axle" (an idea borrowed directly from Boehm's flute), which then causes still another hole, somewhere else on the clarinet's body, to be covered by a padded key. Probably because the Boehm flute was so well known, this new clarinet key system became known as the "Boehm-system clarinet," even though Boehm himself actually had nothing directly to do with the instrument. In short, the Klose-Buffet clarinet, known as the Boehm-system clarinet and developed in 1843, is the one known almost universally today in a form almost completely unchanged. The clarinet today has seventeen keys and six rings, just as the one developed by Klose and Buffet had.

It is ironic and unfortunate that there are apparently no remaining examples of those earliest "Boehm" clarinets of 1843. It seems incredible that some Paris museum does not have one of the original copies of that clarinet, but such is the case. Even the present Buffet-Crampon Company in Paris (probably today's leading manufacturer of professional-level clarinets, named for Buffet and his nephew) does not have any of the clarinets made in the 1840s. The invention of the seventeen-key, six-ring clarinet remains the single most remarkable development in clarinet history since the introduction of the instrument itself. The Boehm-system clarinet is by no means the only system in the world today, but it is by far the most widespread.

The great French Romantic composer Hector Berlioz was an enthusiastic supporter of Adolphe Sax, the instrument maker who patented the saxophone in 1846. Berlioz wrote and conducted a performance of a sextet, since lost, for trumpet in high B-flat, cornet, flügelhorn, clarinet, bass clarinet, and saxophone in 1843. The famous French trumpeter Arban played the trumpet in that performance, and Sax himself played his new, still very experimental saxophone. It is a great pity that such a crazily scored sextet has been lost; it would be marvelous fun, I am sure, if a copy of it should happen to be found.

In any case, that sextet is of small historical significance when it is compared to what Berlioz did for wind music three years earlier. Richard Franco Goldman, in his book on wind band history, stresses the Berlioz *Funeral and Triumphal Symphony* of 1840. I want to mention this work here rather than in Chapter 15, "The Clarinet Literature," because although it is not specifically clarinet literature, it was a work of great historical importance not only for all wind instruments but also for its *use* of the clarinet.

In those days it had become customary for bands to play at ceremonial events and funerals, and Berlioz, as usual, was not to be outdone. Here is what Goldman says about this piece of music:

> This amazing work, almost without a doubt the greatest ever written for wind band, deserves a chapter by itself. It was written for the tenth anniversary of the Revolution of July, 1830, and was first performed in Paris on July 28, 1840. Wagner wrote of this work that it finally convinced him of the greatness of Berlioz. . . . The symphony is in three parts: Funeral March, Prayer, and Apotheosis, and the score calls for 108 players, with a string orchestra of 80 and a chorus of 200 (in the last movement only) *ad libitum*.

As though that were not enough to whet our appetite for the piece, Goldman goes on to list the instrumentation. Some highlights of that include five oboes, eight bassoons in two parts, six ophicleides (which were, in effect, bass keyed bugles, forerunners of today's tubas) in two different keys, eleven trombones in four parts, and twelve trumpets and horns; all of this, and more, in addition to thirty-one clarinets, thirty-three counting the two bass clarinets. The upper thirty-one clarinets break down into five E-flat clarinets, fourteen first clarinets in B-flat, and twelve seconds.

It is clear from this that such an instrumentation, with or without the optionally added orchestra and chorus in the last movement, is a monumental undertaking in more ways than one. The sheer size is staggering, and the work probably represents the first time in the history of music that wind instruments were called upon in the particular numbers and groupings necessary for them actually to *replace* the usual string sections in Romantic-period symphonic music. If that is true, it marks, in effect, the beginnings of our modern symphonic band.

The whole point of all this, for the development of the clarinet, is that the instrument was called upon to replace the violin sections of an orchestra, even to the extreme of carrying two more clarinets in the first section than in the second, a practice normal then, as today, in symphonic violin sections. This Berlioz symphony may mark a more important milestone in band history than it does in clarinet history, but it is interesting in either case, particularly because most American clarinetists today play in bands rather than in orchestras. It is interesting, too, that Goldman goes on to report that, in spite of the size of the ensemble called for in the score, Berlioz conducted performances of the work in Germany and in Russia as well as in France. At the time of his writing (1946), Goldman sadly states that, to his knowledge, no performance of the Berlioz work had ever been done in America, but he performed it later himself and it has often been done since.

I will finish our discussion of that great era of clarinet development in the 1830s and 1840s by saying that, in addition to the important introduction of the Boehm-system clarinet, all clarinets were refined and greatly improved. Wooden bores were carefully studied and reshaped to clear up a certain lack of evenness from one note to the next, and the sizes of the various clarinets became more or less standard, at almost the same sizes they are built in today. Instruments of that era were still made from boxwood, or ebony, and with keys of brass or silver. The applied craftsmanship was at a very high level, and the instruments lost, at last, their generally antique appearance.

THE LATE 1800s

In the first several years after its introduction, the Boehm-system clarinet was by no means universally used; its adherents were definitely a minority and were to be found mainly in France. Willman was succeeded in England by a younger virtuoso named Henry Lazarus, who by 1860 was playing an Albert-system clarinet which had been developed in Belgium. The Albert system was a refined version of the earlier "simple" systems and owed much to Ivan Müller's thirteen-keyed clarinet of 1812.

During the 1870s, however, the Boehm system made significant inroads in Italy, Belgium, and America, and almost no other type of clarinet was used any longer in France. Lazarus in England continued to use his Albert-system clarinet, but recommended the Boehm-system clarinet to his students. Finally, around 1890, a Spaniard named Manuel Gómez became a prominent clarinetist in London; Gómez not only used the Boehm-system clarinet but used one that has become known as the *full* Boehm, due to its extra keys beyond the normal seventeen. Henceforth, the Boehm system was well established in England. Gómez himself, in fact, is interesting as an influence upon contemporary British clarinetists; he taught Charles Draper who, during the first part of the 1900s, taught the still-famous Frederick Thurston and Reginald Kell. The latter two men were the teachers of today's finest British clarinetists.

In Germany, meanwhile, Müller's clarinet of 1812 was being experimented with; Carl Bärmann, who was the son of the famous Heinrich Bärmann, is credited with having made several improvements in Müller's clarinet. It was apparently this Müller-Bärmann clarinet that was played by Richard Mühlfeld during the 1890s; Mühlfeld, an amazing musician, was the man for whom Johannes Brahms wrote his clarinet chamber music. More will be said of him when we discuss the Brahms works in Chapter 15, "The Clarinet Literature."

There is an important factor concerning the development of clarinet technique that should be remembered: Up to the middle of the 1800s, clarinet technique always received its main forward thrust from solo concertos. We have already seen that from about 1790 to about 1820 there was an era of popular demand for solo performers on wind instruments, and we even have the Molter concertos that date from the 1740s. At that early date the clarinet could hardly be considered to have been primarily an orchestral instrument. However, from the middle of the 1800s onward, the clarinetists' technique was mainly forwarded by symphonic and operatic orchestral parts. The composition of solo concertos practically came to an end until well into the 1900s. Many solo concertos were written, of course, during the last half of the 1800s, but practically all of them were for piano, violin, or cello, instruments that totally eclipsed the clarinet and all other wind instruments in a solo capacity. The clarinet continued to be given beautiful solos in symphonic and operatic writing, however, and in fact it may well be that the great majority of what are considered famous orchestral clarinet solos come from the symphonies and the operas of the late 1800s.

The clarinet's transition from a primarily solo status to a primarily orchestral ensemble status is perhaps heralded by the appearance of *The Ring of the Nibelung,* that great cycle of four operas, or "music dramas," of Richard Wagner. Weber, Beethoven, Schubert, Berlioz, and others of that era used the clarinet extensively and to good effect in both symphonic and operatic music

(Beethoven, in fact, was the first great composer to use the clarinet in all of his symphonies), but Wagner's *Ring* gives us the first instance of clarinets being used in greater numbers than pairs, in a "normal" orchestral setting, at least. Indeed, Wagner actually doubled that number by calling for three clarinets and a bass clarinet. By using the clarinet and all other instruments in the orchestra in greater numbers, Wagner firmly established the clarinet once and for all as an indispensable, beautiful, and *complete family* of ensemble instruments. Berlioz, earlier, had called for both the clarinet and the bass clarinet, but never in numbers greater than could be played by two players.

As technical demands on clarinetists grew, attempts were continually made to build the "perfect" clarinet, one that would make all music, no matter how technically difficult to play, much easier for the player to handle. Most attempts were made upon clarinets related to, or direct descendants of, the "simple" systems, which in turn were descended from the Ivan Müller clarinet of 1806–1812. Very few attempts were made to change the Boehm, or "French," clarinet simply because its players were generally satisfied with it already; in fact, all attempted "improvements" on the Boehm-system clarinet have been doomed to failure. We will see in a moment what changes were effected in the "German" clarinets, but first we will deal with a problem that plagued the makers of all clarinets on a worldwide basis during the 1800s.

Today, clarinetists are not particularly bothered by the fact that they must use at least two different instruments in symphony orchestras and in some chamber music, namely, the B-flat and the A clarinets. Most clarinetists, in fact, myself among them, love to play on the A clarinet just as much as they do on the B-flat; because we relish the ever-so-slight, and yet definite, difference in tone quality between the two instruments. Today we are accustomed to having to use these two clarinets in all types of music except in band work, where the A clarinet is never used. But a century ago, the distinguishing characteristics were not so well appreciated.

During the 1800s some clarinetists were so bothered by having to change back and forth between the B-flat and the A, with a C clarinet thrown in for good measure on some occasions, that they began to try to develop what were called "combination" clarinets, or clarinets that were alterable within themselves. This was done to facilitate playing in all keys on the same instrument. A Frenchman named J. F. Simiot, as early as 1808, tried to fix a C clarinet so that it would take ten equally spaced extension joints in order to lower it to B-flat. Removing and replacing ten separate joints must have required the skill and agility of a juggler in an orchestral situation, however, and the invention never caught on. Even with enough time to exchange all those joints, the player had no way to put the clarinet into A.

That is the only known attempt to lower a clarinet a whole step, but several experiments were conducted with an eye toward making a combination clarinet that would go back and forth between B-flat and A. At least two of these experiments occurred in Germany during the 1830s. In one instance, the clarinet mouthpiece and barrel joint were connected by screw threads so that the instrument could literally be unscrewed from B-flat to A. In another instance, a slide joint was installed in the middle joint of the clarinet; when extended, the slide joint lowered the instrument from B-flat to A.

Later in the century, more elaborate combination clarinets were built. No less a maker than Buffet himself, in 1862, built a clarinet containing two separate metal tubes inside the bore, but as usual it had only one set of keys. By turning the bell joint, the player could line up the keys and tone-holes with either the B-flat or the A bore, whichever was his choice at the moment. This was a good idea and it worked amazingly well mechanically, but, as any modern clarinetist would soon guess, that clarinet had overwhelming problems with tone and pitch. An Englishman named James Clinton built a similar instrument and obtained a German patent on it in 1891.

The most amusing attempt of all to make a combination clarinet occurred in the early 1900s. Someone got the bright idea of simply dropping a length of string into the bore of a B-flat clarinet, hooking it onto the shoulder of the barrel joint with two little metal hooks, and ending up with a clarinet that blew so "flat" that it played in A. The string was about 15 inches long and had the approximate thickness of the average rope-type clothesline, and it did indeed lower the pitch of the clarinet a half step. When I was in high school, my band director gave me a string-tuning device which he had had for a number of years, as a sort of curiosity. I still have it, and to this day it occasionally affords me and my students a good laugh. As might be expected, a clarinet with a clothesline in its bore blows like, well, a clarinet with a clothesline in its bore.

Also in the early part of the 1900s, some attempts were made at building a clarinet that would play in quarter tones. New ideas in musical composition at that time exemplified by Gustav Mahler, Igor Stravinsky, Arnold Schönberg, Alban Berg, Anton von Webern, and others gave rise to more "modern" adaptations of the standard instruments. A Berlin musicologist named Dr. R. H. Stein developed the most successful of the quarter-tone clarinets, but the idea itself was soon abandoned as impractical, and no such clarinet is in use now.

All of these modifications and adaptations of the clarinet were indeed temporary and transitory, and none of them has survived.

I have mentioned that while the Boehm-system clarinet, or the one mainly identified with the French, has scarcely altered since the original Klose-Buffet prototype of the early 1840s, the "German" and/or "simple" systems, which trace back to a common ancestor at least as early as Ivan Müller's clarinet of about 1812, have gone through many changes and forms. The most important forms of "non-Boehm" clarinets are the Albert system, the Clinton model, and various other, slightly different versions of what are commonly called "full German models." Each one of these systems is a direct descendant of Ivan Müller's clarinet of the early 1800s. I will briefly describe them one at a time.

The Albert system is the best known non-Boehm clarinet in America today. Most American clarinetists, however, do not know exactly what the Albert system is, although, they are aware of its existence. There are very few Albert-system clarinets left in America, and even fewer of them are in use. Furthermore, almost no American students are learning to play that system. Thus the Albert system is becoming a curiosity more than anything else, even though some German or Czech "polka bands" are still using it. Ironically, the Albert system was not developed in Germany, but rather in Belgium. J. B. Albert himself was an instrument maker in Brussels who more or less remodeled the Müller clarinet sometime during the 1840s or 1850s. No particular advances or specific improvements were made over Müller's clarinet, but Albert did refine the mechanism somewhat, and his clarinet made significant inroads in both Germany and Czechoslovakia. In Belgium itself, the Boehm system prevailed in spite of Albert.

The Clinton-model clarinet, developed by James Clinton and built by Boosey in England in 1885, was another permutation of the old Müller clarinet. A few of these instruments were still in use in England a generation ago, and there may be a handful of them around yet. England during the latter part of the 1800s must have been a rather confusing place for clarinetists, because so many key systems were apparently in use. At that time, the English were using many varieties of these "simple" systems and were importing ideas from all over the European continent. This was either further confused or cleared up, depending on your point of view, by the arrival of the Spaniard Gómez, mentioned earlier, playing on his full Boehm system in the 1890s.

Perhaps I should clarify the use of the term "simple" in this context; to call a key system "simple" means that the mechanism itself is simply constructed. It does not mean that it is a key system designed in a way that would necessarily be easier to play upon. Nearly all American clarinetists, in fact, would be appalled by non-Boehm systems since they are used to the Boehm clarinet. The "forked F" and the fact that there are rarely any duplicate little-finger keys on any of the "simple" key systems are two factors that would, by themselves, give American clarinetists nightmares. Nevertheless, there are players, even today, in many other parts of the world (mostly in Germany and in eastern Europe) who are capable of playing the same music on simple systems that America's best clarinetists play on the Boehm system, and they play it just as well.

Concerning the third and final main category of non-Boehm clarinets, we must turn our attention to Germany itself and to the various types of "full-German" key systems. In this category there are three types: the Schmidt clarinet, the German Normal clarinet, and the Oskar Oehler model.

After extremely careful and very scientific research, the German clarinetist Ernst Schmidt, with the maker Louis Kolbe, developed a clarinet based on the Boehm system in 1912. It is still constructed today and is usually referred to as the "Schmidt Reform Boehm System." In spite of its careful design, it is not tremendously popular today even in Germany, probably because it is neither fish nor fowl; that is, it is close to the Boehm system and yet it isn't Boehm, and it is close to other German varieties of clarinets without being exactly like any one of them either.

The German Normal clarinet also used some ideas from the Boehm system, but fewer of them, and it was earlier than the Schmidt Reform clarinet. It dates from 1890, and was developed by the clarinetist Hermann Kunze and by the instrument maker Thomas Mollenhauer.

The most successful German clarinet, and the one still in use today by most German and eastern European clarinetists who do not play on the Boehm system, is unquestionably the Oehler model. Oskar Oehler of Berlin was a clarinetist whose playing was highly respected, but he became so interested in the mechanism and the construction of clarinets that he stopped his performing career sometime around 1890 to devote his full time to research and manufacturing clarinets. He began work at about that time on the same, great old "simple" stand-by, Ivan Müller's thirteen-keyed clarinet of 1812, to see what improvements he could effect. Eventually he evolved an instrument using twenty-two keys, five rings, and one full finger plate. It is reported that Oehler himself was a fine gentleman, much admired by the German circle of clarinetists; he apparently spent much time with younger professionals and students in an effort to help them and to find out what they wanted in a fine clarinet.

When today's American clarinetists realize that Germany has a great clarinet history and tradition beginning with Denner around 1700, continuing with Ivan Müller around 1810 and Oskar Oehler around 1890, and well into the 1900s, they can perhaps understand a little better the reasons why the Germans are not as taken by the Boehm system as are clarinetists farther to the west.

THE VARIOUS SIZES OF CLARINETS

Today, most American clarinetists have at least one Boehm-system clarinet, the one in B-flat. Nearly all professionals and a few students also own a similar clarinet in A. A smaller clarinet in E-flat is sometimes called for in both bands and orchestras and so it is also fairly common; nevertheless, compared with the B-flat clarinet, the E-flat is a rarity. Occasionally, a symphonic composer (notably Richard Strauss in his several tone poems) calls for a clarinet in D, which is to the E-flat what the A is to the B-flat. The D clarinet is so rare today, however, that parts scored for it are almost always played on the E-flat, transposed. From the Mozart-Haydn era up through Mahler (as late, then, as about 1910), composers sometimes called for the C clarinet, especially in music of the early 1800s. Much of the Beethoven and Schubert orchestral music demands a C clarinet, for example. Therefore the C clarinet was much more common before the earlier part of the 1900s than it is today. If an orchestral part calls for a C clarinet, the modern clarinetist nearly always plays it on his B-flat, transposing the part up a whole step, the reason being that the C clarinet is just enough smaller than the B-flat and the A to require the use of a different mouthpiece and reed. The B-flat and the A do very well while interchanging the same mouthpiece from one to the other, but to keep another reed wet, and to find a suitable reed of a smaller size in the first place, has proven itself too impractical a task for the contemporary clarinetist. Two clarinets are one thing, but two different mouthpiece-and-reed combinations are too much. Having said that, however, I should mention that some players in major orchestras do maintain C clarinets in addition to their other clarinets; some conductors, in fact, insist upon it, just as Berlioz told them to in his *Treatise on Orchestration* years ago.

The four clarinets in B-flat, A, E-flat, and D are generally called "soprano" clarinets; one clarinet is even smaller, the "sopranino" in high A-flat. This instrument is so small that it is tremendously difficult to control. Its use today is almost entirely confined to Italian military bands.

The "alto" clarinet is pitched a perfect fifth lower than the soprano B-flat; it is therefore an E-flat instrument exactly an octave below the E-flat soprano clarinet. It is generally built slightly bent because it is large; the bent joints are usually at the barrel and at the bell, just as they are in the bass clarinet. Those two joints are made of metal. The alto clarinet has more or less gone out of fashion, and even though many works for concert band call for them, the conductor often does not include them in his ensemble, leaving that particular part to be picked up by other instruments such as the saxophones and the horns. The alto clarinet may not add too much to the total band sound, but my own feeling is that in the hands of a good player there is no reason why the alto clarinet cannot carry its own musical weight. Perhaps an even more important reason for keeping the alto clarinet alive today is that it is a wonderful substitute for the basset horn in F, now almost extinct, but for which there are many important parts written in chamber music of the Classical era.

Interestingly, there is no member of the clarinet family called a "tenor"; the bass clarinet in B-flat is only a perfect fourth below the alto instrument. During the Romantic era of the 1800s, parts were written for bass clarinets in A. Wagner nearly always wrote his bass clarinet parts in whichever key his soprano clarinets were in at that moment, either in B-flat or in A, but today the bass clarinet in A is no longer manufactured. All of its parts are played on the B-flat bass, transposed by the player.

Finally, there are two sizes of contrabass clarinets, one in E-flat (an octave below the alto clarinet, and therefore sometimes called the "contra-alto" clarinet) and the B-flat, pitched an octave below the bass clarinet. The E-flat contrabass is generally preferred by band directors and players today because it can be made successfully of wood or plastic just as the smaller clarinets are. The B-flat contrabass is so large that it must be made of metal and its tubing must be bent back on itself in such a contorted manner that it makes me think of a giant paper clip. Nevertheless, it is a perfectly good and legitimate instrument and is used to advantage in wind ensembles and in symphonic bands throughout the world. Athough all of the smaller clarinets (except the alto) are used extensively in orchestras as well as in bands, neither of the two contrabasses are used in orchestras.

THE CLARINET IN FOLK MUSIC

Like the chalumeau before it, the clarinet, even today, does play the role of a folk instrument in some parts of the world. In the Balkan countries, and in several Mediterranean countries, the clarinet is used as a high melodic instrument in some ensembles that accompany folk dancing. The players are usually musicians who are completely unschooled in formal music training and who have become masters of improvisation. Their finger technique is often so astonishing that it makes the formally trained clarinetist wonder whether the printed page can be a significantly inhibiting influence.

In Czechoslovakia, some people have even called the clarinet the national instrument, so widespread is its use in music for folk dancing. In Hungary, the "Gypsy," or Magyar, clarinetist can be every bit as impressive technically and musically as his colleagues on the violin can be.

Besides the clarinet, the saxophone, and the chalumeau before them, only one other single-reed instrument is to be found in significant numbers anywhere in the world, or in any time going back for several centuries: the Hungarian *tarogato*. The tarogato has been a folk instrument for many years in Hungary, and it was a *double-reed* instrument until almost up to the 1900s. As such, it probably doesn't even qualify as a clarinet-type folk instrument; it is more similar to a soprano saxophone in most ways, with a conical bore instead of a cylindrical one. The fingering system is similar to that of the oboe. It was only recently remodeled with a single reed and mouthpiece.

Turning to American jazz, the clarinet played a prominent part in Dixieland's New Orleans-to-Chicago journey up the Mississippi River in the latter part of the 1800s. In this connection, a British music historian named James A. MacGillivray makes an interesting statement in his section on woodwind instruments in Anthony Baines's *Musical Instruments Through the Ages:*

The wild *glissandi* and general conception of improvisation compel one to speculate whether some players from the Balkans were present in the St. Louis area in the embryonic period of jazz, as the influences known to have affected the Southern Negroes at this time provide no antecedent for the type of clarinet playing they adopted. At least one record of a Rumanian player was issued in America before 1914, which suggests that there may have been a vogue for the idiom. The underlying feeling of the music, however, is quite unlike that of jazz, despite the technical resemblance.

MacGillivray, however, does not account for the fact that black clarinetists were playing in the Dixieland style in New Orleans and elsewhere before the style ever reached St. Louis. On the other hand, it is entirely possible that Dixieland clarinetists were influenced to some extent by the playing of Balkan musicians in America, whether that may have occurred specifically in St. Louis or not.

By the early 1900s, there were some Dixieland bands that earned much fame for themselves. Originally, these groups had been called "brass bands" despite the presence of a clarinetist, and were made up of five players who held forth on the following instruments: cornet (or trumpet), clarinet, trombone, piano, and drums.

A clarinetist who achieved early fame in Chicago playing Dixieland was Alcide "Yellow" Nunez. Several of his fellow musicians soon moved to New York, this time with the clarinetist Larry Shields. In 1917, this new group, calling itself The Original Dixieland Jass Band, recorded for the Victor label. It could well be that these records of jazz music were the first ever recorded.

Also in 1917, "King" Oliver left New Orleans for Chicago (leaving his old group to the leadership of the young trumpeter Louis Armstrong), taking with him a clarinetist named Jimmie Noone. Two years later the famous Sidney Bechet, who was noted for his abilities on both clarinet and soprano saxophone, made some concert appearances in Europe where interest in jazz was, in some ways, more intense in those days than it was in America.

There was a Dixieland group in Chicago in 1921 called the New Orleans Rhythm Kings. This group featured some very fine jazz clarinet playing by a man named Leon Rappolo. Johnny Dodds also flourished in the early 1920s, having had his fame as a jazz clarinetist established during his years with the King Oliver band. In the mid-1920s, a very popular jazz group led by Red Nichols numbered Jimmy Dorsey among its members; he played mainly clarinet at that time, changing almost exclusively to saxophone at a later date.

Jazz clarinetists who gained fame during the late 1920s were Frank Teschemacher and a man who is still well known today, Pee Wee Russell. During that same era the drummer Ben Pollack introduced a band that contained the very young Benny Goodman on clarinet.

In 1934, Benny Goodman started his band that would, more than any other single factor, usher in the "swing" era. This band played a series of radio programs, each one an hour long, and Goodman became famous. Two years later, Artie Shaw also became very well known, and Woody Herman was organizing his first famous group at that time. So, during the "big band era," three of the biggest of them all were led by clarinetists. It was in 1938 that Benny Goodman put on the first highly publicized jazz concert in the very citadel of "serious" music, New York's Carnegie Hall.

The popularity of clarinetists' big bands, particularly those of Goodman and Herman, continued into the 1940s and, with much publicized revivals, even into the 1950s. In 1956, the State Department began a program of authorizing trips abroad for some of these famous big bands, and once again, the bands of Goodman and Herman were among them.

Now, however, the clarinet's jazz era is a thing of the past. No jazz player since the 1930s has won and kept fame through playing jazz clarinet, with the exception of some younger Dixieland players such as Pete Fountain. But the difference is very great between Goodman's rise to fame and Fountain's; Benny Goodman became popular because he synthesized a new jazz style. Pete Fountain has risen to fame by playing Dixieland, without establishing a style that is particularly new.

In recent years, the clarinet has lost the firm hold it formerly had on the position of a much-used jazz solo instrument. Today, the clarinet is used in jazz almost entirely as a "doubling" instrument by saxophonists.

THE CLARINET TODAY

Clarinets are found in every nation on the globe today, and are used to some extent at least in nearly every musical style. In America, there are two great training grounds for clarinetists: the instrumental music programs in the nation's public schools and the colleges, universities, conservatories, and institutes of music. The tremendous influence of the educational institutions on American clarinet playing is attested to by the vast numbers of young people playing the instrument today. Most public school clarinetists do not have the benefit of private teachers, and it is a tribute to the nation's instrumental music teachers that their students' high quality in performance is possible in America's educational system.

This brings to mind the famous American clarinetist Benny Goodman. Goodman learned to play clarinet in the Chicago public schools and never had a private teacher on a regular basis. Yet, he went on to influence not only popular music and jazz for which he was so famous, but also classical music. Many people will be surprised to hear that Benny Goodman was responsible in varying ways for the clarinet concertos of both Aaron Copland and Paul Hindemith, as well as for chamber music of which Béla Bartók's is the most notable example. The only other American clarinetist who can make such a claim is Woody Herman, for whose group Igor Stravinsky wrote his *Ebony Concerto*.

With such widespread study of the clarinet occurring throughout this century in America, it is terribly difficult to come up with the names of our nation's most influential clarinetists and clarinet teachers. There are literally dozens of excellent men and women playing and teaching the clarinet in this country today, and to list a manageable number of these people is necessarily to leave out others. Nevertheless, few clarinetists could question the fact that these artists have been (some still are) an overwhelming influence on the American "school" of clarinet playing today: Daniel Bonade of Philadelphia and Cleveland, Gustave Langenus of New York, Simeon Bellison of Philadelphia, Bernard Portnoy of Indiana, Stanley Hasty of Rochester, George Waln of Oberlin, Robert Marcellus of Cleveland and Chicago, Himie Voxman of Iowa, William Stubbins of Ann Arbor, Keith Stein of East Lansing, Anthony Gigliotti of Philadelphia, Elsa Ludewig-Verdehr of East Lansing, Mitchell Lurie of Los Angeles, Harold Wright of Boston, and Lee Gibson of North Texas. The British clarinetist Reginald Kell exerted considerable influence on American clarinetists, too, chiefly from the standpoint of musicianship, sensitivity, and interpretation.

One of the world's finest clarinetists today is the man currently playing first clarinet in the Berlin Philharmonic, Karl Leister. Leister sounds, on his recordings of solo, chamber, and orchestral music, like a clarinetist who is completely in control of his instrument. Obviously his control of the clarinet indicates a prodigious technique, but Leister never flaunts his technique for its own sake; his musicianship is directed toward the spirit of the music itself, no matter what the character of that music may be. Every aspiring clarinetist should listen to the artistry of Karl Leister as a model almost without peer.

NATIONAL "SCHOOLS" OF CLARINET PLAYING TODAY

Whereas schools of thought, varying from nation to nation, have largely disappeared from the scene among pianists and violinists, the players of wind instruments seem to cling to nationally identifiable styles, at least to some extent. My own theory about this is that the piano and violin were the two main instruments for which the majority of solo concertos were written during the high Romantic period of the 1800s, which resulted in international reputations for certain virtuoso performers of all the Western nations. Wind players of the same era remained in relative obscurity in their own national orchestras and conservatories; they did not usually make international tours. The situation seems to have promoted provincialism to some extent in that players of one nation rarely heard players of other nations even on their own instrument. When they did hear players of other nations, they were sometimes shocked by what they heard, and they withdrew quickly, with noses in the air, to the warm security of the musical companionship of their own compatriots. Much of this provincialism has disappeared in the last half-century, mostly because of the advent of electronic sound reproduction. With the proliferation of broadcasts and recordings in today's world, we may reasonably expect provincialism to decline more and more. Players of all nations will become more open-minded and will be able to pick and choose what they like from the various styles without unduly condemning what they do not particularly care for. At this point, however, some distinctively different national styles remain. Perhaps the most meaningful way to discuss those styles would be to confine ourselves to the prevailing schools of clarinet playing in Germany, England, France, and the United States.

It is always difficult, at best, to describe any sound in words since words are really inadequate. This problem is especially obvious when one attempts to describe such a studied and refined thing as the musical style of various players of various nations. The best we can do is to compare those styles with each other, to what extent the printed word will allow.

The word heard most often, perhaps, in connection with the prevailing tone quality of German clarinetists, is "dark." Darkness, in this sense, is taken to mean a sort of deep fullness of sound, and a sound that lacks a penetrating, almost harsh, "edge." We can say, then, that the prevailing German clarinet tone quality is dark and full, as opposed to being "bright" or "edgy." At the same time, however, the German sound is compact and "contained"; that is, it is not what could be called a "spread" sound. The Berliner mentioned above, Karl Leister, is a prime example of that sound, although he exhibits a more "international" sound than most Germans did a generation ago.

Most good German clarinetists are quite expressive in their musical style; they shape their phrases very beautifully. This is often accomplished within a relatively small dynamic range, however, since the player relies on subtle contrasts as opposed to extreme, obvious ones. Sometimes this dynamic range seems so small, in fact, that there can appear to be little or no "shading" audible to the listener on any one given tone, even at the end of a phrase. German tonguing can be rather heavy, too, and it causes some tones to end abruptly. If this is to be considered a fault, however, Karl Leister does not possess it.

The English seem to have had a hard time evolving a national style, which is perhaps to their credit. Their difficulty stems from a rugged individualism; that individualism in clarinet playing was brought on mainly because London is, and has been for centuries, a truly cosmopolitan center of culture. We have already seen how clarinetists from France and Germany were prominent in London during the 1800s, and those players were finally eclipsed by the Spaniard Gómez around 1890. His student Charles Draper was probably the most influential British clarinetist in the early 1900s, and Draper, in turn, "fathered" a whole line of British clarinetists, as did his colleague George Anderson. By the middle of the 1900s, the great British clarinetists and teachers Reginald Kell and Frederick Thurston had solidified what we may now call a definitely English style of clarinet playing.

That style is never forced or brash. The prevailing mood in English clarinet playing is calmness. The sound could be described as mellow and sweet; it has no "edge" as a rule, nor does it possess any great depth. Instead, it is so mellow and "spread" that some have referred to the sound as possessing a sort of "epic" quality, a sense of timelessness. Especially since the influence of Reginald

Kell, English clarinetists often reach great heights of musical art-istry, particularly in phrasing. On the other hand, other English clarinetists do not always keep that broad, mellow sound under control; when that happens, a certain "chirping" can occur on the beginning of various tones in the phrase which is, to say the least, detrimental to the desired effect. I hasten to add, however, that England does not have a monopoly on players who do not mea-sure up to the ideal.

One other noticeable characteristic of English clarinet playing is in their approach to playing in different types of musical ensem-bles. What seems to matter most to English clarinetists is whether there is a conductor present or not. In solos and in chamber works, English clarinetists often play with such relaxed abandon that the resulting sound is almost what we would consider "jazzy." Then, sometimes it is exactly those players who can be heard in one of London's great symphony orchestras, playing with such a beautifully controlled sound that it is truly marvelous to hear. At such times, the artistic blending of the wind sections of those or-chestras is absolutely unsurpassed.

Anyone interested in listening to a current, prime example of British clarinet playing would do well to hear Jack Brymer, who has recorded an abundance of chamber music. A particular favor-ite of mine is his series of recordings of the complete wind music of Mozart, on which he leads the London Wind Soloists. It is mas-terfully done.

Any consideration of contemporary French clarinet playing must be approached with great caution because, when today's American players discuss their French colleagues, they often do so while laboring under certain misconceptions; they may even be debating two totally different playing styles. The reason for this is that, during the current century, there have been two main French styles of woodwind playing, one that prevailed from early in the century until approximately the 1950s, and another that sup-planted it at about that time.

When I was a young student, I was given the impression, not only by my teachers but also through my own observation, that the French clarinetists were absolutely first-rate. I learned about how the French had, by the time of the 1920s and 1930s, estab-lished a school of clarinet playing that remained unsurpassed. French clarinetists' technique, their beautiful clarity of sound, their fluid "binding" of one tone to the next during exquisitely shaped phrases, and their generally artistic approach to all music made French clarinet playing the ultimate model for us to emu-

Reginald Kell, who came to America frequently to teach and to perform during the middle years of the century.

The main influence on American clarinetists was indeed French, but the melting pot was thoroughly stirred early in the game. Italian clarinetists arrived in Boston early in the 1900s and began studying with other clarinetists who had been trained at the Paris Conservatory, for example; and by the time a single generation had passed, one could no longer predict what a player would sound like just by learning his national origins. Nearly all orchestral clarinetists who taught lessons on the side had their students use primarily the study materials of the French clarinetists; those students, in turn, later often taught in American universities and continued to use the same primarily French materials.

The advent of recorded sound, as already noted, significantly influenced American clarinetists. After all, recordings enable musicians to hear the playing styles of Europeans and Americans. It could be that we are now evolving a uniquely American style. Even if that is true, however, and I hasten to add that it may not be, such an identifiable American style of clarinet playing must be less easily defined than that of either France or Germany. Too many Americans play in too many differing styles for the truth to be otherwise.

Having said that, I must, nevertheless, attempt a description of what may be the prevailing American style. Most American clarinetists carry on the primarily French tradition characterized by a certain bright, fluid clarity. That simple statement must be viewed, however, only as a point of departure. And the departures are many.

During the period since 1950 in particular, I sense that a more Germanic approach to clarinet tone quality has gained ground, though the mainly French thrust has continued to prevail. In other words, a primarily bright, fluid, and clear American sound has been deepened and darkened to some extent by truly first-rate American clarinetists. Brightness, in the French sense, has been replaced or at least tempered by an element of that wonderful "woody" darkness heard in German playing. What makes the particular American version of this German woodiness so marvelous to hear, however, is that it is coupled with that equally delicious French "edge"; the resulting sound is rich, full, and expressive with just enough of that tonal edge to carry the sound across a symphony orchestra with ease.

In recent years, however, I have become disappointed in the fact that some prominent clarinetists in this country are leaning toward a sound that has a considerable degree of thinness. The fine old French clarinet sound may have been primarily bright, but it was not *thin* to any great extent. The rather unfortunate trend I hear in America today is literally a thinning out of that rich, full, and slightly edgy ideal described in the last paragraph. In instances where this has occurred, the result is a sound that is just a little too harsh to do justice to the clarinet's tremendous tonal potential.

No doubt there are many reasons for this trend, and I can do no more than to guess them. One primary reason probably is the increasingly thin playing qualities of today's commercially made clarinet reeds. I mention this trend here not to criticize American clarinetists but rather simply to alert them to what may be an unnoticed but lurking danger. I still believe that American clarinet sound has the potential aesthetically to surpass the various styles that gave rise to it, if only because it has already shown that it can take the best qualities of all the other styles and blend them very well. I merely warn my fellow American clarinetists that we must be very watchful, that we must constantly listen to the tone we produce, and that we must never allow ourselves to lose that priceless and artistic tonal treasure that is already ours.

FOR FURTHER STUDY
IN CLARINET HISTORY

In this chapter on clarinet history I have tried to cover the truly important events, names, and dates that affected the clarinet without delving into great detail. There are far more complete histories of the clarinet written by scholars who have set out to be as thorough as possible, a task that is beyond the scope of this book. For readers who are interested in clarinet history in greater detail, I would strongly recommend the works of both Oskar Kroll and Anthony Baines listed in the Bibliography. Baines and Kroll are not only thorough, they are also good and interesting writers; at times, Baines is downright amusing. Students who want to do research projects on clarinet history should read the doctoral dissertations of D. T. Bogart, Jr., and Robert Austin Titus, available through major university libraries, as well as Kroll and Baines.

CHAPTER
15

The
Clarinet
Literature

We have seen that the clarinet is "younger" than nearly all of the other instruments. When J. C. Denner developed the clarinet around 1700, he was already a well-established maker of double-reed instruments, though the only single-reed instrument he had known was the old chalumeau. The clarinet's relative newness means that its body of literature is smaller than that of many of the other instruments. It is fortunate, then, that the clarinet can boast of very high quality, if not of quantity, in the music composed for it. I do not exaggerate when I say that some of the world's greatest music has been written for the clarinet, and even more of the greatest music was written to feature the clarinet, however briefly.

Since this high quality does make up for a lack of quantity, it is difficult to know where to start, and where to end. There is no way that I could discuss all of the clarinet's music in detail in this chapter; I could not hope to discuss it all even in the sketchiest way. All I can do is to concentrate on the clarinet music that is historically important, artistically excellent, or both. Much of the well-known clarinet music fits both categories.

While historical facts tell the story of the clarinet, the literature tells us the way the clarinet was used; therefore, it also tells us what musical *meaning* the clarinet has had, both to composers and to listeners. The clarinet has gone through four general phases of use and development. The first phase, roughly from 1700 to 1790, was a struggle for recognition, the period of the earliest solo concerto music, and an era that saw the clarinet join in wind chamber music and in the orchestra. The second phase, roughly from 1790 to 1820, was truly a golden age of wind music, and it was particularly fruitful for the clarinet: Wolfgang Amadeus Mozart, Ludwig van Beethoven, Carl Maria von Weber, and Louis Spohr all used the clarinet to tremendous advantage during this period, and it came into its own as an equal member of the woodwind family. The third phase, roughly from 1820 to 1910, included the high Romantic era in which no wind instrument was featured much in solo music or in chamber pieces, but during which most of the greatest operatic and symphonic clarinet music ever written was immortalized in orchestral scores. From Hector Berlioz to Gustav Mahler, passing through the music of Richard Wagner, Robert Schumann, Felix Mendelssohn, Anton Dvořák, Johannes Brahms, Richard Strauss, and others along the way, the great preponderance of Romantic music was either written for huge orchestras and/or choruses or it was written for the most intimate of all forms, the solo song accompanied by piano. The contemporary chamber music was written almost entirely for strings, or for strings and piano. In spite of that, however, clarinetists are luckier than are most other wind instrumentalists: The great chamber music of Brahms includes four very late, mature works, all of which feature the clarinet. The fourth and final phase of clarinet literature from 1910 to the present time is a period during which nearly every possible musical use of the clarinet has been explored. No aspect of the clarinet's potential has been ignored in this century.

Just as there are four general time frames of clarinet literature, so also there are *three* general categories of clarinet music: solo, orchestral, and chamber music. The solo category consists of concertos or other solo pieces for clarinet that are accompanied by orchestra, solo pieces that are accompanied by piano, and *unaccompanied* solo pieces. The orchestral category includes the use of the clarinet in the orchestral woodwind section and in the prominent solos it has been given in orchestral music. All of this occurs in both symphonic and operatic orchestras. The third category, chamber music, encompasses the clarinet parts in pieces of music that call for two or three to thirteen to fifteen players (usually three to eight), each instrument being solely responsible for its own part (there are almost never two or more players playing the same part in chamber music). Chamber music is usually performed without a conductor.

PRE-CLARINET WIND LITERATURE

Music for winds, during most of the musical history before (and even for a good while after) the clarinet's time, was usually written without the composer's specification concerning just *which* wind instruments should be used. Even the books written to teach the player how to play the instruments did not specify the exact instruments, mainly concerning themselves with how to read and interpret the music itself. Concepts of blowing, embouchure (where required), and technique were left entirely up to the player to figure out for himself. If such concepts were referred to at all, it was done very generally and briefly. Three Renaissance wind "tutors" exemplify this limitation: Martin Agricola wrote the *Musica Instrumentalis Deudsch* in 1529; wind instrument "instruction" is included in the 1619 *Syntagma Musicum,* volume 2, by Michael Praetorius; and the abbé Marin Mersenne wrote the *Harmonie Universelle* in 1636. These books have highly significant historical value and must have been adequate for their day, but by today's standards they could never teach a player how to play, so highly specialized have we become.

PERIOD I: 1700 to 1790—BEGINNINGS

Instructions for the clarinet were written shortly after its first appearance. Sometime during the first half of the 1700s two German musicians named Eisel and Majer each wrote instruction books for the clarinet that were inadequate and rather poorly conceived. It is said that Abrahame of Paris wrote an excellent clarinet method book in 1788, but no copy of it has been found. Then there are the "mock trumpet" books of around 1700, mentioned in Chapter 14, "A Look at the Life Story of the Clarinet." Doubt remains, of course, whether those books have anything to do with the clarinet.

The first music that we think was meant to include clarinets was Reinhold Keiser's opera *Croesus* of 1710, in which he calls for the chalumeau in the score. The manner in which the part itself is written suggests that he may have had the clarinet in mind, and in that case we have run up against the old problem of confusion of terms.

The Antwerp organist J. A. J. Faber wrote a setting of the Mass in 1720 that gives rise to the same confusion; in this case he called for the clarinet, but the part may just as well have been played on the old chalumeau.

Both Georg Philipp Telemann and Antonio Vivaldi wrote for the clarinet rather early. In a cantata for Whitsunday in 1721, Telemann called for the clarinet, and Vivaldi called for the clarinet to be included in three concertos for mixed woodwinds, all of which were probably written during the 1730s.

This brings us to the first known music that actually featured the clarinet: four concertos written by Johann Melchior Molter, of Durlach. These works seem to have been written during the 1740s, probably the late 1740s, and for a long time they were thought to be unique; since then, however, two more clarinet concertos have been found, written by F.-X. Pokorny during the same era.

For its first seventy-five years or so, the clarinet was thought to be related musically to the trumpet, and composers treated it as such. The Molter concertos are prime examples of this notion: They are triadic and closely resemble "bugle calls" in their melodic structure. The concertos are all written for the D clarinet, and the music lies mostly in the high register of the instrument.

The next significant concerto compositions for clarinet were composed by the Mannheimers, most notably by Karl Stamitz. His *many* clarinet concertos represent a significant early contribution to the literature; unfortunately, they are not of truly great quality. Nearly all of them were played, at one time or another, by the great clarinetist Josef Beer. Karl's father, Johann Stamitz, appears to have written one clarinet concerto himself, and some historians feel that it is of much higher musical quality than any of the many later ones written by his son. Ernst Eichner was another Mannheimer who wrote a clarinet concerto but that one seems to be simply a transposed oboe concerto.

Later in the century, as we approach the 1770s and 1780s, the musical scene becomes dominated by Joseph Haydn and Mozart. Haydn left us no solo works of any description, which is not only disappointing but also surprising when it is known that Haydn had clarinetists available to him from the 1760s onward. (Perhaps their playing did not please him, or his various patrons.) Mozart, of course, is another story.

I observed in Chapter 14, "A Look at the Life Story of the Clarinet," that Mozart was attracted to the clarinet during the early or middle 1760s while he was still a small child (his dates are 1756–1791). The first work of his that included clarinets was written in 1771, the Divertimento, K. 113. By 1773, he was demonstrating a more thorough knowledge of the clarinet's musical capacities in two more divertimenti, K. 166 and 186. In December of 1778, he was in Mannheim and wrote to his father that he fervently wished that they (the Mozarts themselves) had access to clarinets. He told his father of the wonderful sensation of a symphony of flutes, oboes, and clarinets.

His operas show notable use of the clarinet. He gave the clarinet prominent solos in *Idomeneo, Così fan tutte, Die Entführung aus dem Serail, Le Nozze di Figaro,* and *La Clemenza di Tito;* these solos were placed where Mozart felt that the clarinet's expression of poignancy and delicacy would have its greatest effects.

Mozart did not neglect the clarinet in his later chamber music; he is, in fact, one of the few (but great) composers who wrote mature chamber music that included or featured the clarinet. The light but beautiful *Kegelstatt* Trio, K. 498, was written for clarinet, viola, and piano in 1786. On a higher musical level yet is the famous Quintet for Clarinet and Strings, K. 581, written in 1789 to feature his friend Anton Stadler on clarinet. Today, musicians usually refer to this great work as, simply, the Mozart Clarinet Quintet.

The Quintet is in four movements; the first of those, as may be expected, is in the classical sonata form, a form that was most usual in the opening movements of instrumental works of that day. Mozart's particular stamp of greatness, however, is unmistakable in the Quintet's first movement. The second movement, a beautiful "Larghetto," is a sort of instrumental "song" sung by the clarinet to the delicate accompaniment of the muted strings. It is written to convey the same mood to the listener as would a soprano operatic aria designed to project a quiet, pleasant feeling of joy. Nearly the entire range of the clarinet is used in this "aria," and that factor, when combined with the infinite beauty of the melody itself, makes this movement a masterpiece. The third movement is basically an example of the classical "minuet and trio," but it is distinguished by having two different trio sections, one in minor and the other in major. The fourth movement departs from the norm; whereas the fourth and final movements of major works of that day were usually rondo-allegro forms, Mozart ends this Quintet with a set of variations on a sprightly tune. The Quintet ends in A major as it began, but on a lighter musical level.

Some of Mozart's greatest clarinet writing is found in his last three symphonies, Nos. 39, 40, and 41. I enjoy listening to the earlier two of those, in particular, if only to hear the marvelous way Mozart fit the two clarinets into the orchestral fabric, and to hear the brief but wonderful moments when the clarinet is allowed to soar out of that fabric in an unforgettable solo.

The last great work of Mozart that features the clarinet was very nearly the last work that he wrote. It is one of his most famous masterpieces, the Clarinet Concerto. In the Köchel listing of Mozart's works, the Concerto is assigned No. 622, and the complete list goes little further. I will include the discussion of this piece in the next section, not only because it was written in 1791 but also because, as a great clarinet concerto, it fits in better with the aesthetic of the next phase of clarinet literature.

PERIOD II: 1790 to 1820—
THE GOLDEN AGE OF WIND MUSIC

The Mozart Clarinet Concerto, K. 622, in A Major, is a most appropriate place to start a discussion of the golden age of music featuring wind instruments. We have already seen how popular the early wind soloists of this era were; they were in almost as much public demand as were the later (Romantic-period) soloists on piano and violin. During this era, 1790–1820, wind instrument virtuosos pleased and amazed their audiences with their technical skill; they were truly amazing, considering that most clarinets then had only six keys. The musical form made to order for showing off an instrument and its player is, of course, the solo concerto; where the clarinet is concerned the first great concerto is the one by Mozart. The work remains the most famous clarinet concerto in the world, and it may well be the greatest of them all.

Mozart wrote his clarinet concerto, like his clarinet quintet, for his friend, the clarinetist Anton Stadler. The piece was composed during the last year of Mozart's life, 1791. Surprisingly, it was originally conceived for Stadler's basset horn, and not for his clarinet; the performer was well known as a virtuoso on both instruments. Even when the concerto was rewritten for the clarinet, it was written to show off the entire range of Stadler's specially built clarinet, one that was extended down to its low C rather than to its low E as were most clarinets. Stadler had commissioned this concerto apparently so that he could enjoy the same low-range benefits on his clarinet that he had on his basset horn. The modern clarinet, for acoustical reasons, extends only to its low E just as did the normal clarinets of Stadler's day, and it could be that his extended-range clarinet was the only one of that type ever built. In any case, a slight reworking of some of the low-range passages in the Mozart Concerto was necessary in order for the piece to be played on a normal clarinet, and it is that slightly reworked version that has come down to us as the "original" version.

The Mozart Concerto is distinguished by, among other things, its length. Conceived in proportions that are well beyond the usual ones for concertos of that day, it takes roughly half an hour to perform completely, give or take several minutes depending upon the performers' tempos. It has three movements; the first is a very large concerto-sonata form. That is, the orchestra states all of the movement's thematic material in a long introduction, and then this material is repeated with the solo clarinet in the lead. A development section follows, and a restatement, or recapitulation of the original material, rounds out the movement. A beautiful "Adagio" constitutes the second movement, which is characterized by long, liquid melodic lines. There is a cadenza, or improvised passage for the soloist alone, in the middle of this movement, the only cadenza to be found in the entire concerto. The third and final movement is a rondo-allegro of absolutely massive proportions; a recurring bright and joyful section alternates throughout with several varied sections, each one of which contrasts with the others and with the main recurring section. The result is that Mozart managed, in that movement, to explore nearly every mood that the clarinet is capable of establishing, and yet he did so in a unified manner. The entire concerto is so contrasting and yet so unified, in fact, that on that point alone the work would have earned its place as one of the great musical masterpieces of all time.

The next great composer who had a profound effect on clarinet literature is Beethoven. He was about a generation later than Mozart (his dates are 1770–1827), and his musical genius was of a completely different type.

In one sense, it is something of a struggle even for us today to see Beethoven's magnificent influence on clarinet literature; nevertheless that influence is there. The difficulty of seeing it immediately is twofold: First, Beethoven wrote no solo clarinet works, and second, he was indeed a composer who stood with one foot in the Classical era of Mozart and Haydn and the other in the later Romantic period. These difficulties are more than set aside, however, when any thoughtful person takes a look at the really fabulous clarinet writing that occurs in Beethoven's nine symphonies. While clarinetists may well wish that this great composer had written a solo piece (at least a sonata, if not a concerto), all is forgiven when they sit down in an orchestra and play a Beethoven symphony.

The fact is that Ludwig van Beethoven is the first great composer to include clarinets in all of his symphonies, right from the start, beginning with No. 1. He obviously loved the clarinet and wrote very well for it. One of his best friends was the Viennese clarinetist Joseph Friedlowsky, whom he consulted about writing clarinet parts. That may account partially for his fine orchestral clarinet writing.

In Chapter 14, "A Look at the Life Story of the Clarinet," I mentioned the popularity of the wind octet (made up of pairs of oboes, clarinets, horns, and bassoons) during the latter part of the 1700s and extending for some few years into the early 1800s. Beethoven's first exposure to the clarinet was hearing, probably, just such a wind octet play at the court of the Elector of Cologne while he was still a boy. He wrote a magnificent wind octet of his own, Opus 103, in E-flat major. In spite of its high opus number (it was catalogued much later), he wrote it while still a very young man. Earlier composers of wind octets, of whom Mozart is a prime example, left the first oboe to handle the main, leading melodic parts, but Beethoven's octet forces the first oboist to share the honors equally with the first clarinetist, and the entire ensemble gains immeasurably by it, if only from the standpoint of tonal variety. It has been speculated that this octet, along with a shorter Rondino for the same instrumentation, plus the three very fine Duos for Clarinet and Bassoon, were all written by Beethoven specifically for the mealtime performances presented at the court of the Elector of Cologne. Another fine chamber piece for winds is Beethoven's Sextet for two clarinets, two horns, and two bassoons, Opus 71, written during the 1790s. Several arrangements of that work have been done for the modern woodwind quintet.

I should mention three of Beethoven's chamber works involving clarinets and strings. Opus 11, No. 4, is a fine trio for clarinet, cello, and piano; Opus 16 is the great Quintet for oboe, clarinet, horn, bassoon, and piano in E-flat major; and finally there is the Septet, also in E-flat major, Opus 20, for three winds and four strings: clarinet, horn, bassoon, violin, viola, cello, and double bass. Particularly the latter two works, the piano quintet and the septet, are among the greatest pieces of chamber music ever written. The septet is, incidentally, almost a violin concerto accompanied by the other six instruments.

This brings us to a more specific discussion of the clarinet writing in Beethoven's nine symphonies; nearly all of his symphonies were written later than the chamber works involving the clarinet.

It has always seemed interesting to me that Beethoven's odd-numbered symphonies, particularly Nos. 3, 5, 7, and 9, have enjoyed more popularity than have the even-numbered ones. There seems to be no especially good reason for this; it could be that the odd-numbered symphonies are easier to listen to with a relatively untrained ear. The fact remains that all nine of the symphonies are masterpieces. The most spectacular clarinet writing, however, occurs in the even-numbered symphonies, especially in Nos. 4, 6, and 8.

In Beethoven's First Symphony, we find particularly significant clarinet parts in the first and last movements. The first movement has a drawn-out solo for the clarinet which dovetails a similar solo for the oboe. The last movement does not contain any particular clarinet solo, but the clarinet is forced to join the other instruments in playing a theme most difficult to execute. Performed by a fine orchestra this movement is, as a result, spectacular.

The Second Symphony contains prominent and beautiful clarinet parts in its second movement, a slow, romantic Larghetto. The clarinet solos are beautiful in themselves, though many such passages are actually duets for the two orchestral clarinetists who play, for the most part, in thirds.

The famous *Eroica* Symphony, Beethoven's Third, has some long, soaring clarinet solos in the first movement, followed by some fairly prominent passages in the Funeral March, which is the second movement.

Beethoven's Fourth is a big one for clarinetists. The lyrical first movement has the solo clarinet playing with and around the other solo woodwinds. The slow second movement brings us some more beautiful clarinet duets along with some truly memorable solos. The fourth and last movement can scare the daylights out of clarinetists; it contains a solo that moves in rapidly articulated sixteenth-notes, and there are passages of fast-moving triplets, in the low register, for both clarinetists. Those triplets must also be tongued very rapidly.

By the time we get to the Fifth Symphony it becomes obvious

that clarinet duets, in thirds, are a favorite device of Beethoven's in his slow movements. The second movement of the Fifth, an Andante con moto, contains beautiful clarinet duets.

The *Pastoral* Symphony, the Sixth, is unique among Beethoven's symphonies in that it borders on program music, or music that is intended to paint a visual image for the listener. And with the possible exception of the oboe, what instrument can sound more "pastoral" than the clarinet? Beethoven's Sixth abounds in gorgeous clarinet solos, especially in the first two movements, where nearly the whole range of moods is expressed by the solo clarinet. The third movement has one particularly spectacular long solo run for the clarinet, and the fifth and final movement actually begins with a clarinet solo. Perhaps the most famous orchestral clarinet solo of all time is the one found in the second movement of the Sixth, where the clarinetist is called upon to imitate the call of the cuckoo bird.

In the first movement of Beethoven's Seventh there are some very nice, but brief, solo clarinet passages; mostly these passages are in response to a solo by some other instrument. Probably the nicest solo in this symphony is found in the second movement, in the form of a couple of long, lyrical lines. The third and fourth movements resemble the first again, with the clarinet surfacing for solos only occasionally, and then very briefly.

It is a great shame that Beethoven's Eighth is not more widely known than it is. It is gradually becoming my favorite among all the Beethoven symphonies, and not just because of its magnificent clarinet parts. Nearly all the themes exude cheerfulness and brilliance; they are used by a great master at the very height of his powers. The clarinet is used most artistically in all four movements of the Eighth, but it is the third movement, a Menuetto, that practically *features* the solo clarinet. This particular solo must be played in a singing, yet very delicate, manner which is most difficult to accomplish because it is in a very high register of the clarinet. The solo ends on the clarinet's high G, very softly; that in itself can be a nightmare for the clarinetist, but the whole passage is so beautiful that it is worth the effort.

The clarinet occasionally surfaces in a solo passage during the first movement of Beethoven's Ninth (the famous *Choral* Symphony), but these passages are not particularly distinguished when compared to the solos of the other woodwinds. There are a couple of very nice solos in the third movement, which in this case is the slow one; and there again we have some fine, beautiful clarinet duets in addition to the solos. The last movement is where the chorus comes in, of course, and with the vocal soloists, the chorus manages to put all woodwind solos pretty much in the background.

I could sum it up by saying that anyone who wishes to listen to some especially fine clarinet writing would do well to listen to any of the Beethoven symphonies, but particularly to Nos. 6 and 8, in which such writing reaches brilliant artistic heights both musically and technically.

An event that occurred during the period between 1790 and 1820 was the establishment of the modern woodwind quintet as a commonly used instrumental combination in chamber music. Since the wind section of the "classical" orchestra was made up of pairs of flutes, oboes, clarinets, bassoons, and horns (trumpets and trombones were treated more as "extras" during this period), it was natural for the first-chair players of those five main wind instruments to be called upon occasionally to play wind chamber music. To this day, as a result, a "woodwind" quintet consisting of flute, oboe, clarinet, horn, and bassoon is a standard instrumental combination and represents to the wind players what the string quartet does to the players of string instruments.

One prominent, early composer of woodwind quintets was Anton Reicha, a Czech who lived from 1770 to 1836. He was born the same year as Beethoven, and he was apparently a friend of Beethoven's in later years. Reicha played flute in a chamber group for a while, and Beethoven played viola in the same group. The Czech composer wrote a few operas and a few symphonies, but the only music he is remembered for is that which he wrote for woodwind quintet. Reicha was, during his own time, noted more as a theory teacher than as a composer, and late in life, he taught both theory and piano at the Paris Conservatory. The younger composers Franz Liszt and Charles Gounod studied with Reicha.

Reicha's quintets are remarkable on at least two counts: their very high quality and their great quantity. The composer wrote at least twenty-four woodwind quintets, in four sets of six quintets each. Since these quintets are nearly all standard, full-length works with approximately four movements each, they represent a highly significant contribution to the woodwind quintet literature. In style, Reicha composed very much in the manner of Beethoven, and it does not in any way detract from Beethoven's reputation to say that Reicha's quintets stand up very well when they are compared with most of Beethoven's wind chamber music.

A Swedish composer, Bernhard Henrik Crusell, wrote a fine concerto for clarinet very early in the 1800s. In style it is somewhat reminiscent of Weber and Spohr, but it is good in its own right. Crusell was a clarinetist himself, and he also wrote some worthwhile chamber music that involves the clarinet.

Carl Maria von Weber (1786–1826) stands alone, really, in his effect on clarinet literature. There is no question that he was a musical genius of the first order, and while he never has had the historical status of Mozart or Beethoven, there are two ways in which Weber's genius remains absolutely unsurpassed throughout the entire history of music: his incredible sense of drama and his brilliant use of the instruments themselves.

Drama depends so much upon just the right *timing,* and Weber's operas are masterpieces from that standpoint. He knew just exactly how long to make a dramatic pause in any particular case, and he knew just exactly how to come out of that pause to establish the new mood. Apparently this uncanny sense of timing never failed him, either in the stage action or in the music itself. Obviously the operas of Mozart, Wagner, and Giuseppe Verdi exhibit a most artistic sense of timing, but I reiterate that for sheer drama Weber remains unsurpassed.

Weber's instinctive, brilliant rapport with musical instruments has only occasionally been matched. The composer's natural genius enabled him to write for all the orchestral instruments as though he had been a virtuoso performer on each of them. It enabled him to combine them in musical groupings so that his sense of drama might find its proper expression. In short, when we are confronted with the combination of Weber's sense of the dramatic and his abilities in orchestration, we are up against something very special indeed.

Weber is credited with the virtual founding of the German Romantic opera. That he deserves this credit was established in 1821 by the appearance of his first highly successful opera, *Der Freischütz.* The overture to that opera is such a masterpiece that it has been held up as a model of its kind. It is mentioned here, of course, because it contains a masterful clarinet solo, a solo so great that it has become famous in its own right. Throughout the opera, in fact, Weber uses the clarinet soloist to magnificent advantage. The composer's operas *Euryanthe* and *Oberon,* particularly the latter, also demonstrate Weber's consummate command of clarinet writing.

Clarinetists are even more interested in the six works this composer wrote for the solo clarinet. The opus numbers are all mixed up chronologically so that they do not indicate the order in which these pieces were written, but that need not bother us. The first five of the six works were all written for the man who, at that time, was known as the greatest clarinet virtuoso, Heinrich Bärmann. The composer met Bärmann in early 1811, and before that year was out, he had written *four* of those eventual six works for him; he had even begun work on the fifth one. First there was the Concertino for clarinet and orchestra, Opus 26, which caused a sensation when Bärmann first performed it. By the middle of the summer of 1811, Weber had completed the two clarinet concertos, Opus Nos. 73 and 74. In December, the composer was on a concert tour with Bärmann and, while on tour, composed a set of Variations, Opus 33, on a theme from his opera *Sylvana* for clarinet and piano. Bärmann, with Weber himself on the piano, performed the variations in concert the very same day the composition was finished.

The fifth work for solo clarinet, begun in 1811 but not finished until 1815, was Weber's quintet for clarinet and string quartet, Opus 34. Unlike Mozart's piece for that instrumentation, this clarinet quintet is not really chamber music as such, but is more another clarinet concerto accompanied by the string quartet.

The sixth work was the Grand Duo Concertant, Opus 48, for clarinet and piano, written in 1816, not for Bärmann, but rather for Johann Simon Hermstedt. Hermstedt was the clarinetist for whom Spohr wrote most of his clarinet solo works. In this case, Weber performed the Grand Duo with Hermstedt in Prague shortly after the piece was completed.

The Concertino, Opus 26, is often performed today and is probably Weber's best known solo clarinet piece. The orchestral part has been transcribed for piano and also for symphonic band, making the piece accessible to students as well as to orchestral clarinetists. This work is characterized by Weber's customary sense of high drama. The entire piece is magnificent, but the slow opening section of the concertino, the introduction, is a perfect musical gem. In a few short bars, that introduction allows the clarinetist to express fully his instrument's entire range of musical color.

Of the two concertos, my favorite is No. 1 in F minor. It is in the standard three-movement concerto form; the first movement is a fine Allegro with much fire and drive, and the final Rondo is of a brilliant character. The slow, middle movement is beautifully expressive. The composer has included recurring sections wherein the solo clarinet plays the lead part of a quartet, the other members of which are three horns. I myself have made a transcription of this F Minor Concerto for clarinet and wind ensemble.

The second concerto, in E-flat major, follows the same general format, but in this case the slow movement is a veritable soprano aria, complete with recitative sections. There are only two differences between that movement and typical soprano arias found in Weber's operas: In this concerto movement, the soprano is a clarinet, and there are no words. The movement is actually a recitative and aria for clarinet and orchestra, and a beautiful one at that. The third and final movement is a Polacca, which unfortunately is often nearly destroyed by performers who try to play it too fast; it should be characterized by a certain playful stateliness, for it is a real masterpiece when it is not rushed.

The Variations for clarinet and piano, Opus 33, is a theme and seven variations followed by a return of the theme at the end. The second and fourth variations are for piano alone. The whole piece is in a sprightly B-flat major with the exception of the sixth variation, which is very slow, in B-flat minor. A similar piece for clarinet and piano was written, by the way, by Gioacchino Rossini.

I have already mentioned that Weber's clarinet quintet is, in a way, another clarinet concerto, this one accompanied by a string quartet. There really is nothing of interest in the string parts, but the solo clarinet part is conceived by the composer along his usual, dramatic lines.

The Grand Duo Concertant, Opus 48, has been called "the hardest piece ever written for the clarinet." It *isn't* that, but it certainly makes great technical demands on the player. The piano part is extremely tough also, and shows that Weber was concerned with not being "outshone" by Hermstedt's prodigious clarinet technique. By the time a pianist has learned this piece he will be able to do whatever is humanly possible on a keyboard in E-flat major!

The Grand Duo follows the usual three-movement pattern, and again, the slow middle movement is particularly beautiful, while the outer two Allegro movements are full of fire, brilliance, and rhythmic drive. I have recorded this piece with Frances Mitchum Webb, a truly fine pianist and accompanist.

Despite his flair for the dramatic Weber was, in general, very cautious in his use of the clarinet's highest register. In his solo clarinet works he seldom carried the instrument up to its highest G, although that G is called for fairly often in the F Minor Concerto. I think there are only three notes higher than G in all six pieces put together: There is a high A and a high B-flat in the first movement of the Second (E-flat) Concerto, and there is one high A near the end of the Grand Duo. All three of those notes are approached very carefully and are positioned at the very end of ascending arpeggio lines. Apparently Weber's superior knowledge of the instrument prevented him from using the clarinet's extremely high notes to excess. The same cannot be said of Spohr.

Ludwig (Louis) Spohr, who lived from 1784 to 1859, was a violinist and conductor who wrote four clarinet concertos as well as some other, smaller works for the instrument. Hermstedt was his main inspiration, but Spohr was never able to grasp the clarinet's nature to the same extent that Weber, Spohr's contemporary, was able. Spohr did have great respect for Hermstedt's abilities and often consulted him; as a result, he gradually increased his knowledge of the clarinet. And, although the writing is quite "violinistic," Spohr's four clarinet concertos are all very good musically. The general style is similar to that of Weber; both composers present us with good examples of the beginnings of the "Grand Concerto" approach of the early Romantic period. One striking feature in Spohr's clarinet concertos, however, is that he sometimes ended the first movements with the clarinet playing softly in its low register; far more usual, of course, was the practice adopted by Weber and others of that time of ending the first movements of concertos with the clarinet playing loudly in its high register. Spohr's approach was different but effective.

Looking through the pages of Spohr's clarinet concertos, however, one is immediately struck by his use of the instrument's extremely high notes. Before he was very far into the first movement of the first concerto, Spohr wrote an arpeggio that ends on the clarinet's highest C. That is the note traditionally considered the absolute top of the clarinet's range, although now we know that it is possible to "squeak out" some higher sounds. Often Spohr did not take any particular care at all with the manner in which he approached those high notes; on several occasions he included the highest notes in the middle of long, fast runs. In the third movement of the third concerto, in fact, there is a long run downward that *begins* on the clarinet's highest B-natural!

One of Spohr's finest pieces is a set of Six German Songs, Opus 103, for soprano, clarinet, and piano. The clarinet part is most rewarding; sometimes the instrument joins the piano in accompanying the voice and sometimes the soprano and the clarinet join in a duet accompanied by piano. There are some introductory and transitional passages for clarinet and piano alone which possess a very rare beauty.

The most famous song for soprano, clarinet, and piano is, of course, *Der Hirt auf dem Felsen (The Shepherd on the Rock)* by that incomparable song composer, Franz Schubert. This song was one of Schubert's last works (written at the ripe old age of thirty-one in the year of his death, 1828), and it is one of the most exquisite of his more than 600 songs.

The song begins with a rather long clarinet introduction to a supremely beautiful Andantino section during which the clarinet complements and echoes the singer. There is a bridge to the second and final section of the song in the form of a cadenza for the clarinet. At the end of this final Allegretto section, after the singer finishes, there is a coda-like ending to the song that is an absolute burst of virtuosic clarinet writing. This final passage in *Der Hirt auf dem Felsen* is one of the most difficult passages in clarinet literature; but when it is played really well the effect is nothing short of spectacular.

Schubert is famous for his gorgeous melodies, which generally are models of beautiful simplicity. His rhythmic figurations, also, are always "just right," and again are characterized by a sort of beautiful simplicity. One of the most remarkable aspects of Schubert's music, however, is his harmony. Schubert's harmonic movement (that is, his choice of exactly which chord should follow a preceding one, and so on) is both surprising and original, and *Der Hirt auf dem Felsen* is a prime example of his harmonic genius.

Schubert's originality was, in fact, one of his basic traits, manifested in another context that we should look at: the opening of his famous *Unfinished* Symphony, No. 8. Nearly all of today's textbooks on the study of orchestration recommend that an orchestrator should avoid calling for the oboe and the clarinet to play in unison, at least in prominent passages. The reason is that unison oboe and clarinet tone qualities, due to acoustical causes, obscure each other's individuality. The two tone qualities tend to absorb each other, resulting in a combined sound that somehow lacks focus. At the very beginning of Schubert's *Unfinished* Symphony, however, the famous melody is first introduced by the solo oboe and the solo clarinet in unison! In this case the effect was what Schubert wanted, even though it broke "the rules," and the result is marvelous. Listen to the *Unfinished,* and rejoice in Schubert's original genius.

I shouldn't leave the subject of Schubert without mentioning one of his finest chamber works: the Octet for clarinet, horn, bassoon, string quartet, and double bass. The first violin part is slightly more virtuosic than is the clarinet part, but not by much; the clarinet, since it is the highest wind instrument in the ensemble, is prominent throughout this fine, six-movement work. The second movement features a long, sustained melody for the clarinet which is typical of the great charm often found in Schubert's music. The last movement is a fiery rondo in which the clarinet and first violin take turns in playing dashing displays of their technical prowess. If you know and love Schubert's *Trout* Quintet, but are not acquainted with this octet, you owe it to yourself to discover this fine piece; the Octet, like the *Trout,* offers some of the most pleasant listening in the literature, and in this case the three winds and the five strings offer an instrumentation that brings to mind a miniature classical orchestra. It's perfectly delightful.

During this "golden age" of wind music, many composers besides the famous ones I have mentioned so far contributed to the clarinet literature. Noteworthy solo clarinet music was written by Franz Danzi, who is mainly remembered today for his woodwind quintets; in that respect he is historically similar to Anton Reicha. A clarinetist-composer named Franz Tausch wrote concertos for clarinet that were so technically demanding that they are very rarely heard even today. And, since audiences demanded solo wind music during that era, more musicians decided to learn to play the clarinet; this inspired the writing of several "tutors" or "method books" for the instrument. Clarinet instructional materials were written during this period by such clarinetists as J.-X. Lefèvre, J. G. H. Backofen, Ivan Müller, John Mahon, and T. L. Willman.

But the Mozart concerto and the works by Beethoven, Weber, Spohr, and Schubert retain their positions as the high points of this altogether remarkable era in the life of the clarinet.

PERIOD III: 1820 to 1910—
THE HIGH ROMANTIC ERA

In Chapter 14, "A Look at the Life Story of the Clarinet," I mentioned Berlioz in connection with his *Funeral and Triumphal Symphony* for huge wind band, and with his now lost sextet which included clarinet as well as saxophone, but that isn't all that needs to be said about Berlioz.

One of his contributions to the development of the orchestra and of the specific instruments was his *Treatise on Instrumentation,* written in 1844. This treatise represented the first time that a composer attempted to put down sensibly in words a description of the various characters of the different instruments. Berlioz achieved this by resorting to phrases that sound typical of the Romanticism of that era, but he did such a good and sensitive job that we should forgive him. In the section of the *Treatise* devoted to the clarinet (and the same holds true of Berlioz's treatment of the other instruments), we find a description of the clarinet's range, what types of passages are found to be easy or difficult for clarinetists to play, wonderfully chosen musical examples generally given in full orchestral score, all interspersed with Berlioz's sagacious remarks. In discussing the registers of the clarinet, he says:

> Each of these has its own distinct quality of tone. The high register has something piercing, which can be used only in the fortissimo of the orchestra or in the bold runs of a brilliant solo. (Some of the very high notes can, however, be sustained *piano* if the tone has been properly prepared.) The medium and chalumeau registers are suited to cantabile melodies, arpeggios and runs. The low register, especially in sustained notes, produces those coldly threatening effects, those dark accents of quiet rage which Weber so ingeniously invented.

It will be seen from this quotation, by the way, that Berlioz considered the chalumeau register to be that area of the range today known as the "throat tones"; he called the notes below that simply "the low register."

Berlioz says the medium (clarion) register "is imbued with loftiness tempered by a noble tenderness, appropriate for the expression of the most poetic feelings and ideas." And at a later point he refers to the clarinet as "this beautiful instrumental soprano, so resonant, so rich in penetrating accents when employed in masses, gains as a solo instrument in delicacy what it loses in power and brilliance." And later still: "There is no other wind instrument which can produce a tone, let it swell, decrease and die away as beautifully as the clarinet. Hence its invaluable ability to render distant sounds, an echo, the reverberation of an echo, or the charm of the twilight."

Berlioz's *Treatise* was used as a guide to instrumental combinations and colors throughout the remainder of the 1800s and it still makes its influence felt in our own century. There is no question that it helped later composers toward better usage of the clarinet and the other instruments of the orchestra. It influenced Liszt and Richard Strauss in particular.

Berlioz wrote, of course, marvelously expressive clarinet solos. His huge work *The Trojans,* which is actually two operas (*The Conquest of Troy* and *The Trojans in Carthage*), contains excellent examples. The best example of all is found in the second scene of the second act of *The Conquest of Troy*. The music is gathered around the solo clarinet during the entire scene; the high drama of that scene apparently gave Berlioz the idea that nothing less than the clarinet would, or could, serve his purpose. The libretto at that point concerns a widow and her small son who have entered the stronghold of the victorious enemy in order to place flowers on the grave of the woman's husband, who fell in the previous battle. The victors are so amazed and impressed that they fall back from the woman, silently honor her, and share her grief. She is permitted to depart without mishap, leaving her dead husband's enemies stunned by her unexpected visit. Berlioz keeps an exquisitely beautiful clarinet solo going throughout to emphasize the widow's brave loneliness and loyalty.

By this time we are well into the Romantic era, a period that caused virtually all chamber music involving the clarinet to come to an end, a period that also completely discouraged the creation of solo clarinet pieces, but one that did give rise to the writing of masterful clarinet parts in orchestral music.

Rossini is famous among opera composers for his very difficult but beautiful woodwind solos; the best known of these are found in his operas' overtures. He especially favored the clarinet and the oboe for such prominent solos, and the most famous ones of all are found in the overtures to *The Barber of Seville* and *Semiramide*.

Mendelssohn wrote frequent clarinet solos in his symphonies and overtures, but perhaps the most famous Mendelssohn clarinet part is not really one that involves solo work at all. During the Scherzo from the music for *A Midsummer Night's Dream,* the composer calls for the clarinetists to execute tremendously difficult passages characterized by fast, agile, and light tonguing.

Schumann's symphonies are not known for their orchestration; as a composer Schumann apparently remained more comfortable writing for the piano. Nevertheless, his orchestral music contains some gratifying clarinet parts. Clarinetists think of Schumann in connection with the *Fantasy-Pieces,* Opus 73, for clarinet and piano and a couple of other small chamber pieces involving clarinet. The *Fantasy-Pieces* were, however, written originally for cello and piano, even though they are probably performed today more often on clarinet than on cello.

Wagner wrote so much for the solo clarinet during his output of opera music that it would be impossible to single out any particularly notable passage. One could easily find a beautiful clarinet solo nearly anywhere in any Wagnerian music drama. Wagner was the first composer to use the bass clarinet in the orchestra extensively and almost continuously; in fact, he was the first composer to call for *more than two* clarinetists simultaneously to help augment the size and the coloristic capabilities of his huge orchestras.

The opera music of Giuseppe Verdi is noted for, among other things, its profound musical sensitivity. When Verdi wrote his opera *Rigoletto,* he included a long, beautiful solo for the clarinet. In this, the composer was apparently influenced by the presence in the opera orchestra of a most virtuosic and flamboyant clarinetist named Ernesto Cavallini. Cavallini himself was an interesting character; later in life he spent much of his time teaching clarinet in a Russian conservatory. In any case, the *Rigoletto* solo was written especially for Cavallini, and it became so well known in its own right that it was separately published. Since that time it has been played so often by clarinetists with piano accompaniment that it is considered a standard, old "warhorse" in the solo clarinet literature.

Ernesto Cavallini, by the way, wrote some clarinet studies himself as a conservatory clarinet teacher. These studies show a remarkable resemblance to Verdi's own melodic style, probably because Cavallini had played in opera orchestras for such a long time. These studies are very good within that style, however, and are still in use today.

Dvořák's *New World* Symphony is well known for its English horn solo, but it also contains more than one fine clarinet solo. Dvořák wrote a *Serenade,* a large chamber piece for strings and winds, in which oboes and clarinets are more or less featured. The instrumentation is remarkable in that a major composer used it at the height of the Romantic era. Much more common for that time would have been a piece for strings only, or for strings and piano.

For sheer finger speed, it is hard to beat the spectacular effect of the famous clarinet solo found in the Presto section of Alexander Borodin's *Polovtsian Dances* from *Prince Igor.*

Nikolai Rimsky-Korsakoff was famous as an orchestrator, and like Berlioz, he wrote a treatise on the subject. He was a master of clarinet writing; his most famous examples are found in *Scheherezade* and especially in the *Capriccio Espagnol.*

Meanwhile, as the need for more and better clarinetists grew, there appeared more and more books designed for teaching purposes. I have mentioned Ivan Müller's "tutor" of 1825, a book aimed at players of the thirteen-keyed clarinet; in 1836, Frederic Berr revised the Müller book and adapted it for users of fourteen-keyed clarinets. All earlier clarinet teaching books were made obsolete in 1843, however, by the appearance of the great clarinet method book by H. E. Klose. Klose's book was the one designed for users of the "Boehm-system" clarinet (seventeen keys, six rings) which is the predominant type of clarinet in western Europe and in America today. The Klose book is considered the most important "old standard" teaching book even for today's clarinetists. During the 1930s, when that book was ninety years old and when much new clarinet music was being written, several French clarinetists revised and updated the Klose book so that they could continue to make profitable use of it. Some sections of the book will never be out of date.

Because the Germans and the eastern Europeans have not traditionally used the Boehm-system clarinet, they have not used the Klose book. The most prevalent "tutor" in those areas is the one written by Carl Bärmann between 1864 and 1875, in five sections.

Another composer who contributed much to clarinet literature was Richard Strauss. Strauss lived from 1864 until halfway through this century (1949), but the works that made him famous, his symphonic "tone poems," were all written during the period from 1889 to 1898, when he was still very young. The tone poems *Don Juan, Til Eulenspiegel, Death and Transfiguration,* and *Don Quixote* contain masterful clarinet parts and solos conceived by Strauss, a composer who was famous as a brilliant orchestrator. He felt secure enough in his abilities in the art of orchestration to take upon himself the task of revising and updating the Berlioz *Treatise* on the subject, and he completed that project in a manner that shows his genius. Perhaps the most famous Strauss clarinet solo occurs in *Til Eulenspiegel* in the part written for the D clarinet (now always performed on the E-flat clarinet, transposed) representing the antics and the pleadings of prankster Til himself.

In the summer of 1891, Johannes Brahms provided the world's clarinetists with two of the greatest pieces of chamber music ever: the Brahms Trio, Opus 114, and the Quintet, Opus 115. In November of that year, Brahms and his clarinetist friend Richard Mühlfeld, along with the Joachim String Quartet, tried out both works and performed them in December to the great delight of the assembled listeners.

The Trio, Opus 114, in A minor for clarinet, cello, and piano, is a four-movement work on a grand scale. It is really a much better work than the short, light, three-movement trio written for that combination of instruments by Beethoven. As usual, Brahms adhered to his own brand of Romantic conservatism in this trio. The first movement is a fine sonata-allegro form in A minor, and it is followed by a beautiful Adagio in D major. The third movement is a gorgeously flowing Andante grazioso in A major, which contains a middle section (in D major) that resembles, in character, one of the Germanic folk-music forms, the "Ländler." The fourth movement, a rondo-allegro, makes use of one of Brahms's favorite rhythmic devices, the "three-against-two"; it does so generally, however, *not* in the usual "hemiola" fashion, but by abrupt changes all at once for all three instruments. This is somewhat startling to the listener; no sooner does he get used to the beat flowing in twos and fours than he hears it flowing in threes. Brahms's application of this device is of course beautifully effective.

The Clarinet Quintet, Opus 115, is harmonically ambiguous; it is difficult to know whether it is in D major or in B minor because it vacillates throughout between the two keys. Brahms uses the five instruments (clarinet and string quartet) as musical equals, too; that is, the clarinet part is not "accompanied" by the string quartet. All five parts participate in the musical fabric on an equal basis.

After a marvelous opening sonata-allegro form movement, there is a most unusual Adagio movement. It begins serenely enough and later ends that way, but a middle section, although it too is played at a very slow tempo, contains the most technically difficult clarinet passages in the entire Quintet. Long, fast, and flashing lines cover the entire range of the clarinet. It is most unusual, and very effective.

The third movement is also unusual since it is *not* written in a triple meter, and thus it is not related to either the early minuets or to the later scherzos usually found in Classical and Romantic third movements. Instead it is an Andantino movement in a flowing "four," with a "Presto" middle section. Here too the clarinet has some long, agile runs, but not at all of the type found in the previous movement.

The Quintet ends with a fine set of variations, developed and unfolded in a highly subtle manner. At the very end, a Coda uses thematic material from the Quintet's *first* movement, an especially beautiful finishing touch, bringing the listener's memory back to the very beginning of this magnificent piece of music. Many historians feel that this Brahms Clarinet Quintet represents the finest achievement in Romantic chamber music, and few clarinetists would disagree.

Three years later, in 1894, Brahms wrote for himself and Mühlfeld the last two works of his that resemble instrumental chamber music: the Clarinet Sonatas, Opus 120, No. 1 in F Minor and No. 2 in E-flat Major. Mühlfeld played these sonatas with Brahms on a clarinet of the type that Carl Bärmann had improved from the old Müller model. Whereas both the Trio and the Quintet were written for the A clarinet, Brahms wrote both sonatas for the B-flat instrument. In passing, it is interesting to note that the clarinet sonatas were almost the last thing that Brahms ever wrote. He did write two more works at the very end of his life, both very introspective: Opus 121, the *Four Serious Songs* for voice and piano; and Opus 122, a set of eleven chorale preludes for pipe organ.

The F Minor Sonata is a four-movement piece that follows the usual format. The opening theme is an extremely angular one that shows off the clarinet's ability to move around its long range with seeming ease. The first movement ends with a "sostenuto" coda that contains a tremendous amount of quiet, but powerful and intense, passion.

The slow movement is designed to show off the clarinet's powers for long, sustained lines, which it does beautifully. The third movement is a scherzo-like section that has a wonderfully light and carefree atmosphere about it. The character of the last movement could perhaps be best described as triumphant; the main theme, in fact, possesses the flavor usually associated with powerful trumpet calls in orchestral music.

The E-flat Sonata has only three movements. The first one is another example of Brahms's mastery of the sonata-allegro form, though it is not followed by a slow movement. The second movement is, instead, written in a fast "three"; it would be incorrect, however, to refer to it as a scherzo. The movement is too deadly serious for that. This second movement is a very earnest, passionate dance with much Hungarian flavoring, another of Brahms's favorite styles. It has a slower middle section, whose harmonies are truly exquisite.

The third and final movement is a theme with variations, and here Brahms makes up for his previous lack of a slow movement. The theme and most of the variations are played at a slow tempo, but then the last variation forms a "finale" for the piece in every sense of the word. With that final variation, Brahms finishes the sonata with a blazing passion, most gratifying to play and to hear.

Brahms's four clarinet works perhaps represent the greatest output of music for the instrument written by any one composer. We clarinetists are most fortunate that such an unusual person as Richard Mühlfeld became a friend of Brahms because he probably inspired Brahms's clarinet pieces. Mühlfeld must have been an amazing musician himself. After establishing his musical career as a violinist, Mühlfeld decided that the clarinet offered him more variety of expression. He changed to clarinet and pretty much taught himself how to play the instrument. Brahms was able to write, in a letter to Clara Schumann, that it was impossible to play the clarinet any more beautifully than it was played by Mühlfeld. Clarinetists should never forget that although Brahms wrote this magnificent music he might never have done so without Mühlfeld's influence. Justice demands that the career of Richard Mühlfeld, of Meiningen, Germany, become much better known throughout today's music world.

Brahms also wrote beautiful clarinet parts, of course, in his orchestral works, especially in all four symphonies. My favorite example is the solo that opens the third movement of Symphony No. 1.

Any discussion of the Romantic period should include Max Reger, who, upon hearing the two clarinet sonatas by Brahms, said, "I too must write a couple of those!" The actual result of that desire was *three* clarinet sonatas and some other chamber works involving the clarinet. The Reger sonatas are all very long and complex pieces, but each one contains some excellent musical moments.

An American imitator of Brahms, Daniel Gregory Mason, also wrote a rather nice clarinet sonata, but it is far too long and complex in proportion to its musical worth. It too, however, has some fine moments.

PERIOD IV: 1910 TO THE PRESENT— FROM MAHLER AND DEBUSSY ONWARD

In much the same way that Beethoven bridged the gap between the Classical and the Romantic eras, Mahler was a transitional figure between the high Romanticism of the late 1800s—embodied by Wagner, Verdi, Anton Bruckner, Brahms, and Richard Strauss—and several of the new styles that developed in our own century, such as those of Claude Debussy, Arnold Schönberg, Stravinsky, and others. (Since Mahler composed until 1910, he should technically be mentioned in the previous section of this chapter. Stylistically he influenced the new period, however. By the same token, Daniel Gregory Mason wrote for the clarinet around 1920, but he was included in the previous section because of his very Brahmsian style.)

Gustav Mahler (1860–1911) was a great conductor who became famous as a specialist in operatic work in Europe before arriving to conduct the New York Philharmonic late in his life. His extensive conducting experience made it easy for him to apply his genius to writing for orchestra. Like his predecessors and his contemporaries, Mahler scored his orchestral music for a vast array of instruments. But Mahler had an urgent, driving tendency toward experimentation, the results of which set him apart from his contemporaries but which also made Mahler the stylistically transitional figure that he is.

From his almost limitless orchestral palette, Mahler created and used completely new colors. He "pulled" new sounds from the orchestra by altering and mixing the old, traditional instrumental combinations. The full orchestral sound does not prevail in Mahler's music; instead, the listener hears what amounts to an ever-changing succession of chamber-sized instrumental groups as the music unfolds. Mahler influenced the later twelve-tone composers with his experimentation, as well as the later Impressionists with his ever-changing color combinations. He influenced all later musical styles with his small and unique instrumental combinations.

Mahler's symphonies and orchestral song cycles are full of brilliant clarinet writing. For anyone who would like to listen to Mahler's music with an ear toward the clarinets, I would recommend the First and Fourth Symphonies in particular, along with the *Song of the Earth*. Pay close attention to the first two movements of the Fourth Symphony, and to the first and third movements of the First. If I were to attempt to be any more precise, I would be doing Mahler an injustice, since all of his clarinet work is excellent.

The chief Impressionist was Debussy, and what he accomplished in 1910 marks another milestone in the history of clarinet literature. In that year Debussy was asked to write the contest pieces for clarinetists at the Paris Conservatory. The result was two compositions for solo clarinet and piano: the *Première Rhapsodie* (which means "First" Rhapsody, but unfortunately there never was a second one) and the *Petite Pièce*.

The rhapsody for clarinet and piano is a masterpiece in itself, but it takes on further importance simply by being the first major work for the solo clarinet written in this century. It begins with an atmosphere of tranquility that is somewhat deceptive because, before long, it becomes obvious that this tranquility masks an underlying power and suspense. From there, the piece goes through virtually every mood that the clarinet and piano are capable of expressing within the context of the Impressionist style. The rhapsody constantly ebbs, flows, and changes, and finally culminates in an absolutely blazing and unusually dramatic finish. It is tremendously difficult to perform the piece well, not only because of the technical demands it makes on the player but also because of the high degree of sensitivity that it requires simultaneously.

It is important to reemphasize that the *Première Rhapsodie* was originally written for clarinet and piano; it was *not* meant to be accompanied by orchestra. Later, however, Debussy orchestrated the piano part, and it is the version for clarinet and orchestra that is most widely known today—so much so, in fact, that today many clarinetists believe the orchestrated version to be the original. This misapprehension is a shame because the piano-accompanied version, for economic reasons, is played far more often than is the orchestrated one. I think it is a shame also because the version for clarinet and piano is the superior one, in my opinion, and it should be recognized as the original. The Impressionist style demanded that the composer write his music in a way that its very nature would merge with the natural idiom of the instruments that perform it. This in itself would indicate the superiority of the clarinet and piano version, but in addition to this, I feel sure that if Debussy had originally wanted a piece for clarinet with orchestra, he would have written a substantially different piece of music. Listen to both versions with an open mind, and I believe you will agree with me. However, both versions make a beautiful work of art, definitely not to be downgraded for any reason. I simply feel that the version with piano is "closer to home" both musically and artistically than is the one with orchestra.

The clarinetist contestants at the Paris Conservatory in 1910 had to play not only that great rhapsody, which they worked on and studied at great length, but also they were called upon to "sight-read," to play a shorter piece that they had never seen before. For that purpose Debussy wrote his *Petite Pièce* for clarinet and piano, a little gem that lasts only for a minute or two. For that short space of time Debussy conceived a wonderfully fine work; it is rhythmically complex, yet it conveys a mood of tranquil simplicity. Harmonically, Debussy maintains a somewhat suspenseful interest by having the clarinet hover around a leading tone on F-sharp, continually leaving it and coming back to it; the melodic line does not resolve itself a half step upward to the tonic note G until near the very end, making it all the more effective.

I said earlier that it was Mahler who provided the transition from the Romantic period to the more diverse styles of our own century. That is true, but what Mahler began, Igor Stravinsky completed. Between 1909 and 1912, Stravinsky gave us *The Firebird, Petrushka,* and *The Rite of Spring,* all monumental works that are great not only in themselves but also in what they have meant, stylistically, to succeeding generations of artists and composers.

Shortly after the completion of those three great ballets, Stravinsky went into a much more scaled-down phase of artistic expression which has become known as his "neoclassic" period. During this period he wrote *The Soldier's Tale,* which more or less features a solo clarinet along with the solo violin, and the *Pulcinella Suite, The Wedding,* and the *Octet for Winds.* The latter work also contains a prominent clarinet part, and is one of the finest chamber pieces ever written.

Clarinetists will always be grateful to Stravinsky for the new ground he broke in 1919: In that year he wrote his *Three Pieces* for unaccompanied clarinet, a piece that contains elements of Stravinsky's neoclassic style and also elements of jazz. By this time jazz, of course, had come to Europe, particularly to Paris, where Stravinsky had spent a good deal of time. The *Three Pieces* represent such rhythmic and melodic complexity and sophistication that it remains difficult to believe that the work was written as early as 1919.

Another neoclassicist at that time was the rather puzzling Ferruccio Busoni, an Italian-German concert pianist, composer, theorist, and philosopher. He was a great intellectual and a great artist, and he paid considerable attention to the possibilities of the clarinet. He wrote an *Elegy* for clarinet and piano and a *Concertino* for clarinet and orchestra; neither work is performed very often today. Busoni included a prominent clarinet part in his opera *Arlecchino* in 1917, but that will also no doubt remain obscure. Donald J. Grout, in his *Short History of Opera,* says of Busoni's opera *Doktor Faust* what may well be said of nearly all of Busoni's work:

> Despite moments of dramatic force and musical beauty, the general style of *Doktor Faust* is so compressed, so complex in both its dramatic and harmonic implications, and so rooted fundamentally in the late German romantic sound-world that the opera is unlikely ever to become a permanent work in the repertoire.

The twelve-tone or serialist composers of the early 1900s were led by Arnold Schönberg and his two most prominent students, Anton Webern and Alban Berg. All three wrote compositions that are interesting to clarinetists, but I will mention only two of their works here. First, Schönberg's Opus 43a is a theme and variations written for a modern-day concert band. The clarinet parts are very interesting because Schönberg at times splits up the clarinet section into so many different parts that nearly every member of the band's clarinet section plays what amounts to a solo part. We need not stretch our imaginations too far to see, again, the influence of Mahler on Schönberg's use of that device.

The second twelve-tone composer's work that should be mentioned is Alban Berg's *Four Pieces* for clarinet and piano. This is a highly intellectualized work, brilliantly conceived. It is terribly difficult to perform well, and terribly difficult for both players and listeners to fathom. However, the piece is well worth the effort demanded. Berg broke new ground, too, with this piece, in calling for what has been referred to as either "avant-garde" techniques, or "extended" techniques, on the part of both players. Berg calls for harmonics, tone clusters, and the toneless depression of keys from the pianist, and for tremolos and "flutter-tonguing" from the clarinetist. Once a player or a listener is thoroughly acquainted with the work, it is obvious that none of those techniques was used by Berg as a "gimmick"; every one of them is in the proper place and the proper context to contribute to a great work of art.

In France, meanwhile, the teacher-composers at the Paris Conservatory had been greatly influenced by Debussy, and later by Ravel. Clarinetists are lucky because one of the clarinet teacher-composers at the Conservatory was Paul Jeanjean. This man contributed clarinet quartets and much study material to the literature still used today. All of Jeanjean's work was influenced by the French Impressionism of his day, and although it is probably a good thing that he did not in any way try to compete for the status enjoyed by Debussy and Ravel, his clarinet music has remained in the forefront of the modern clarinetists's literature.

Jeanjean and the other Conservatory clarinetists were called upon yearly to present music for their own use and for that of their students. As a result, we have today a great body of solo and small ensemble literature for clarinet which, even if it is less than great, constitutes a fine contribution to the literature. Also, the general level of Paris Conservatory compositions for clarinet seems higher than it does for most of the other woodwind instruments.

Paul Hindemith was a musical giant of this century. There was a sort of crusty, German pragmatism about this man that led him to create instrumental music characterized by a lack of pretension.

There is no nonsense or romanticism about Hindemith's music; he wrote, instead, what amounted to yet another form of neoclassicism. In the 1920s, Hindemith wrote his now-famous woodwind quintet in which there is no question that the clarinet part is featured; it is also very difficult to play technically. This piece, Hindemith's Opus 24, No. 2 in five movements, is a treasured part of contemporary woodwind quintet literature.

In 1939, Hindemith wrote his Clarinet Sonata, a work that has always disappointed me in many ways. Hindemith wrote sonatas and concertos for almost every instrument and more than one work for several of the instruments. Somehow I feel that the clarinet sonata is not as good, overall, as are most of his other sonatas. It is in many ways a good, solid work, however, and it is one of the more frequently performed works for clarinet and piano; apparently most clarinetists enjoy the work more than I do. The more I play it, and the more I teach it to others, the more I am able to see its merit. And although much of my disappointment stems from what I perceive as a rather uninspired treatment of themes, the themes themselves are definitely among Hindemith's better ones.

In 1947, Hindemith wrote a clarinet concerto. This concerto is not only one of Hindemith's very best works but it is also the greatest clarinet concerto of this century. It is a magnificent work, and like so many other clarinet solo pieces of the middle part of this century, it was written for clarinetist Benny Goodman.

The Hindemith Clarinet Concerto is a piece that is entirely too little known. Most clarinetists, even some of those who have played that composer's sonata for the instrument, have no idea that Hindemith wrote such a concerto. That fact is a terrible pity. This particular concerto (written for the A clarinet rather than for the B-flat) gives the clarinet soloist ample opportunity to display his virtuosity, and possesses a musical power matching that of the composer's *Mathis der Maler* or his *Symphonic Metamorphoses of Themes by Weber*. The concerto opens with a fine, serious, and powerful sonata-form movement. The second movement, a sort of scherzo, is short, very fast, stunningly clever and brilliant. The third movement is a slow one of great beauty; however, if the concerto has any fault at all, it is that this third movement is perhaps a bit too long. The fourth and last movement is a concerto-rondo form that ends the concerto on a note of lighter character, while maintaining an atmosphere of great musical power.

There is an old recording of Hindemith's Clarinet Concerto on Angel Records, with Hindemith himself conducting a British orchestra. What makes the recording so remarkable is that it offers the listener an excellent opportunity to hear the solo clarinet play-ing of that great old French clarinetist I mentioned in Chapter 14, "A Look at the Life Story of the Clarinet," Louis Cahouzac.

Bernhard Heiden, who has taught for several years at Indiana University, was a student of Hindemith. His Sonatina for clarinet and piano is frequently played, and justifiably so.

Another student of Hindemith should be far better known than he is, the British composer Arnold Cooke. Cooke writes in the Hindemith style, but there is somehow a warmth in his music that is missing from Hindemith's own. I feel that the Arnold Cooke clarinet sonata is a better piece than Hindemith's sonata; I whole-heartedly recommend this piece to clarinetists.

The music of Alvin Etler is probably influenced by Hindemith, but it has a definite stamp of originality. Etler, who died in the early 1970s, wrote what I consider to be one of the best clarinet sonatas of this century. It is a very solid piece, expressed with excellent craftsmanship. Etler also wrote two first-rate woodwind quintets along with several other chamber works involving both strings and winds. Etler even wrote a clarinet concerto that has a unique accompanying ensemble made up of brasses and string bass. Etler was an oboist as well as a theorist and composer, and his music reflects an intimate acquaintance with what woodwind in-struments can do best. I have performed the Etler sonata on sev-eral occasions, and it has been my pleasure to include it on one of my recordings with the pianist Frances Mitchum Webb.

The Australian-born composer Arthur Benjamin wrote a piece for clarinet (or viola) and piano called *Le Tombeau de Ravel—Valse Caprices,* a series of connected waltz-type movements in the style of Ravel. It is a very good work, but it makes strenuous demands on the clarinetist's endurance.

Antoni Szalowski wrote an excellent sonatina (which Frances Webb and I recorded on the same record that contains the Etler Sonata); Szalowski was a Polish composer, a student of Nadia Boulanger in Paris. His sonatina is written in a good, clean, neo-classic style.

Another Polish composer was Witold Lutoslawski; his *Five Dance Preludes* for clarinet and piano is an excellent work. This piece is another version of one Lutoslawski originally wrote for solo clarinet with strings, harp, piano, and percussion.

The works of four different British composers should be men-tioned next. The great Ralph Vaughan Williams wrote a piece called *Six Studies in English Folksong* originally for cello and piano. He made alternative versions of the solo part for clarinet and violin. In any case, this is a beautiful work which I believe is performed more often today with clarinet and piano than it is with either a solo cello or solo violin. This piece makes a wonderful "opener" for a clarinet recital.

The British composer Gordon Jacob has two fine pieces for clarinet. One is a sonatina for clarinet (or viola) and piano, and the other is a quintet for clarinet and strings.

For sheer originality it is hard to beat the music of Malcolm Arnold. He wrote a concerto and a sonatina for clarinet, both of them most interesting pieces. The sonatina is perhaps even better than the concerto.

Gerald Finzi, the last British composer to be mentioned in this series of four, also wrote a clarinet concerto, but his best piece is the *Five Bagatelles* for clarinet and piano.

The great French composer Francis Poulenc wrote his clarinet sonata near the end of his life, in 1962. He wrote several other chamber pieces involving the clarinet (including one duet for a B-flat clarinet and an A clarinet), but it could well be that the Poulenc clarinet sonata is not only the best of those works, but also the best such piece written in this century. I loved it from the outset of my acquaintance with it, and the longer I play it and teach it, the more fond of it I become. Poulenc has brilliantly conceived a work with ever-changing moods, one that has the artistic nerve to alternate without warning between serious concert music and clever satire on serious music. It is a wonderful piece, full of fun and beauty; as I said, it may well be the greatest clarinet sonata of our century.

Two friends of Poulenc wrote clarinet pieces, although both of these pieces are of far less musical significance. Arthur Honegger wrote a Sonatine for A clarinet and piano, and the Frenchwoman Germaine Tailleferre wrote a piece for unaccompanied clarinet.

Darius Milhaud wrote both a Sonatina for clarinet and piano and a Duo Concertant for the same instruments; both pieces are pleasant and light-hearted without, however, carrying much musical weight.

A very fine piece for unaccompanied clarinet is Willson Osborne's *Rhapsody*. This work is written in a sort of post-Romantic style and is really very beautiful with its long, flowing, melodic lines and its expertly shaped form.

Another excellent unaccompanied piece for clarinet was written by the Hungarian-American composer Miklós Rózsa. It is a fairly long piece in two movements, all of it of very high quality. Rózsa himself is an interesting composer because he has made his living by composing the sound track music for such films as *Ben Hur;* at the same time he is capable of writing very serious, first-rate, "classical" music in a style very similar to that of his fellow countryman, Béla Bartók.

In 1976, Russell Riepe finished one of the finest pieces ever written for unaccompanied clarinet, entitled *Three Studies in Flight.* The composer wrote this work especially for me after hearing a performance I gave of Stravinsky's *Three Pieces.* Riepe's work is characterized by a tremendous musical power that makes his work a major contribution to clarinet literature and to the musical world in general. While Riepe is a personal friend of mine and I might be considered to have a bias, I feel sure that many professionally competent musicians would readily confirm my estimation of this fine composition. I have recorded Riepe's piece on the same record that contains the Etler and Szalowski works.

I mentioned Bartók a moment ago; this great Hungarian composer wrote a trio for clarinet, violin, and piano called *Contrasts.* It is a three-movement piece based on Hungarian peasant dances, and like all of Bartók's music, it is of extremely high quality and is technically very difficult. The composer wrote the piece to be played originally by himself on piano, Benny Goodman on clarinet, and Joseph Szigeti on violin. The clarinet part calls for both the B-flat and the A instruments, and the violinist has to use a *second* violin at the beginning of the third movement because an unusual tuning of the strings is called for at that point.

One of the musical masterpieces of this century is the Bartók *Concerto for Orchestra.* All music lovers should acquaint themselves with this work. Clarinetists may want to pay special attention to the second of the five movements; this movement is characterized by duets played by identical instruments. The clarinet duet constitutes a brilliant passage, written almost entirely in parallel minor sevenths. The *Concerto for Orchestra* has been recorded by nearly every major orchestra in the world, so it is readily available to the listener.

The works of Dimitri Shostakovich for orchestra are full of interesting woodwind parts. Perhaps the most interesting clarinet solos to be found in that particular composer's music are in his Symphonies Nos. 1 and 5.

Sergei Prokofiev was a master orchestrator. A famous clarinet part is found in his *Peter and the Wolf,* of course, and he wrote well for the clarinet in all of his other works. One of his chamber pieces that is not well known at all, however, is his *Overture on Hebrew*

Themes for solo clarinet, string quartet, and piano. That sextet is a marvelous piece and should be heard more often.

I mentioned earlier the clarinet study books written during the 1920s and 1930s by Paul Jeanjean and others; two other composers of clarinet study materials in our century should be remembered. One of them is Gustave Langenus, who brought out a "method" book in 1913 that was mainly a continuation of the old Romantic period study books by such men as Klose and Lazarus. Langenus added material of his own making, and his work remains a mainstay in modern clarinet study.

The other clarinetist-composer is Rudolf Jettel, who teaches at the conservatory in Vienna. His series of books entitled *The Accomplished Clarinetist* is a wonderful work, full of enough virtuosity and musical interest to keep the *most* accomplished clarinetists busy for the rest of their lives. These studies became available in about 1950, and they are written in a more contemporary idiom than are the earlier, more famous ones from the Paris Conservatory. With Jettel, as with Jeanjean, clarinetists have been very lucky in having been "written for" by such a high-quality composer.

I would like to mention three more clarinet concertos written in this century, two of them French, and then there is "that Danish one." I will explain in a moment what I mean by "that Danish one," for those who have not guessed yet.

The clarinet concerto by Jean Françaix is a good one; it is nothing spectacular, but it is very difficult to play. My feeling is that it would be made considerably easier to play if much of it were transposed to the A clarinet. Even though Françaix has written it entirely for the B-flat clarinet, we know that the French clarinetists are used to transposing, and it would not surprise me to hear that most of the Françaix concerto is played in France on the A clarinet. In any case, it would be a good idea for the rest of us to do so.

The clarinet concerto by Henri Tomasi is much better known than is the Françaix, and it is a better piece. It requires a tremendous amount of virtuosity, of course. The opening theme is a very clever musical device; it is obviously a parody of the main theme from Bach's "double-violin" concerto in D minor. Tomasi has parodied the melody but has maintained rhythmic patterns practically identical to the ones originally used by Bach. The result is very pleasing. The Tomasi is a good piece; most clarinetists need to know it better than they do.

"That Danish" concerto is the one by Carl Nielsen—his Opus

57, written in the late 1920s. I want to single it out for special attention. First of all, most clarinetists who have studied for any length of time have heard of the Nielsen clarinet concerto, many of them have attempted to play it (hardly anyone has ever played it really *well*), and it is always spoken of with a great sense of awe. In truth, it is an awesome piece. The published solo clarinet part is ten pages of solid, beastly difficult passages. To say that the concerto presents a technical challenge to the player and his A clarinet is to make a gross understatement. It is as though Nielsen set out to punish all clarinetists for having the temerity to take up the instrument in the first place. Furthermore, the concerto is all but formless. Nielsen loaded his work with thematic ideas, but he failed to develop many of them in any meaningful way. The concerto moves from idea to idea without warning, without connection, and with an almost total absence of effective recapitulation and development. The opening theme comes back rather nicely throughout the concerto generally (this work is in one long movement), but when there are as many as eight or ten other definite, identifiable themes that remain virtually undealt with, the result has to be one of musical imbalance. And musical imbalance, or a lack of form, is sure to undercut the quality of a composition, no matter how inspired its themes are.

Every one of the themes is excellent, however, cleverly conceived and inspired. Nielsen was obviously a master of melodic construction and melodically implied harmony. But there is enough thematic material in this concerto to have done for several concertos. It is a shame that a work of such immense potential wealth was left so undeveloped by its own composer.

The piece opens with what sounds like a most promising fugue; the "subject" or theme of this fugue is stated three times. The third time is the opening of the solo clarinet part, but then this very fine theme drops almost completely from sight for too long a period of time. That is an example of its lack of development. As an example of the piece's technical difficulties, I have counted five places on the first page alone that require the clarinetist to resort to some kind of unusual and/or undesirable fingering technique. (Incidentally, there is a marvelous story, perhaps a true one, to the effect that a bassoon-playing friend of Nielsen's told the composer that if he wrote a bassoon concerto, *he,* the bassoonist, wouldn't play it!) In short, this clarinet concerto is too difficult in comparison to its musical value to occupy a pedestal of the height of the one it sits on in the minds of many clarinetists.

Does this mean the Nielsen concerto deserves to be forgotten?

Definitely not. But it should be put into its proper perspective. I have already mentioned the Hindemith concerto, saying that it may well be the greatest clarinet concerto of this century. The Aaron Copland concerto (another work written for Benny Goodman and one which I *haven't* mentioned yet) is also a contemporary concerto of much greater value than the Nielsen. I highly recommend it to clarinetists and to listeners alike. The point is that clarinetists should not be measured by whether they "have played the Nielsen."

A vast amount of clarinet literature in our century, of course, comes from the music for the symphonic band and the wind ensemble. Examples of such music are too numerous to mention specifically, but there are (and there have been for several decades now) many fine composers of music for band and for wind ensemble. These composers have contributed some great things to music in general as well as to clarinet literature. Even though the clarinet is not used anymore as a substitute for the orchestral violin (except when a band is performing old orchestral transcriptions), the band's clarinet parts remain in the forefront of the leading, high woodwind section of these ensembles. By definition, then, good-quality band music will always have clarinet parts of great technical and musical interest. Many of today's high school and college clarinet students never play any music except band literature, and some of them never will. It is highly important, therefore, that fine young composers continue to write serious, high-quality music for band and for wind ensemble. Band literature has become, perhaps, the chief instrumental music teaching medium of our century.

In recent decades a new kind of music has emerged, one that departs from any of the other styles both past and present. Much music written today contains elements of "chance," "indeterminacy," and "extended techniques" and is described as being "aleatoric" or, more vaguely, as "avant-garde." These various terms are not actually interchangeable and have specific meanings of their own, meanings that are beyond the scope of this book. I would like to point out to musical conservatives that a piece of music is not automatically a bad one just because its composer wrote in extra-musical instructions for the performer. And I would say to musical radicals that a piece of music is not automatically bad, reactionary, or outmoded just because it does *not* contain such instructions! No piece of music should be judged by the artistic materials used in its construction; it should be judged by how aesthetically effective the result is. Here is an example: If musicians claim that a clarinet part calling for toneless blowing, along with intentionally noisy key rattling, is "bad" or "unmusical" by definition, then those musicians are no better off than would be the art critic who claimed that the color "red" has no place in the world of art. In other words, many painters have used the color red to tremendous effect, and many have used it badly. By the same token it would be artistic and intellectual poppycock to claim that no art is any good without the color red.

I trust that I have made my point. I have played and heard several pieces of music using "extended techniques" (harmonics, multiphonics, playing sections of a clarinet instead of the whole instrument, key rattling, singing, or speaking into the clarinet, and so on), and the fact is that some of those pieces of music are good and some are musically worthless. Low quality versus high quality in art is not new to our own century, and never hinges upon the specific techniques used during its creation. It hinges instead, as always, upon the inherent artistic talent of the artists involved. I hesitate to mention examples of pieces of music using such techniques simply because of all the controversy surrounding this music; however, I will name two composers who have used experimental techniques for clarinet. The American William O. Smith is a clarinetist-composer who has written several pieces involving such techniques, and the British composer Peter Maxwell Davies has a most ambitious work of this type for clarinet and piano entitled *Hymnos*. The question in a listener's mind always should be: Is this music artistically effective or is it just so much technical posturing?

To conclude this chapter on clarinet literature I will say again that it has been very difficult to know what to talk about and what not to bother with, when books could be written on the subject of clarinet literature. I have discussed only what I consider to be some of the highlights. At the end of this book, in Appendix I: "A Selected List of Clarinet Literature," there is a list of music for the clarinet; even that is not "complete," of course, but it is far more so than is the list of works I have discussed in this chapter.

Where will clarinet literature go in the future? No one knows, but new, high-quality music will always be recognized and performed if clarinetists and listeners alike forge ahead with open minds in whatever direction the best composers lead them.

APPENDIX

I

A Selected List

of

Clarinet Literature

By definition, selected lists are incomplete lists. This one is no exception to that rule, as I have had to come up with certain criteria. While the body of clarinet literature is much smaller than that for piano or violin, it is still vast.

I have selected the music for the following list in this manner: I asked myself a question concerning any particular piece of music, "Does this music, or its composer, possess greatness, fame, or both?" There are several comprehensive lists available (although only one of those, that of *The Music Register,* is *truly* comprehensive); there are lists based on sales volume; and of course, there are lists printed by publishers giving only the music published by them. But I think I have come up with a uniquely selected list by adhering to the criteria of greatness and/or fame of the piece of music and/or its composer. That greatness and that fame are, of course, judged solely and subjectively by me.

I reduced the size of the list further by eliminating some categories of clarinet literature; I omitted, for example, the music for woodwind duets, trios, and quartets on the grounds that there are far too many such compositions, and far too few of them are either great or famous. There are some fine old clarinet duets, but these are generally included in the old method books. Both Beethoven and Poulenc have written excellent duets for clarinet and bassoon, and a transcription of Beethoven's Opus 87 makes a fine clarinet trio, but I felt that none of this would warrant a separate category if I am to avoid extending the list beyond feasible bounds.

Likewise, for example, I have left off the music for solo clarinet and band; there is really only one good piece for that combination: the Weber *Concertino,* and even that is a transcription of the original orchestral version. Chamber ensembles requiring more than eight players have been ignored, too, on the grounds that they are relatively unwieldy to perform and few of them, with the exception of Mozart's *Serenade for Thirteen Instruments,* K. 361, amount to much.

I have confined myself to clarinet study materials, unaccompanied solos, music for clarinet and piano, trios, quartets, and quintets for clarinet with strings and/or piano, chamber pieces including clarinet and voice, quintets, sextets, septets, and octets that include clarinet, and finally, a category of great music for solo clarinet and orchestra.

I have listed publishers of this music but I have not listed more than two publishers for any given piece of music. Many of the works of Mozart, Weber, and Brahms, for example, are available from more publishers than I have listed. To save space I have abbreviated the names of some of the publishers:

A.C.A.	American Composers Alliance
A.M.P.	Associated Music Publishers
B. and H.	Breitkopf and Haertel
Boosey	Boosey and Hawkes
A. Broude	Alexander Broude
Broude	Broude Brothers
Int.	International Music Company
M. and M.	McGinnis and Marx
Southern NY	Southern Music Company of New York City
Southern TX	Southern Music Company of San Antonio, Texas
U.E.	Universal Editions
W.I.M.	Western International Music Company

Here, then, follows a list of what I believe to be clarinet music of a very high quality:

COMPOSER	TITLE	PUBLISHER

Clarinet Methods

COMPOSER	TITLE	PUBLISHER
Bärmann-Bettoney	Method, Opus 63	C. Fischer
Gabucci	Breve Metodo	Carish
Gay	Grand Method	Billaudot
Jettel	School for Clarinet	Doblinger
Kell	Clarinet Method	Boosey
Klose-Williams	Clarinet Method	C. Fischer
Klose-Prescott	Clarinet Method (excerpts)	C. Fischer
Lazarus-Langenus	Modern Method	C. Fischer
Thurston	The Clarinet: A Comprehensive Tutor	Boosey

Clarinet Studies

COMPOSER	TITLE	PUBLISHER
Bitsch	12 Rhythmic Studies	Leduc
Bona	Rhythmical Articulation	G. Schirmer
Brahms-Kucinski	Brahms Studies	Fox
Cavallini	30 Caprices	C. Fischer
Gillet	Exercises for Advanced Clarinet Technique	Leduc
Hamelin	Scales and Exercises	Leduc
Jeanjean	16 Modern Etudes	Leduc
Jeanjean	25 Melodic and Technical Studies	Leduc
Jeanjean	18 Etudes	Alfred
Jettel	The Accomplished Clarinetist	Shapiro-Bernstein
Kell	17 Staccato Studies	Int.
Langenus	27 Original Studies	C. Fischer
Perier	Studies in Style and Interpretation	Leduc
Polatschek	Advanced Studies	G. Schirmer
Rose	32 Studies after Ferling	C. Fischer
Sarlit	25 Virtuosic Etudes	Leduc
Uhl, Alfred	48 Studies	Schott

COMPOSER	TITLE	PUBLISHER

Clarinet Orchestral Excerpts

COMPOSER	TITLE	PUBLISHER
Bonade	Orchestra Studies	Leblanc
Drucker (ed.)	Orchestral Excerpts, vols. 5–10	Int.
	(This Drucker edition is a continuation of the following McGinnis edition.)	
McGinnis	Orchestral Excerpts, vols. 1–4	Int.
Waln	Clarinet Excerpts from Orchestral Literature	Belwin

Unaccompanied Clarinet Solos

COMPOSER	TITLE	PUBLISHER
Apostel	Sonatina, Opus 19, No. 2	U.E.
Frohne	Study, Opus 17	Bote and Bock
Genzmer	Fantasy	Peters
Heussenstamm	Monologue 1973	Seesaw
Jacob	5 Pieces	Oxford
Jettel	5 Grotesques	Peters
Karg-Elert	Sonata, Opus 110	Peters
Křenek	Monologue	Broude
Martino	A Set for Clarinet	M. and M.
Osborne	Rhapsody	Peters
Riepe	Three Studies on Flight	Southern TX
Rozsa	Sonatina, Opus 27	Rongwen
Smith	5 Pieces	U.E.
Stravinsky	3 Pieces	Omega; Int.
Sydeman	Sonata	Peters

Clarinet and Piano

COMPOSER	TITLE	PUBLISHER
Arnold	Sonatina	Lengnick
Arnold	Concerto	Lengnick
Avon	Fantasie de Concert	Alfred
Bartók-Balassa	3 Hungarian Songs	Boosey
Bartók-Balassa	Sonatina	Boosey
Bax	Sonata	Chappell
Beethoven-Langenus	Minuet from Opus 22	Boosey

COMPOSER	TITLE	PUBLISHER
Clarinet and Piano (continued)		
Beethoven-Andraud	Adagio Cantabile	Southern TX
Benjamin	Le Tombeau de Ravel	Boosey
Berg	4 Pièces	U.E.
Berlioz-Weston	Solo from The Trojans	Schott
Bernstein	Sonata	Witmark
Bitsch	Pièce Romantique	Leduc
Brahms	Sonata, Opus 120, No. 1	C. Fischer; Int.; Boosey
Brahms	Sonata, Opus 120, No. 2	C. Fischer; Int. Boosey
Busoni	Concertino, Opus 48	B. and H.
Busoni	Elegy	B. and H.
Butterworth	Pastorale	Boosey
Cahuzac	Variations sur un Air du Pays d'Oc	Leduc
Carter	Pastoral (clar. in A)	Presser
Castelnuovo-Tedesco	Sonata	Ricordi
Cavallini	Adagio and Tarantella	C. Fischer
Cimarosa-Benjamin	Concerto	Boosey
Cooke	Sonata in B-flat	Novello
Copland	Concerto	Boosey
Crusell	Concerto in F Minor	Sikorski
Debussy	Première Rhapsodie	Durand
Debussy	Petite Pièce	Durand
Delmas	Fantasie Italienne	Alfred
Dukas	Alla Gitana	Leduc
Etler	Sonata	A.M.P.
Ferguson	4 Short Pieces	Boosey
Finzi	Concerto	Boosey
Finzi	5 Bagatelles	Boosey
Genzmer	Sonatina	Peters
Hamilton	Sonata, Opus 22	A.M.P.
Hamilton	3 Nocturnes, Opus 6 (clar. in A)	Schott
Heiden	Sonatina	A.M.P.

COMPOSER	TITLE	PUBLISHER
Clarinet and Piano (continued)		
Hindemith	Concerto (clar. in A)	Schott
Hindemith	Sonata	Schott
Honegger	Sonatine (clar. in A)	Salabert
Horovitz	2 Majorcan Pieces	Mills
Ibert	Aria (clar. in A)	Leduc
Jacob	Sonatine (clar. in A)	Novello
Karg-Elert	Sonata in B-flat	Peters
Leclair-Waln	Musette and Scherzo	Kjos
Manevich	Concerto	Int.
Martinů	Sonatina	Leduc
Mason	Sonata	C. Fischer
Maxwell Davies	Hymnos	Boosey
Milhaud	Sonatine	Elkan-Vogel
Mozart (ed. Kell)	Concerto	Int.
Mozart (ed. Catelinet)	Quintet, K. 581 (arranged)	Peters
Nielsen	Concerto, Opus 57 (clar. in A)	Peters
Piston	Concerto	A.M.P.
Pokorny-Becker	Concerto in B-flat	B. and H.
Poulenc	Sonata	Chester
Rachmaninoff	Vocalise	Int.
Rameau-Ettinger	Suite	Boosey
Ravel	Pavane for a Dead Princess	C. Fischer
Ravel-Hamelin	Pièce en forme de Habanera	Leduc
Reger	Sonata, Opus 49, No. 1	U.E.
Reger	Sonata, Opus 49, No. 2	U.E.
Reger	Sonata, Opus 107	Bote and Bock
Reinecke	Introduction and Allegro Appassionata, Opus 256	C. Fischer
Rochberg	Dialogues	Presser
Rossini	Introduction, Theme and Variations	Oxford; Sikorski
Rossler	Concerto in E-flat	Peters
Rueff	Prelude and Toccata	Leduc
Rueff	Concertino	Leduc

COMPOSER	TITLE	PUBLISHER

Clarinet and Piano (continued)

COMPOSER	TITLE	PUBLISHER
Saint-Saëns	Sonata	Durand
Saint-Saëns– Langenus	The Swan	C. Fischer
Scarlatti-Drucker	4 Sonatas	Int.
Schönberg-Greissle	Sonata (arranged from the Quintet, Opus 26)	U.E.
Schubert-Bellison	Introduction, Theme and Variations	C. Fischer
Schubert-Davis	Themes from the First Movement of the Unfinished Symphony	Rubank
Schubert-Simon	Sonatina	Boosey
Schubert-Perier	Impromptu, Opus 90, No. 3	Leduc
Schubert-Roth	Andante from the Octet	Boosey
Schumann	Fantasy Pieces, Opus 73 (clar. in B-flat *or* A)	Peters
Schumann	Romances, Opus 94	Peters
Searle	Suite, Opus 32	A.M.P.
Seiber	Concertino	Schott
Siegmeister	Concerto	Fox
Simon (ed.)	Masterworks (containing music of Weber, Mendelssohn, Schumann and both Brahms sonatas)	G. Schirmer
Spohr	Concerto No. 1	C. Fischer; Int.
Spohr	Concerto No. 2	C. Fischer; Int.
Spohr	Concerto No. 3	B. and H.; Int.
Spohr	Concerto No. 4	B. and H.; Int.
Spohr	Potpourri	Musica Rara
Stamitz, Johann	Concerto	Belwin
Stamitz, Karl	Concerto in F Minor	Peters
Stamitz, Karl	Concerto in B-flat	Int.
Starer	Dialogues	Belwin
Stravinsky	Excerpts from the Ballets	Edition Musicus

COMPOSER	TITLE	PUBLISHER
Clarinet and Piano (continued)		
Sydeman	Duo	Southern NY
Szałowski	Sonatina	Omega
Tartini-Hite	Sonata in G Minor	Southern TX
Tomasi	5 Sacred and Profane Dances	Leduc
Tomasi	Concerto	Leduc
Vanhal	Concerto	Boosey
Vaughan Williams	Six Studies in English Folk-Song	Galaxy
Verdi	Operatic Solos	Franco Colombo
Verdi-Armato	Andante	C. Fischer
Wagner (Bärmann)	Adagio (later proven to have been composed by Bärmann)	B. and H.
Weber (C. M. von)	Concerto No. 1, Opus 73	Peters; Int.
Weber	Concerto No. 2, Opus 74	Peters; Int.
Weber	Concertino, Opus 26	Peters; Int.
Weber	Variations, Opus 33	Peters; Int.
Weber	Grand Duo, Opus 48	Peters; Int.
Weber	Quintet, Opus 34 (arranged)	Peters
Wellesz	Two Pieces, Opus 34	U.E.
Weston (ed.)	Four Clarinet Albums	Schott
Clarinet, Violin, and Piano		
Bartók	Contrasts	Boosey
Berg	Adagio	U.E.
Ives	Largo	Southern NY
Khatchaturian	Trio	Int.; Peters
Milhaud	Suite	Salabert
Smith	Four Pieces	MJQ Music
Stravinsky	Soldier's Tale (arranged by Stravinsky himself)	Chester; Int.

COMPOSER	TITLE	PUBLISHER

Clarinet, Viola, and Piano

Bassett	Trio	A.C.A.
Bruch	8 Pieces, Opus 83 (clar. in A)	Simrock
Jacob	Trio	Musica Rara
Mozart	Trio, K. 498	B. and H.; Int.
Reinecke	Trio, Opus 264 (clar. in A)	Simrock; Int.
Schumann	Fairy Tales, Opus 132	B. and H.; Int.
Uhl	Kleines Konzert	Doblinger

Clarinet, Cello, and Piano

Beethoven	Trio, Opus 11	Peters, Int.
Beethoven	Trio, Opus 38 (arranged by Beethoven himself from the Septet, Opus 20)	Peters; Int.
Brahms	Trio, Opus 114 (clar. in A)	Peters; Int.
d'Indy	Trio, Opus 29	Elkan-Vogel; Int.
Mendelssohn	Concert Piece No. 1, Opus 113	Int.
Mendelssohn	Concert Piece No. 2, Opus 114	Int.
Muczynski	Fantasy Trio, Opus 26	G. Schirmer
Starer	Trio	Southern NY
Sydeman	Trio Montagnana	Seesaw

Clarinet and String Quartet

Bliss	Quintet	Novello
Brahms	Quintet, Opus 115	Peters; Int.
Cooke	Quintet	Oxford
Hindemith	Quintet, Opus 30	Schott
Jacob	Quintet	Novello
Moore	Quintet	C. Fischer

COMPOSER	TITLE	PUBLISHER
Clarinet and String Quartet (continued)		
Mozart	Quintet, K. 581 (clar. in A)	Peters; Int.
Reger	Quintet, Opus 146 (clar. in A)	Peters
Reicha	Quintet in B-flat	Musica Rara
Reicha-Merka	Quintet, Opus 107	Peters
Weber	Quintet, Opus 34	Peters; Int.
Weber	Introduction, Theme and Variations	Bote and Bock; Peters

Chamber Music Including Clarinet and Voice

Copland	As It Fell Upon a Day (for soprano, flute, and clarinet)	Boosey
Hindemith	Die junge Magd, Opus 23, No. 2 (for alto, flute, clarinet, and string quartet)	Schott
Meyerbeer	Hirtenlied (for high voice, clarinet, and piano)	M. and M.
Mozart	Parto! Ma tu ben mio (for soprano, clarinet, and piano)	Schott
Rorem	Ariel (for soprano, clarinet, and piano)	Boosey
Schubert	Der Hirt auf dem Felsen (for soprano, clarinet, and piano)	G. Schirmer
Schubert	Romanze from Die Verschworenen (for soprano, clarinet, and piano)	Peters
Schubert-Lancelot	Le Patre sur la Montagne (for soprano, clarinet, and piano)	Billaudot

COMPOSER	TITLE	PUBLISHER

Chamber Music Including Clarinet and Voice (continued)

COMPOSER	TITLE	PUBLISHER
Spohr	Six German Songs (for soprano, clarinet, and piano)	B. and H.
Stravinsky	Elegy for J.F.K. (for medium voice and three clarinets)	Boosey
Stravinsky	Three Songs from Shakespeare (for mezzo, flute, clarinet, and viola)	Boosey
Tippett	Victoria Rules an Autumn Land (for alto, clarinet, cello, and piano)	Schott
Vaughan Williams	Three Vocalises (for soprano and clarinet)	Oxford
Villa-Lobos	Poema da Crianca e sua Mama (for mezzo, flute, clarinet in A, and cello)	Eschig

Woodwind Quintets

COMPOSER	TITLE	PUBLISHER
Amram	Fanfare and Processional	Peters
Andriessen	Quintet	Peters
Arnold	Three Shanties	C. Fischer
Barber	Summer Music	G. Schirmer
Barrows	March	G. Schirmer
Beethoven-Stark	Quintet, Opus 71	A.M.P.
Berger (Arthur)	Partita	Belwin
Berger (Jean)	6 Short Pieces	Peters
Bergsma	Concerto	Galaxy
Bozza	Variations on a Free Theme	Leduc
Brahms-Rosenthal	Capriccio	W.I.M.
Carter	Quintet 1948	A.M.P.
Chavez	Soli No. 2	Mills
Cowell	Suite	Presser
Dahl	Allegro and Arioso	M. and M.

COMPOSER	TITLE	PUBLISHER
Woodwind Quintets (continued)		
Danzi	3 Quintets from Opus 56	Leukart
Danzi	Quintet, Opus 67, No. 1	Leukart
Danzi	Quintet, Opus 67, No. 2	Peters; Int.
Danzi	Quintet, Opus 67, No. 3	Peters
Danzi	Quintets, Opus 68, Nos. 1 and 2	Peters
Danzi	Quintet, Opus 68, No. 3	Musica Rara
Diamond	Quintet 1958	Southern NY
Douglas	Dance Caricatures	Peters
Dvořàk-Haufrecht	Serenade, Opus 44	A.C.A.
Etler	Quintet No. 1	A.M.P.
Etler	Quintet No. 2	A.M.P.
Fauré-Williams	Berceuse from Dolly	Southern TX
Fine	Partita	Boosey
Foss	Quintet	Salabert
Françaix	Quintet	Schott
Genzmer	Quintet	Peters
Grainger	Walking Tune	Schott
Handel-Bauer	Six Little Fugues	A.C.A.
Hartley	Two Pieces	Crescendo
Haydn-Philadelphia Quintet	Divertimento No. 1	Presser
Heiden	Sinfonia	A.M.P.
Heiden	Quintet 1965	A. Broude
Hindemith	Kleine Kammermusik, Opus 24, No. 2	A.M.P.
Ibert	Three Short Pieces	Leduc
Jongen	Quintet	CeBeDeM
Kingman	Quintet	W.I.M.
Klughardt	Quintet, Opus 79	Peters
Milhaud	La Cheminée du roi René	Southern TX
Mozart-Baines	Divertimento No. 14	Oxford

COMPOSER	TITLE	PUBLISHER

Woodwind Quintets (continued)

COMPOSER	TITLE	PUBLISHER
Mozart-Bryant	Divertimento No. 12	Galaxy
Mozart-Jensen	Divertimento in E-flat	Crescendo
Mozart-Rottler	Divertimento in C Minor	Leukart
Mozart-Weigelt	Divertimento No. 8	Leukart
Mozart-Weigelt	Divertimento No. 9	Leukart
Mozart-Weigelt	Divertimento No. 13	Leukart
Muczynski	Movements	Shawnee
Nielsen	Quintet, Opus 43	Hansen
Persichetti	Pastorale	G. Schirmer
Pierne	Pastorale	C. Fischer
Pijper	Quintet	Peters
Piston	Quintet	A.M.P.
Powell	Divertimento	C. Fischer
Ravel	Pièce en forme de Habanera	Leduc
Reicha	Quintet, Opus 91, No. 1	Peters
Reicha	Quintet, Opus 91, No. 2	Peters
Reicha	Quintet, Opus 91, No. 3	Peters
Reicha	Quintet, Opus 91, No. 4	Billaudot
Reicha	Quintet, Opus 91, No. 5	Peters
Reicha	Quintet, Opus 99, No. 2	Musica Rara
Reicha	Quintet, Opus 100, No. 4	Peters
Reicha-Seydel	Quintet, Opus 88, No. 5	Leukart
Reicha-Wise	Quintet, Opus 88, No. 2	W.I.M.
Reizenstein	Quintet	Boosey
Riegger	Quintet	Scherchen
Rosetti (Rossler)	Quintet in E-flat	Presser; Peters
Schönberg	Quintet	Belmont
Schubert-Schoenbach	Shepherd Melody	Presser
Schubert	Rosamunde Ballet Music	C. Fischer

COMPOSER	TITLE	PUBLISHER

Woodwind Quintets (continued)

Schuller	Quintet 1958	A.M.P.
Schuller	Suite	M. and M.
Seiber	Permutazioni a Cinque	Schott
Sibelius-Langenus	Pastorale	C. Fischer
Szałowski	Quintet	Omega
Tomasi	Quintet	Baron
Washburn	Quintet	Oxford
Washburn	Suite	Elkan-Vogel

Two Clarinets, Two Horns, and Two Bassoons

Beethoven	Sextet, Opus 71	Peters; Int.
Beethoven	Minuet and March	E. B. Marks
Michael (one of the early Moravians)	Parthias IV and VI	Boosey
Mozart	Serenade, K. 375	Schott
Weber	Adagio and Rondo	Schott
Weber	Two Pieces	Musica Rara

Septets

Beethoven	Septet in E-flat, Opus 20 (for clarinet, horn, bassoon, violin, viola, cello, and string bass)	Peters; Int.
Kreutzer	Grand Septet, Opus 62 (for the same instruments)	Musica Rara
Revueltas	Octet for Radio (for clarinet, bassoon, trumpet, two violins, cello, string bass, and percussion)	Southern NY

Wind Octets

(For the classical instrumentation: two oboes, two clarinets, two horns, and two bassoons)

Beethoven	Octet in E-flat, Opus 103	Musica Rara

COMPOSER	TITLE	PUBLISHER

Wind Octets (continued)

Beethoven	Rondino in E-flat	Presser; Int.
Beethoven-Sedlak	Fidelio (in 2 volumes)	Musica Rara
Haydn	Octet in F Major	Peters; Int.
Hummel	Octet-Parthia	Musica Rara
Jacob	Divertimento	Musica Rara
Mozart	Divertimento No. 11	B. and H.
Mozart	Divertimento No. 12	B. and H.
Schubert	Minuet and Finale (*not* the *famous* Schubert Octet)	M. and M.

Octets

(For mixed instrumentation)

Badings	Octet (for clarinet, horn, bassoon, and string quintet)	Peters
Ferguson	Octet (for clarinet, horn, bassoon, and string quintet)	Boosey
Hindemith	Octet (for clarinet, horn, bassoon, violin, two violas, cello, and bass)	Schott
Reicha	Octet (for oboe, clarinet, horn, bassoon, and string quartet)	Musica Rara
Schubert	Octet in F Major, Opus 166 (this *is* the famous Schubert Octet: for clarinet, horn, bassoon, and string quintet)	Peters; Int.
Spohr	Octet, Opus 32 (for clarinet, two horns, violin, two violas, cello, and bass)	Musica Rara

COMPOSER	TITLE	PUBLISHER

Octets (continued)

COMPOSER	TITLE	PUBLISHER
Stravinsky	Octet (for flute, clarinet, two trumpets, two bassoons, and two trombones)	Boosey
Sydeman	Divertimento (for flute, clarinet, bassoon, and string quintet)	Seesaw

Solo Clarinet and Orchestra

COMPOSER	TITLE	PUBLISHER
Debussy	Premiere Rhapsody	Presser
Goossens	By the Tarn (for clarinet and string orchestra)	Chester
Hindemith	Variations (for clarinet and string orchestra)	Schott
Horovitz	Concertante (for clarinet and string orchestra)	Chester
Manevich	Concerto	A.C.A.
Mozart	Concerto, K. 622	B. and H.; Peters
Nielsen	Concerto, Opus 57	Peters
Rogers	Pastorale Mistico (for clarinet and string orchestra)	Galaxy
Rossini	Variations	M. and M.
Stamitz, Karl	Concerto No. 3	Peters
Tartini-Jacob	Concertino (for clarinet and string orchestra)	Boosey
Wagner (actually Bärmann)	Adagio (for clarinet and string orchestra, or for clarinet and string quintet)	Lucks

APPENDIX

II

Clarinet

Fingerings

This is not really a "fingering chart"; it is not made up of pictures and drawings. This is more of a catalog, or list, of some clarinet fingerings that I have found useful. If some of your favorite fingerings have been left out, write them in yourself, so that this list may be more useful for you and your acquaintances. I have not attempted to compile a comprehensive list. The clarinet world is full of fingering charts, many of them excellent; some of them are more comprehensive than this list is, but many fingerings that I have here do not appear on those larger lists. In any case, these are the fingerings that I use, and many of them were "discovered" either by me or by one of my students, or a student and I together "developed" a fingering that has stood the tests of time and usage.

I have included no multiphonic fingerings (fingerings that give more than one tone at once), no "microtones" (fingerings that give notes closer together than a half step), and no tremolos. For all of those I recommend the Rehfeldt book that is listed in the Bibliography. I have, however, included a few trill and harmonic fingerings, some of which I have never seen anywhere else. This fingering list adheres to conventional clarinet playing, in short, but it is through experimentation with these conventional fingerings that more "extended" techniques can be and have been found.

All of these fingerings, even the extremely high ones, can be obtained using the regular clarinet embouchure, assuming a rather long mouthpiece facing with a rather close tip-opening and a reed that has a good, firm heart.

All fingerings given are for the Boehm-system clarinet, in its most standard form: seventeen keys and six rings. All things considered, the fingerings given will work more often on the B-flat instrument than on the A (especially the extremely high notes), but these differences between the B-flat and the A are so slight that they are negligible. We all need to continue experimenting with those highest fingerings, anyway, on all our clarinets.

KEY TO SYMBOLS
USED IN FINGERING LIST

Thumb (Left Thumb):

T	Thumb on its tone-hole
R	Thumb on the register key

Left-Hand Fingers:

A	Index finger (side of first knuckle) on the top key that gives "throat A," written on second space of staff
G#	Index finger (side of second knuckle) on the top key that gives "throat G#," written on second line of staff
1	Index finger on top tone-hole
2	Middle finger on second tone-hole
D# – A#	Small key between second and third tone-holes, played with ring finger
3	Tone-hole covered by ring finger
C# – G#	Key that gives chalumeau C# and clarion G#, played by the little finger
F – C	Key that gives chalumeau F and clarion C, played by the little finger; an alternate for the right-hand F – C key

F# –C#   Key that gives chalumeau F# and clarion C#, played by the little finger; an alternate for the right-hand F# –C# key

E –B   Key that gives chalumeau E (lowest E) and clarion B (B on the middle line of staff), played by the little finger; an alternate for the right-hand E –B key

Right-Hand Fingers:

SK1   Bottom "side key," which can be used for some of the same purposes as the D# –A# key in the left hand, played by the side of the index finger (of the right hand)

SK2   Second-from-the-bottom side key, played with the side of the index, practically always simultaneously with SK1

SK3   Third-from-the-bottom side key, played with the side of the index finger

SK4   Fourth-from-the-bottom (the top one) side key, played with the side of the index finger

4   Index finger on its tone-hole, the top tone-hole of the clarinet's lower section

5   Middle finger on middle tone-hole of clarinet's lower section

B –F#   Small key between the last two tone-holes (or ring keys) of the clarinet's lower section, played by the ring finger

6   Third and last tone-hole on the clarinet's lower section, played by the ring finger

G# –D#   Key that gives chalumeau G# and clarion D#, played by the little finger

F –C   Key that gives chalumeau F and clarion C, played by the little finger; an alternate for the left-hand F –C key

F# –C#   Key that gives chalumeau F# and clarion C#, played by the little finger; an alternate for the left-hand F# –C# key

E –B   Key that gives chalumeau E and clarion B, played by the little finger; an alternate for the left-hand E –B key

lowest E   T/123,E –B/456
(three ledger lines)   T/123/456,E –B

lowest F (three ledger lines)	T/123/456,F–C T/123,F–C/456
lowest F# –G-flat (two or three ledger lines)	T/123/456,F# –C# T/123,F# –C#/456
lowest G (two ledger lines)	T/123/456
lowest G# –A-flat (two ledger lines)	T/123/456,G# –D#
lowest A (two ledger lines)	T/123/450
lowest A# –B-flat (one or two ledger lines)	T/123/400
lowest B (one ledger line)	T/123/050 T/123/40,B –F#,0
lowest C (one ledger line)	T/123/000
lowest C# –D-flat (one ledger line or on space below staff)	T/123,C# –G#/000
lowest D (space below staff)	T/120/000
lowest D# –E-flat (space below, and first line of, staff)	T/120/SK1,000 T/12,D# –A#,0/000 T/100/400 T/100/050 T/100/006
first-line E	T/100/000
first-space F	T/000/000
first-space F#, and second- line G-flat	0/100/000 T/000/SK1,SK2,000

second-line G	0/000/000
second-line G#, and second-space A-flat	0/G#,000/000
second-space A	0/A,000/000
second-space A#, and third-line B-flat	R/A,000/000 R/A,003/006,F–C R/A,003,F–C/006 0/A,000/SK3,000 (this fingering makes a beautifully clear tone, but may be too sharp or too bright; if so, add just the ring around the thumb-hole, leaving the hole uncovered)
third-line B	TR/123,E–B/456 TR/123/456,E–B
third-space C	TR/123/456,F–C TR/123,F–C/456
third-space C#, and fourth-line D-flat	TR/123/456,F#–C# TR/123,F#–C#/456
fourth-line D	TR/123/456
fourth-line D#, and fourth-space E-flat	TR/123,456,G#–D#
fourth-space E	TR/123/450
top-line F	TR/123/400
top-line F#, and G-flat on top of staff	TR/123/050 TR/123/40,B–F#,0 TR/123/006 (this fingering is slightly sharp, but is very handy to use in conjunction with the similar fingering for the D# or E-flat above it)

G on top of the staff

TR/123/000

G# on top of the staff, and A-flat with one ledger line

TR/123/C#–G#/000 (if this tone is sharp on your A clarinet, add the right-hand F–C, or F#–C# key)

TR/120/450 (this should be used only in the most dire emergencies, but it is handy in dire emergencies)

high A
(one ledger line)

TR/120/000

high A#–B-flat (one ledger line)

TR/120/SK1,000
TR/12,D#–A#,0/000
TR/100/400
TR/100/050
TR/100/006

high B
(one ledger line)

TR/100/000
TR/123/SK1,456 (an excellent harmonic)

high C
(two ledger lines)

TR/000/000
TR/123/SK1,456,G#–D# (another very fine harmonic, capable of very soft dynamic levels without going sharp)

high C#–D-flat
(two ledger lines)

TR/023/450
R/100/000 (harmonic)
TR/000/SK1,SK2,000 (harmonic)
TR/123/SK1,450 (this harmonic produces a nice, dark sound, and trills very well *down* a whole step to B-natural through the use of tone-hole 6)

high D
(two ledger lines)

TR/023/400 (G#–D# optional)
R/000/000 (harmonic)

high D# –E-flat
(two or three ledger lines)

TR/023/40,B –F#,0(G# –D#
 optional)
TR/A,000/000 (harmonic; can
 also be used for tremolos
 down to high C by trilling
 the A key)
TR/A,023/450 (the best use of
 this fingering is for trills
 downward to C# or D-flat;
 trill the A key)
TR/023/006,G# –D#

Note:
Please observe that I have *not* included the following fingering for high D# –E-flat: TR/023/
050,G# –D#. This fingering is not even worthy of
consideration under any circumstances; it is miser-
ably flat on all clarinets, and any of the four fingerings given in the preceding list for that tone will
serve the purpose far better. I mention it because
so many young clarinetists use this poor fingering,
usually due to lack of proper supervision. Even for
trills to this note from the C# a whole step below,
avoid that fingering, and instead use the third one I
have listed.

high E
(three ledger lines)

TR/023/000,(G# –D# optional)

high F
(three ledger lines)

TR/023,C# –G#/000 (G# –D#
 optional)
TR/123,C# –G#/456
TR/023/SK1,000(G# –D# op-
 tional) (this is sharp in
 pitch, but is useful for some
 trills up from E)

high F# –G-flat
(three or four ledger lines)

TR/020/00,B –F#,0,G# –D#
 (this is the best fingering of
 all for this note, as long as
 you are sure to allow the
 right-hand ring keys to stay
 all the way up; lowered
 rings will spoil it)

TR/020/000,G# –D#
TR/120/456,G# –D#
TR/123,C# –G#/450

high G
(four ledger lines)

TR/020/450,G# –D# (this is the most widely known high G fingering, but it tends to be sharp)
TR/020/SK1,00,B –F#,0,G# –D# (this is the best high G of all, if it can be obtained handily, such as from the similar fingering for high F# mentioned in the preceding list. The tuning and tone quality of this fingering are excellent, but the right-hand ring keys must be allowed to stay all the way up; otherwise this fingering is spoiled)
TR/020/406,G# –D#
TR/120/SK1,450,G# –D#

high G# –A-flat
(four ledger lines)

TR/023/456,F# –C# (by far the best fingering for this note, full-toned and in tune)
TR/023,F# –C#/456
TR/020/050,G# –D# (handy, but not reliable)
TR/02,D# –A#,0/SK1,SK2,00, B –F#,0,G# –D#

highest A
(four ledger lines)

TR/020/006,F# –C# (a wonderful fingering, closely related to the first one in the preceding list given for high G#)
TR/023/000,F# –C#
TR/023,F# –C#/000
TR/023/000,G# –D#
TR/023,F# –C#/006
TR/023/006,F# –C#

highest A# – B-flat
(four or five ledger lines)

TR/123,C# – G#/456,F – C (if the reed has a good heart, this fingering is miraculously good; it is excellent for slurring up to from the "long F" fingering, a fourth below)

TR/G#,023,C# – G#/000,G# – D#

TR/020,F# – C#/000,G# – D#

TR/123,F – C/456,G# – D# (to slur smoothly from this fingering up a whole step, remove fingers 2, 3, 5, and 6)

highest B
(five ledger lines)

TR/G#,123,C# – G#/456,F# – C# (this fingering is fairly complicated, but very good; this is fortunate, because I have found no other fingerings for this note that work for me in any way that could be called reliable)

highest C
(five ledger lines)

TR/G#(or A),123,C# – G#/SK1,456,E – B (this is obviously complicated, but if it can be obtained handily, it is excellent, the best I have found)

TR/G#,100,C# – G#/400,F# – C# (this one is used for slurring up to from the fingering I gave for highest B)

TR/020/SK1,406,F# – C#

TR/020/SK1,406,E – B

TR/020,406,E – B (the only differences between this fingering and the two preceding ones involve tuning, and will vary from player to player)

TR/A,10,D# – A#,0/400,F# – C#

TR/A,02,D# – A#,0/400,F# –
C#
TR/A,100,F# – C#/SK1,400
TR/A,023,C# – G#/SK1,456,
E – B

highest C# – D-flat
(five or six ledger lines)

TR/023/056,G# – D# (this fingering is incredibly good
and reliable if tone-hole
No. 1 is "half-holed" rather
than completely open)
TR/A,000,C# – G#/SK1,400,
E – B

highest D
(six ledger lines)

TR/A,000,C# – G#/SK1,000,
E – B (this fingering is
especially good when it is
slurred up to from the immediately preceding fingering I
gave for C# – D–flat)
TR/A,003/SK4,006,G# – D#

highest D# – E-flat
(six ledger lines)

TR/A,003/SK4,006,E – B (I admit that this fingering is not
reliable, and is best thought
of as "experimental"; use it
as a point of departure to
see if you can improve upon
it)

Two High-Register Trills:
between high E-flat and F
(three ledger lines)

TR/023,C# – G#/000,G# – D#
(this fingering will give you
high F, of course; to effect
the trill down to E-flat,
"half-hole" the tone-hole
No. 1, and then trill on
tone-hole No. 4)

between high F and G
(three or four ledger lines)

TR/023,C# – G#/000,G# – D#
(this again is the high F; trill
up to G by trilling on tone-
hole No. 2)

APPENDIX

III

Some Mailing Addresses Useful to Clarinetists

Some of the items clarinetists need are so specialized that a major search is often required to discover a source. The following list should help shorten the searching process.

We all know, however, that any such list of addresses can go "out of date," wholly or partly, without notice. As of this writing, the following addresses are known by me to be good, useful, and active ones. The addresses of many other suppliers are known to me, but I have eliminated the ones that I have found to be unreliable and overpriced. Again, if you know of other good suppliers, add their addresses to this list so that the list will be more useful to you and your acquaintances.

SOURCES OF CLARINET MUSIC

Malecki Music, Inc.
4500 Broadmoor, S.E.
P.O. Box 150
Grand Rapids, Mich. 49501

(I have obtained most of my music for many years from Malecki's.)

Southern Music Company
1100 Broadway
San Antonio, Tex. 78206

(Another excellent source.)

Joseph Boonin, Inc.
P.O. Box 2124
South Hackensack, N.J. 07606

(A fine music dealer.)

Joseph Wood Music Company
148 East Main St.
Norton, Mass. 02766

(Specialists in woodwind music.)

SOURCES OF CLARINET REED BLANKS

Charles Ponte Music Company
142 West 46th St.
New York, N.Y. 10036

(Ponte's is interesting; they specialize in double-reed supplies and in *bass* clarinets. They have been my principal source of reed blanks, too.)

C. & L. Woodwind Company
1595 Broadway
New York, N.Y. 10019

(C. & L. has sometimes had reed blanks in stock when no one else has.)

S. Delacroix
5, Rue des Ecoles
94140 Alfortville, France

Glotin
15, Rue du Progres
95460 Ezanville, France

(Both of these Paris-area suppliers give good service and will respond to inquiries. Both demand payment in advance with international bank drafts. Delacroix has prices much less expensive than Glotin, at this writing.)

SOURCES OF NEW CLARINETS

California Musical Instrument
   Company
1019 East Vermont
Anaheim, Calif. 92805

Wichita Band Instrument
   Company
106 South Grove
Wichita, Kans. 67211

(Both of these dealers specialize in mail orders and in very low prices. While the buyer cannot select his instrument, both companies will make exchanges until the customer is satisfied. The low prices may make this an economical process for many players.)

The Clarinet Shop
7115 Alderney
Houston, Tex. 77055

(Owned by a fine clarinetist, who also keeps a huge supply of barrel joints.)

SOURCES OF CLARINET ACCESSORIES AND SUPPLIES

C. & L. Woodwind Company
(see address above)

The Clarinet Shop
(see address above)

Charles Ponte Music Company
(see address above)

Erick Brand
1117 West Beardsley Ave.
Elkhart, Ind. 46514

(Because Erick Brand is one of the nation's largest suppliers for instrument repairmen, he is an excellent source of pads, springs, tools, and so on.)

SOURCE OF A GOOD REED-MEASURING GAUGE

PerfectaReed
c/o Ben Armato
Box 594
Ardsley, N.Y. 10502

(This is the gauge referred to in this book's section on reed making. It is the best product I have yet seen for measuring the thickness of reeds and reed-blanks.)

SOURCE OF A COMPLETE LIST OF CLARINET MUSIC

The Music Register
Wayne Wilkins, Editor
P.O. Box 94
Magnolia, Ark. 71753

(*The Music Register* provides the only "complete" and current list of music and its sources known to me. The current list is always up-dated through annual supplements.)

Bibliography

ALLEMAN, JOHN E. "Significant Psychological and Physical Factors Related to Matching Bore Size of the Clarinet Barrel and Body." Ph.D. dissertation, Indiana University, 1969.

AUSTIN, WILLIAM W. *Music in the Twentieth Century.* New York: Norton, 1966.

BAINES, ANTHONY, ed. *Musical Instruments Through the Ages.* Rev. ed. Harmondsworth, Eng.: Penguin, 1969.

————. *Woodwind Instruments and Their History.* Rev. ed. New York: Norton, 1963. (This is one of the best books ever written on the subject of woodwinds in general.)

BARTOLOZZI, BRUNO. *New Sounds for Woodwind.* London: Oxford University Press, 1967.

BERLIOZ, HECTOR. *Treatise on Instrumentation.* Rev. ed. Enlarged and revised by Richard Strauss. Translated by Theodore Front. New York: Kalmus, 1948.

BOGART, D. T., JR. "A History of the Clarinet as an Orchestral Instrument from Inception to Full Acceptance in the Woodwind Choir." Ph.D. dissertation, Michigan State University, 1968.

CULVER, CHARLES A. *Musical Acoustics.* 4th ed. New York: McGraw-Hill, 1956.

FOSSNER, A. K. "Significant Changes and Improvements in Certain Woodwind Instruments Since 1860." Ph.D. dissertation, Columbia University, 1971.

GOLD, CECIL V. *Clarinet Performing Practices and Teaching in the United States and Canada.* 2nd ed. Moscow, Idaho: University of Idaho Press, 1973.

GOLDMAN, RICHARD FRANCO. *The Concert Band.* New York: Rinehart, 1946.

GROUT, DONALD J. *A Short History of Opera.* 2nd ed. New York: Columbia University Press, 1965.

KROLL, OSKAR. *The Clarinet.* Revised by Diethard Riehm. Translated by Hilda Morris. Translation edited by Anthony Baines. London: Batsford, 1968.

McCORKLE, DONALD M. "Moravian Music in Salem." Ph.D. dissertation, Indiana University, 1962.

OPPERMAN, KALMEN. *Repertory of the Clarinet.* New York: Colombo, 1960.

PINO, DAVID. "Learning and Teaching On-the-Reed Double and Triple Tonguing on Clarinet." Ph.D. dissertation, University of Texas, 1975.

REHFELDT, PHILLIP. *New Directions for Clarinet.* Berkeley, Calif.: University of California Press, 1977.

RENDALL, FRANCIS GEOFFREY. *The Clarinet.* 3rd ed. Edited by Philip Bate. New York: Norton, 1971.

RIMSKY-KORSAKOV, NIKOLAI. *Principles of Orchestration.* Edited by Maximilian Steinberg. Translated by Edward Agate. New York: Kalmus, n.d.

ROBERTSON, ALEC. *Chamber Music.* Harmondsworth, Eng.: Pelican, 1957.

SACHS, CURT. *The History of Musical Instruments.* New York: Norton, 1940.

STEIN, KEITH. *The Art of Clarinet Playing.* Evanston, Ill.: Summy-Birchard, 1958. (This is the best book ever written on how to play the clarinet.)

THURSTON, FREDERICK. *Clarinet Technique.* 2nd ed. London: Oxford University Press, 1964.

TITUS, ROBERT AUSTIN. "The Solo Music for the Clarinet in the Eighteenth Century." Ph.D. dissertation, State University of Iowa, 1962.

ULRICH, HOMER. *Chamber Music.* 2nd ed. New York: Columbia University Press, 1966.

WESTPHAL, FREDERICK W. *Guide to Teaching Woodwinds.* 2nd ed. Dubuque, Iowa: Wm. C. Brown, 1974.

WILKINS, WAYNE. *Index of Clarinet Music.* Magnolia, Ark: The Music Register, 1975.

WILLAMAN, ROBERT. *The Clarinet and Clarinet Playing.* New York: McGinnis and Marx, 1949.

Index